There's No Place Like Washington

BY VERA BLOOM

ILLUSTRATED

FOUNDED 1838

GPPS

G. P. PUTNAM'S SONS   New York

SECOND IMPRESSION

IMPORTANT

*Government wartime restrictions on mate-
rials have made it essential that the
amount of paper used in each book be reduced to a minimum. This volume is
printed on lighter paper than would have
been used before material limitations became necessary, and the number of words
on each page has been substantially in-
creased. The smaller bulk in no way indi-
cates that the text has been shortened.*

Designed by Robert Josephy

MANUFACTURED IN THE UNITED STATES OF AMERICA

CONTENTS

ILLUSTRATIONS

With affection toward most and malice toward none
of those I have mentioned in this book

1. All Aboard for Washington!

Even if Judgment Day is well advertised in advance, I'm quite sure that there will be a party going on in Washington, and that everyone there will feel they had some very good reason why they simply had to go.

When you've watched Washington change from the leisurely, lighthearted town it used to be in the twenties to the highpowered, overgrown place it is today, and seen that even the world's most terrible war has not halted the parties, you realize that surely something beyond frivolity keeps them going; that they are somehow altogether a part of carrying on the nation's and the nations' business.

Of course, the war changed all our lives and our sense of values, and social life was by no means immune. Gasoline and food rationing did away with such timeless Washington phenomena as the daily avalanche of calling cards with which official hostesses were snowed under from four to seven every afternoon. The before-the-war quota of four or five teas or cocktail parties a day gave way to what Mrs. Roosevelt approvingly called "parties with a purpose."

For a while you may have thought that even these were unnecessary; but when you had the opportunity to meet Queen Wilhelmina, or Mme. Chiang Kai-shek, or, perhaps, General de Gaulle, you felt that it was not only a once-in-a-lifetime chance to have a world-famous personality become a *person* to you, but that even if it was just for the second when they greeted you at a mammoth reception, you were, in a way, paying tribute, and not for yourself alone, to the indomitable peoples for whom they stood.

In the old days, I must admit, we kept going round and round the capital carrousel for very different reasons. If any of us stopped to think why we went to a party at all, the reasons were probably one of these:

Because they were very old friends, or very new.

Because you had been there so often that it would seem ungrateful not to accept; or because you hadn't been able to, and to regret once more would be just too much.

Because they outranked you in the official scale and you had to go and pay your respects; or you outranked them, and you knew it would mean something to them to have you there.

Because they entertained so magnificently that it was really an experience to be there—or so simply that you wouldn't have them think for the world that it wasn't grand enough for you.

Or because it was an official party to which you were obliged to go—or an unofficial one where you felt you were really wanted for yourself.

Or you just had to go because you were afraid you might miss something. . . .

Washington has always reminded me of a great waterfall. The glitter, the froth, the sparkle are what we see on the surface, yet all the time it is generating the power, the energy, that runs the greatest government in the world.

And all of us in official life have, you might say, a private waterfall of our own. We are in Washington for a serious purpose—to represent the folks back home as well as we possibly can, and to see that both their big interests and their personal problems are helped and safeguarded. At the same time we enjoy sparkling occasions that we would almost certainly have missed if we had stayed in private life. But the froth is not mere froth, for no one has ever been in Washington long without realizing that a friend made across a dinner table the night before may be truly a friend in need across a desk the morning after.

Yet if it's true that there's "nothing for nothing" in this world, that is especially so in public service. After all, it's a rootless life, although often it may take, as it did with me, many years of watching people come and go, of making friends only to have them scattered again and again to the ends of the earth, having new ones take their places and beginning it all over again, to see at last that it's really just the old, old story of the Lotus Eaters,

2

From a painting by Eulabie Dix

Vera Bloom in Costume for the Bicentennial Ball

and that lotus leaves, even prepared by the best embassy chefs, are not the most nourishing things in the world.

When I heard the news that my father had been asked to run for Congress from the Nineteenth—the Columbia University—District in New York City in the special election of 1923, I was utterly horrified!

A cartoon I had seen as a child—the bulging, leering politician, big cigar in mouth, derby on one side, diamond stickpin, positively reeking of vulgarity and ill-gotten gain—rose up life-size before my eyes. This was a Congressman! This was what they wanted my "Daddy" to become! It was unbearable; and Father put off accepting the nomination in view of my ridiculous young unhappiness.

The difficulty was solved, as all deep troubles should be, by a tall, dark, handsome prince. His unwitting emissary was Nini Tolentino, a dear Italian friend of ours, who asked me one day to go down to the pier with her to greet the new Italian Ambassador about to arrive.

It was a wet, blustery day, and I couldn't see anything very tempting in the idea of waiting on a drafty pier with a welcoming committee; but Nini begged, and I went. After all, my feelings for Italy were very special. We had spent much time there, and the fact that I had, though accidentally, "discovered" Mussolini for America, had made the whole Italian colony in New York consider me rather as an adopted daughter, in those days when he seemed a great leader. I felt quite ambassadorial, myself.

The long, cold wait on the Italian Line pier was just what I had expected, and I began to wish I had resisted Nini's persuasiveness, when the boat finally docked, and down the gangplank strode the Ambassador, Prince Caetani, tall, dark, handsome, and more besides, for he was brilliant and magnetic as well: the very embodiment of a Roman noble.

Suddenly it dawned on me that Washington was not merely a city of Boss Tweeds, it was also one grand series of ballrooms filled with glamorous diplomats, and there was more than a little to be said in its favor. After the Ambassador had exchanged a hasty, charming word with each of us, explaining that he was hurrying to catch the next train to Washington, I rushed off also—to telephone my father with the fervent hope that it was not too late for him to accept the nomination.

Of course he did accept it, and I shall never forget the night he was officially notified that he had been named.

Mother was entertaining. Someone had been improvising at the piano, and tall, dapper Raoul Tolentino, Nini's husband, a great expert on Italian art, was just holding forth on the comparative beauties of French and Italian primitives when the Congressman-to-be arrived with fifty or sixty wildly enthusiastic future constituents from the district Democratic clubhouse.

Raoul put his monocle in his eye and stared at them. They stared back, completely enchanted. I don't think most of them could believe there was such a thing as a monocle in real life. And then someone called out, loudly and cheerfully, "Say, when does that guy start pulling the rabbits out of his hat!"

Whereupon the party broke up—and I suddenly realized how foppish and funny he must have appeared to them. I'm ashamed to confess that I burst into tears as soon as they had all gone. Young and foolish I was, and I felt as if the practical politicians had come in and toppled my ivory tower. Life seemed to have two incongruous departments, now that we were in politics, and I couldn't see how I was going to learn to cope with the one and enjoy the other. But the die was cast!

Later I came to enjoy both, and to appreciate heartily the boundless good humor, loyalty, and enthusiasm of those stalwart backers without whom neither the serious work nor the pleasures of our Washington experience could have happened. I came to know their special domain, the district clubhouse, so important not only as a political headquarters but as a real social center for the neighborhood; and it was fascinating to learn the ropes of the ramified feudal system through which a large city's votes are rallied, from the boss down to the district leader and co-leader, without whose support no would-be candidate can hope to be nominated or renominated, and the block captains, who are supposed to know every voter in their one block and to see that every last one gets to the polls on Election Day, whether it means taking care of the baby or any other odd job that has to be done.

That first campaign, a special midwinter election which meant that only one office was being voted on, was a terribly anxious time. I was sure I had no flair for politics, and lived in constant dread of

4

doing the wrong thing. Mother and Father had no such inhibitions; campaigning came as naturally as breathing to them, though certain fine points were a surprise. In those days Father's advisers were very careful about having him take the London labels out of his hats, and his favorite black ribbon off his eyeglasses, and reminding him that he could get along perfectly well without a walking stick crooked over his arm—at least until after election.

We had to get used to riding all over New York with a huge banner tied across the back of the car: an enlargement of the legend that appeared in every store window and on every hoarding in the district, begging one and all to

ELECT
SOL BLOOM
TO
CONGRESS

It didn't take us long to learn that no modest violet could survive a political campaign. And we learned as promptly that, once you enter public life, there is no such thing as a small matter, a trivial occasion, an impersonal contact.

At that time the unofficial headquarters for all the political people of both parties in New York was Pomerantz', an unimposing restaurant at Broadway and 95th Street, known far and wide as Pommy's. There one night you might see "Young Teddy" Roosevelt, during his gubernatorial campaign, persuaded to stand up on the table and say a few words. The next night Senator Copeland or some other Democrat might be the star, and any night you could see the big Wall Street bettors calmly putting up colossal wagers on how the elections would go. Everyone had a table reserved where they would wait for the returns after the polls closed on election nights. It was the sort of place where the European café tradition of talking for hours on end over a sandwich and a cup of coffee was still the rule—Pommy would not allow a drop of liquor to be sold in his place—but it must have been an unprofitable one to the Pomerantz family, for Pommy's is no more, and campaigns are much duller without it.

5

It was all a very new New York for us, that we had hardly known existed. Ours had been a New York that anyone with leanings toward an artistic salon would have envied—the parties upstairs at the Lyceum Theater that dear "Uncle Dan" Frohman, the dean of the American theater, gave in relays all day long, from children's parties in the morning to brilliant little stag dinners for William Gillette, William Lyon Phelps, Brander Matthews, or maybe Otis Skinner, with probably a tea for all the current most beautiful Broadway stars thrown in. It was a New York whose highest highlight for me was when that same more-than-elusive great gentleman of the stage, William Gillette, of Sherlock Holmes fame, used to let me call for him at the Plaza Hotel and we would ride round and round the park, and he would say quite seriously that he wanted to adopt me. In any walk of life, in any country, he would have been the greatest gentleman of them all.

It was the New York of musical parties with the Kreislers, the Godowskys, the Kneisels, Ysaye, Chaliapin, and other stars of the Metropolitan Opera, who all used to gather at the Billy Guards' when he was master of all opera press representatives, or at Mme. Calvé's great studio in the Hotel des Artistes, where I went several times a week for my singing lessons with the great Carmen of former days. And in the same building was the Howard Chandler Christy studio that we knew so well. Just across the street at 2 West 67th Street was the wonderful studio the Burton Holmeses had filled with their treasure trove of all his trips to the East for travelogue material, where it was always such fun to be asked. Often we would come home and find that Edwin Markham had taken poetic license and invited himself to dinner. And there were the quite fabulous parties Cobina Wright gave for the musical and social worlds at her huge apartment on Madison Avenue. Then there were my friends among the younger set and all the Italian friends I so specially enjoyed.

It was a nice New York, and as Election Day drew near, I often wondered if Washington, even on part time, would be a good exchange, especially after a former Congressman's wife told us that Congressmen were so plentiful they were merely "hitching posts" down there, and we might stay for thirty years without even a glimpse of diplomatic glamour.

And what had I to offer as an open-sesame? Well, I certainly wasn't a great beauty, as Mother was, with her auburn hair and lovely, lovely face. Nor had I Mother's and Father's easy, California-bred friendliness; but I did have a certain gift of making friends, especially the "difficult" ones, both in Europe and at home.

I didn't play bridge; but I could *talk,* not only in English but in the French and German that Mademoiselle Martin, the governess whose tantrums were the scourge of my childhood, had made almost second nature to me. It was she who had given me, too, my unquenchable taste for the Great World, for she told fascinating tales of her former life in the Hofburg Palace in Vienna, where her father, although a Frenchman, had been one of the court chancellors to the Emperor Franz Josef, and they had lived in an apartment right under the great palace clock, which she had shown me when we were in Vienna. Royal Wonderland to me was a real and discoverable place! And later, even some of the fairy tales in which I entered it myself were to come true. I was to make my curtsey in the Throne Room at Buckingham Palace; I was to be received by the aged Empress Eugénie in Paris; and young Archduke Otto, the exiled heir of the Austrian Empire, was to become a friend of ours in Washington.

Also on the credit side (to get back to my inventory) were the Italian and Spanish I had picked up later; and on the debit side, the fact that I was absolutely no good at sports, and that, although I think a glass of good sherry or a fine French wine is one of the real delights of life, I have never had a highball, and I have never smoked, because I prefer to sing.

How would it all add up?

Well, election night came at last; and as it was a special election, Father had all the spotlight at Pommy's to himself. What a night that was! The results were so close—in the end there had to be a contest in the House before he was finally seated—that half a dozen times he was called upon to get on the table to say a few words of thanks for his election, only to be pulled down again by his campaign manager with a whispered caution that it looked again as if he had lost.

At last it appeared certain that he had won: by exactly 145 votes. We counted each one apart to be sure they were really there, and hoping to find a mistake in our favor; but 145 it was. It seems funny now, when he can pile up a majority of fifty thousand without particular jubilation, but it wasn't funny then! We felt rewarded for the nearly twenty-four-hours-a-day campaigning, and

Mother and I were very glad that we had gone along to the eight or nine speeches he had made each evening, even acting as understudies for him at women's meetings during the day. If we hadn't made good with just 73 of those 145 people, their votes, thrown into the Republican scale, would have given the necessary number to our opponent and have meant defeat instead of victory.

Later, at general elections, when his returns were overshadowed in the suspense of wondering what had happened to the whole ticket from the President down, we always waited at our own headquarters, where we could get direct returns from each captain's territory over a battery of telephones and count them up on charts as they came in. When you realize how many square blocks we had in the district from 86th Street to 125th and from Fifth Avenue to Riverside Drive, you can easily imagine the telephoning and figuring involved. With the state reapportionment in 1944, which gave my father the Twentieth Congressional District instead, including added territory down to 24th Street, there were new charts to study. And there is always the suspense, even after one's own victory is assured, in hearing from all over the country, over the radio, whether official friends in Washington have gotten the political guillotine or not.

Naturally, after that first victory, the inevitable reaction of stage fright set in. Could we help wondering if we would like Washington—and, much more important, if Washington would like us? And, like all New Yorkers, wondering if life could really be worth living off Manhattan Island? And—? And—?

Well, there was nothing to do about it now except to get ready for the new life. We knew no more about Washington than any visiting sight-seer, so we put ourselves in the hands of the New York shops that were supposed to know. First we went to the stationers to have new visiting cards made, and unquestioningly took their advice, as internationally approved arbiters of good taste and good form, to change our new Congressman's card from "Mr." to "Honorable." The result was that as soon as we got to Washington, they all had to be thrown in the wastepaper basket, for they would have made him a laughingstock where even a Senator's cards read simply "Mr. Smith" (he doesn't use his first name, though a Congressman does) with the name of the state in the corner. We learned right then that the wise thing is always to wait and take advice on the spot.

8

In the meantime Mother and I listened to the dressmakers' siren songs about what perhaps they honestly thought we would need for our very hypothetical embassy parties, and went down to Washington with our luggage full of formal afternoon "costumes" that we never wore. They were worse than useless in a place where to look dressed up at an afternoon party is the unmistakable sign that you are one of those who don't belong, and where the safest rule is, the grander the party, the simpler the clothes. Naturally, evening clothes are about the same everywhere; but for Washington nights too much magnificence, too many jewels, too many orchids are more apt to be amusing than envied. One of the nicest things about Washington to me is that clothes competition as you found it in New York or Paris simply doesn't exist. You get a few things and wear them over and over all season, and so does everyone else. I have known two French ambassadresses—and chic ones, too—who have worn three evening dresses all winter, going to a dinner party nearly every night, and no one gave it a thought.

Feelings of ease. How lovely they are, when attained to! Green-horns newly arrived in the great capital, we called at once on the one couple to whom we needed no introduction: Mother's cousin, Commissioner Lissner of the Shipping Board, and his wife Ermine. They were from Los Angeles, and she was so full of Hollywood glamour that she used to say she couldn't go to the Congressional Club because the members' hats made her seasick!

Ermine took us in hand with the idea that we, coming from New York, would be as amused as she was by the intricate elegance of official calling. And we did laugh with her, though a little nerv-ously, when she picked up the morning paper the Thursday after we arrived, and looked at the society page to make a list of the Senators' wives who would be "at home" that afternoon. We couldn't believe that she was seriously intending to take us into all those strange women's houses to tea.

She explained patiently that we were *expected* to walk into every strange woman's house in Washington whose husband happened to outrank us in the official scale. At least, we were expected to leave cards, whether we found her at home or not. And not only once, but we were expected to call again every year we stayed in official life. These calls were to be made on the established official days at home: the Supreme Court and the Army and Navy wives on Mon-days, the Congressional on Tuesdays, the Vice-President's, the

9

Speaker's, and the Cabinet wives on Wednesdays, the Senate ladies on Thursdays, and the diplomats on Fridays. In all, only about six hundred and six calls to make a year, not counting calls to be repaid on those beneath you in rank, and on unofficial Washingtonians, which usually brought it to over a thousand calls a season. And when you stop to realize that at least three cards had to be left at each place—a "Mr. and Mrs.," a "Mr.," and a "Miss,"—and more if there are more daughters in the family—it's easy to see why the fashionable Washington stationers have such a striking resemblance to the cat that swallowed the canary.

Even the fact that on our rounds that afternoon we met Mrs. Coolidge, so soon to become the First Lady, did not take away our feeling of the futility of the whole thing. Mrs. Coolidge was too delightfully friendly to take advantage of the prerogative of the Vice-President's wife not to return calls in person, and of course we, like everyone else, fell completely under her spell; a spell so hard to define that I am going to leave it until later, or I'll never get on with my story.

That first day taught us that one of the high-priority tasks of New Yorkers in Washington is to develop their stair-climbing muscles, grown soft and useless from life in the greatest apartment-house city in the world, whose elevator mileage if put all together would doubtless reach to the moon. But Washington is primarily a city of houses and gardens—and staircases, which range from the white-marbled splendor of embassy grand-staircases to the smaller ascents of cosy suburban homes.

Eventually we found out that every woman who comes to the Capital takes the question of official calls according to her own temperament. The idea infuriates some, while it terrifies or amuses others. But in the end they all come to submit to it, as the only plan ever devised to turn a city of strangers into a city of friends. To be sure, you may have spent one long, cold winter afternoon after another calling on twenty hostesses in succession who were not "at home"; but the twenty-first may be in, and may become a life-long friend.

Our one other contact besides the Lissners was a letter from a friend of mine at the Italian Consulate General in New York to Celesia, then the counselor of the Italian Embassy. This was to be my open-sesame to that inner Washington world which the former Congressman's wife had told us so few Congressional families ever get to know. As it turned out, I had time to appreciate the truth of her observation. (Incidentally, one of the first things we noted was that a Congressman literally does not exist, socially *speaking*. You never hear the word except in government offices and on Capitol Hill. It is always "Representative John Jones" in the newspapers or in introducing a member of the House to someone; otherwise he's just plain "Mr. Jones." An envelope is almost always addressed "The Honorable John Jones.")

We had been advised that the Hamilton Hotel was the nicest, and although since then it has been far outshone by the Mayflower, the Carlton, and the Shoreham, that was quite true then.

To a long table in the restaurant at the Hamilton every noontime came all the brighter lights of the diplomatic corps, brightest among them the Italian Ambassador, that same tall, dark, handsome Prince Caetani of the pier, all unaware, alas, of his part in having brought certain new guests to Washington. There they would hold merry luncheons, and I would sit, so near and yet so far, wondering if I would ever be one of the American girls who were always with them tossing off first names so casually. I began to realize that while in New York it's more important to "do something," in Washington it's more important to "be someone."

The something I had done in New York had been to write special articles for the *New York Times,* the *Herald,* the *Telegram,* and the Hearst Syndicate; but though I finally gained distinction by being lucky enough to get an interview from Mussolini every year, when he would only give one to a man from the London *Daily Mail* and the one to me, I cannot claim ever to have been a real newspaper woman pounding out a story on an office typewriter amid the bedlam of a paper going to press.

No, I'm afraid a truer picture would be of the time I had a magazine assignment to interview a Broadway star on her Connecticut farm, and we stopped off on our way to Cape Cod by motor. She looked at me in utter amazement as I drove up in an imported car with a mother, a father, a school friend, a chauffeur, and a dog—and asked witheringly what kind of an interviewer I might be? In covering plays, I could take assignments only to those plays that were just what I, as a nice girl in her teens, should see. Yet editors put up with me, and I had all the work I wanted to do.

We weren't long in Washington before we learned that the friends one would make would be very few indeed unless one first mastered the almost endless intricacies of protocol and precedence.

Protocol is as much the law of social Washington as the Constitution is the law of the land. It settles irrevocably who's who in official life; and precedence, protocol's little brother, then decides exactly how much more or less important everyone is than everyone else. Woe betide the green and innocent new Congressman's wife who should happen to pass ahead of a Senator's lady through a door or into an elevator! For, just as in a court of justice, ignorance is no excuse before the law. And similarly, there is no appeal from highest authority: the decisions of the chief of protocol at the State Department. Where he says you rank, you rank; and at a dinner party, where he says you sit, you sit.

"The law" said, for instance, that you had to leave cards within forty-eight hours wherever you had been to lunch or dinner; and that, moreover, every letter or answer to the White House, the Cabinet, an embassy, or a legation could not be mailed but must be left by hand. This was kept up until wartime gasoline rationing put a stop to it, at least for the duration. One thing I had a little part in stopping, by wailing long and loud about it to my friends in the Protocol Division when I got to know them well enough to do it, was the simply idiotic custom of having to motor all over near-by Virginia or Maryland, as likely as not through snow drifts, to return cards on someone whom you probably didn't even know. Finally the Powers That Be were moved and did decide that any calls "past the District Line" could be returned by mail.

While we were beginning to learn the social law, we duly sent around the letter to Celesia, only to find out when we met him that he was about to be transferred to a new post. However, he passed us on to his successor, Augusto Rosso, who was to come back, not so many years later, as ambassador—the first ambassador, incidentally, whom I had ever known "when." So it was Rosso who sent us our first diplomatic invitation, to an afternoon musicale he was giving at the Embassy while Prince Caetani was home on leave and he was chargé d'affaires. And then I had to come down with a miserable cold which kept me in bed while Mother and Father went off in state.

The first invitation, and doubtless the last, I grumbled in head-throbbing misery: my one chink in the charmed circle, closing forever. Little pleasure could I take in the triumph of Frank, our homesick Irish chauffeur from New York. His peers at the garage (so I heard when the family returned) took their own rank from their employers' official status with the solemnity of the caste system in the servants' hall at an English ducal house party, and had turned him quite cold shoulders until they found him waiting in line at an embassy party. From then on he "belonged."

Meanwhile, whether the Blooms belonged in Washington was still, in the most practical terms, a question. That very close election was being contested, and the decision lay with the House itself. The matter did not come up for over a year. We felt that the right thing to do was to stay rather quietly in the background until our official status was assured; which was probably a fortunate thing in the end, for it saved us from rushing in and making foolish mistakes where a wise political angel would fear to tread.

Of course, through all this time my father had his seat in the House pending the final decision, and he immediately began taking lessons in parliamentary procedure from the Parliamentarian—a wise and humble move on his part, that gave him immeasurable advantages when his time came to debate on the floor, where such knowledge is as necessary to a Congressman as his anvil to a blacksmith or his last to a cobbler.

It must have been a very deep happiness to him to realize how far he had come, carving out every step of the way for himself from the time when he was a little boy selling newspapers and violets on the San Francisco streets, a boy who ran away from school when he was eight years old because he was so hurt at the injustice of having "Free Copy" stamped on his schoolbooks, which gave the other children a chance to make him feel the gulf between them simply because their parents had been able to pay for theirs. The steps he was yet to take, when later he would be called on to head the Foreign Affairs Committee of the House as it dealt with the problems of World War II and the peace to come, were unseeable items lying in the balance of the contest decision.

At last the day came, and Mother and I hung breathlessly over the marble railing of the House Gallery while he made his dramatic and successful plea to be entitled to the seat he had been elected to.

It was over—and we really belonged in Washington. Of course, he still had to keep the usual "seen but not heard" attitude expected of a new member for some time to come. It was probably a great experience for him to hold back in deference to his more or less "distinguished colleagues," for he had never in all his life been

13

happy working in harness with a partner. His original mind, his spontaneous humor, his quick sympathy, his hair-trigger temperament, and his complete unpredictability all made him seem born to succeed alone. But now he was merely one—and, under Congressional rules of seniority, the least and latest—of four hundred and thirty-five successful men. He really adjusted himself marvelously. In the meantime Mother kept patiently at her rounds of calls, effortlessly winning all hearts; but, I must admit, I went along with enthusiasm only on Fridays, when the diplomatic hostesses were at home. I was so homesick for New York that any excuse would find me back there again.

We might have been having a brilliantly good time all along through our connection with the Italian Embassy, where Prince Caetani was still the center of all that was gay and glamorous in Washington, except for the ridiculous reason that someone who should have known better had told us—most misleadingly—that it was impossible for a married man to leave his card on a bachelor. On the contrary, it is the inflexible rule that the person of lower rank, married or single, must pay the first call on someone who outranks him. So it was impossible for the Ambassador to recognize the fact that we officially existed, or to invite us to the Embassy, until my father had called on him. And we didn't learn how mistaken we were until after Caetani had gone back to Italy!

Before long, however, the Italian debt settlement came up in Congress, and the debates were so hot that Mother and I, usually the most lukewarm gallery-gods, were up at the Capitol nearly every day. Naturally the Italian Embassy staff were there constantly too. Introductions were soon made, and, a Congressional Cinderella almost before I knew it, I, too, was nicknaming all the younger diplomatic crowd.

The Secretary of the Italian Embassy and Mme. Luciano Mascia —she, the darkly beautiful French Canadian "Toto"—were then the most popular young couple in Washington; perhaps too popular, for they drifted apart and Toto finally caused a front page sensation by "kidnaping" their baby daughter to Canada, so that Luciano could not, as Italian law provided, take the baby back with him to Italy. But at that time they were the happiest and most attractive couple imaginable, their house on Tracy Place the center for all the amusing diplomats in town, and I suddenly discovered

From a portrait by Villarez

Vera Bloom

From a portrait by Villarez

Mrs. Sol Bloom

Congressman Sol Bloom (*second from right*) After Winning the Contest for
His Seat in the House

that I was virtually living there too. It all happened as simply as that, and so it has gone on ever since.

For when one diplomat leaves, he almost invariably brings his successor around to present him before he goes. Sometimes, naturally, neither you nor the newcomer find each other as sympathetic as the one who is going away; but as one meets many, there is always about the same percentage of friendships to be made. And they are friendships, full blown in an amazing moment like the friendships one sometimes makes on shipboard, and probably for the same reason, because you know from the first that they can't last forever. But you know, too, that whenever you may meet again, the friendship will go on as if there had never been a moment's break. Meanwhile, you have the rather cold comfort of knowing you could pick up the telephone in practically any capital in the world, make a local call, and hear a good friend's welcoming voice at the other end of the wire.

I was so absorbed in my international good will that it seemed a flash of great discovery when, turning into Pennsylvania Avenue late one winter afternoon when every window in the State Department was blazing with light, I suddenly realized that there must be at least one terribly nice *American* behind each one of those windows! There was. And I, in time was to know most of them, and to find among them some of the finest people I've ever known and the best friends I've ever had. And then there were the friends Mother and Father were making besides, whom I, because Washington mixes its generations so generously, was to know so intimately too.

They say that New Yorkers are the most provincial people in the country, completely unaware that anything exists west of the Hudson River. If it's true (as I should never be one to admit), a few years in Washington are the best cure I can think of. When you've met charming, cosmopolitan people from Squeedunk or Sioux Falls, and dull, provincial ones from the biggest cities, you begin to take people for themselves. And you learn, too, not to be too beglamoured by "names," when a Hamilton Fish, with a grandfather who was Secretary of State, and with one of the most distinguished backgrounds any American could have, will resort to every trick of demagogery and obstructionism (to put it politely), while a man like Joe Martin, the Republican leader of the House, who makes no claim to such an imposing background, is beloved and respected by

Republican and Democratic members alike because they know that once he gives his word about how he stands or what he will do about any legislative question, they can depend on it to the end.

It seems to me like deliberately locking one's self in a dark room, to refuse to know and like people who don't belong to your own political party or your own particular neck of the woods. I remember, for instance, Mother's telling of a meeting at the Women's National Democratic Club, where Congressional wives were exchanging ideas about their campaign experiences and local political problems. A woman from the Deep South, whose husband had been in the House for nearly thirty years and was chairman of a very important committee, got up when her turn came, and looking straight at all those other Congressional ladies, said in all seriousness, "We'd be perfectly happy with everything in our state exactly as it is, if *you foreigners* would just leave us alone!"

Her daughter, a really sweet girl who had lived most of her life in Washington, was nevertheless almost as narrow-minded as her mother. One day I casually mentioned to her that I had just been over to Baltimore with Mrs. John Q. Tilson, whose husband was then Republican leader of the House; the Tilsons were among our closest friends. Of course, it's only fair to remember that where she came from, a Republican would be about as great a wonder as a two-headed calf. The girl looked at me exactly as if I'd just come back from an expedition with a Hottentot, and said in utter bewilderment, "But what on earth could you possibly find to talk about to a *Republican?*"

Probably the acme of all my Montague-and-Capulet doings was the time I was guest of honor at a luncheon at the Union League Club—the Republican holy of holies in New York—the day before the Roosevelt-Willkie election. With partisanship at the pitch it had reached then, I supposed that such rashness could have no other end than to put me in a cross-fire from allies and "enemies" both.

It happened this way. Among our dearest Congressional friends are the Eaton family of New Jersey. Dr. Eaton, who used to be John D. Rockefeller's pastor, is now the ranking Republican member on the Foreign Affairs Committee—to our great delight, for he and my father have always been able to work together with complete confidence and co-operation, and one of the red-letter days of our lives was when Hamilton Fish betook himself and all his works to the Rules Committee and left his place to Dr. Eaton, since a Congressman can serve only on one major committee.

When we were home in New York during the Roosevelt-Willkie campaign, I had called the Eatons' daughter, my very good friend, Mary Rose His, to see when we could meet for lunch. We had agreed on the Monday before Election Day, leaving time and place open. The day came: and a telegram from Mary Rose saying "Be at the Union League Club at one. I have asked some friends to meet you."

She was already on her way to town from Plainfield, and there was no way to ask her if she really meant to entertain for a "Democratic daughter"—a Tammany one, at that—where the air, which I had never breathed before, is supposed to be too refined for anyone but Blackest Republicans. So off I went. Of course all the taxi drivers on our corner where we had lived so long knew me, and when I got into the cab and that unsuspecting Democratic taxi man asked where to, I had neither the heart nor the courage to tell him. I cravenly said, "The Russian Tea Room, next to Carnegie Hall," which was the first place that popped into my head; and I felt like a lady spy in a movie when I got out there, went inside until he drove off, then took another cab to the Union League.

As we drove up to the austere portal of the Club, forgetting entirely about my unaccustomed political double life I asked the usual, "Well, who do you think will win tomorrow?" I'm sure the driver was a perfectly good Democrat, but he probably expected a fat Republican tip, for he looked up at the imposing facade and said wanly, "Willkie, of course!"

I found Mary Rose waiting with the others, and when we sat down to luncheon, my place the one of honor at her right, I told her that she was really the grandest and most broad-minded girl in the world, but that I would have felt better if she had allowed me to bring my Court Taster along.

She laughed and said, "There's only one rule for today, darling. *No politics.*"

To which, of course, I agreed. Only, knowing that if the Republicans should win, Ham Fish would surely take the chairmanship of the Rules Committee, which would make her father chairman of the Foreign Affairs Committee in my father's place, I asked if she would allow just one toast. She looked a little dubious, but everything was all right when I raised my glass of sherry and proposed: "To the next chairman of the Committee on Foreign Affairs—whoever he may be!"

Yes, we found Washington a city where one can make (and sometimes keep) good friends on both sides of all kinds of fences. With all the impermanence of political comings and goings, it can be a home place.

You might call it an intermittent home town; and to it, no one returns. Oh, of course, someone may be politically "out" a while, then win re-election. Otherwise, those who are "out" are not likely to come back. I used to wonder, especially, why Mrs. Coolidge never visited the Capital after their term was over. Surely she must have known what a royal welcome would have been hers. And it has been so with many another.

Was it, underneath, that feeling of non-return that made me want to write of Washington while we are still there: as if, later, I too might not want to go back even in that way? One doesn't altogether settle in. Our house in Washington is still not deeded but leased.

2. The Coolidges and the Hoovers

All Washington is divided into four parts. Or at any rate you can have a good barometer reading of just how people stand, if you know through which of the four main entrances they enter the White House.

It took us years, as it takes nearly everyone else, to be bidden to anything but the East Gate, where the steps are long enough for the doormen to take care of several cars at the same time, and where inside, in the downstairs corridors, there is a forest of coat-racks in the care of the upper crust of the Capital's colored "extra" maids and butlers, who in peacetime are engaged all over town by-the-function, day after day and night after night, and who invariably invite you with a broad smile to "rest yo' wraps."

Later, our White House invitations read "South Gate," which meant that official position now qualified us to come in with the diplomatic corps and the State Department higher-ups by the door facing the gardens, where there are real coatrooms and a red-carpeted circular hall where gold-braided uniforms, white-plumed hats, and the once-a-year appearance of tiaras made the night of the Diplomatic Reception the one occasion of the year when Washington fully lived up to its fictionized and cinema self. By the South Entrance came guests invited to the larger state dinners, or to the musicales.

Far smaller is the list of those who have entered by the beautiful front door, the North Entrance; for most of Washington never comes nearer to it than to drive up to the wide curving steps where, in peacetime, a liveried footman is always on duty afternoons, silver salver in hand, to receive the calling cards for the President and the First Lady which are everyone's first social gesture in Washington,

19

and without which, ordinarily, no White House door is ever likely to open. (Since Pearl Harbor, of course, no one is allowed past the White House gates without a special dated pass, even when invited to dinner.) The front door is for the Cabinet, other very high officialdom, and the First Family's intimate friends, for whom there is a single, sacred coatrack in the great, round entrance hall where the Marine Band plays on state occasions, right across the long corridor from the Blue Room. And this is the way you come when and if you are eventually invited to a small dinner (small, that is, by White House standards) or to an intimate tea.

But though it is publicly a distinction to enter by the front door, it is secretly far more important to go through the West Entrance —the door used by the President when he crosses through the gardens to the Executive Offices. This is the gateway for the very few: men of such influence that the President prefers to talk to them quietly in his White House study while the newspapermen wait in vain for them to emerge from the Executive Offices. When my father finally went in *that* way, we had encompassed the White House entrances from East to West.

I am glad the first First Lady we knew was Mrs. Coolidge; but I despair of writing about her in a manner fitting.

Somehow, somewhere in the world in each generation, one or two women appear who cast a warm spell over people's hearts. It doesn't seem to depend on beauty, or brilliance, or allure, though she may have them too. Barrie knew what such charm is: he has Maggie say wistfully in *What Every Woman Knows,* "If you have it, you don't need to have anything else, and if you don't have it, it doesn't much matter what else you have." But even he couldn't really describe it. So how am I going to describe Mrs. Coolidge's charm? It was made up of so many things—naturalness, dignity, tact, kindness, vivacity, and sympathy—each in just the right degree. But when you've said all that, it's only more elusive than ever.

Mrs. Coolidge was never beautiful; she wasn't even what you'd call pretty. She just had a pleasant, average face and a slender, average figure; but her genuine interest in you, which shone out through her warm, dark eyes, and her *kindness* (not "graciousness," that horrible word!) seemed to cast a sort of glow around her wherever she went.

Perhaps there are many women who have it, women just as obscure as Mrs. Coolidge would have been if destiny had left her a teacher of the deaf-and-dumb in a little New England town. I can only think of one other woman today who casts the same spell, and she is Queen Elizabeth of England. Has it, I wonder, anything to do with the fact that neither the Queen nor Mrs. Coolidge is typically "modern"?

Mrs. Coolidge, of course, had to have enough charm for two, for the President had absolutely none of the geniality and good-humor that is usually part of the political temperament. He did practically nothing to refute Alice Longworth's classic assertion that he was "weaned on a pickle," except to provide a plausible personality for the caustic Coolidge jokes that swept the country, and that somehow only added to the tremendous confidence the people had in him. Some of them were even true: like the one we heard first hand about the gushing lady who said to him, "Mr. President, I was *so* anxious to hear your speech at the opening of Congress yesterday, that I had to stand the *whole* forty-five minutes!" To which his only answer was, "So did I."

He was probably the most undemonstrative man we've ever had in public life; but his way of showing his affection for his wife was by never letting her out of his sight when he could help it. They told us in Philadelphia that he even insisted on having her with him on the judges' stand at the Devon Horse Show. Respectful protests were ventured, for no woman ever set foot on that stand before or since. His response (unabridged) was, "Come on, Grace."

For all his homespun qualities he had the deepest respect for the office of the Presidency—as distinguished from himself, the man. One day around Christmastime a friend of ours was with him in his office when John Coolidge, home from college for a holiday whirl, came in to ask his father whether it would be all right if he stayed so late at a tea dance that he would not have time to dress for dinner that evening.

The President thought it over a moment and then simply reminded him, quite impersonally, "You are dining with the President of the United States."

However, the Coolidges combined their reverence for White House tradition with a great deal of consideration. For instance, an invitation to the White House is, of course, considered a command;

and this can cause great flustration if you have already accepted something for that evening, or, worse yet, are giving a dinner party yourself. When the Coolidges wanted to ask intimate friends at the last moment, they used to do it in this thoughtful way: one of their secretaries would telephone and inquire, "Would you be quite free for this evening if the President and Mrs. Coolidge *should* ask you to dinner?" In other words, the invitation had not been extended yet; you were expected to say quite frankly whether you were free or not.

While there were often unexpected flashes of the dour Coolidge wit, the only time I ever saw the President in a positively genial mood was the time we took David Belasco to the White House to see him.

For forty years Mr. Belasco had been coming to the Capital to try out new plays. Washington audiences were perennially noted as the coldest in the country; if they liked a play, probably anyone would. And yet in all those forty years, Mr. Belasco had never been to the White House nor to the Capitol. His days in Washington were invariably bounded by the theater and his hotel.

When he mentioned this to us one night back stage after a play opening, we were amazed, and promptly outlined a plan for him to meet the President that week. He agreed, quite nervously, but only on condition that the whole Bloom family go along as escorts and cohorts. So a morning appointment was arranged, and we called for him at the Washington Hotel in plenty of time to get calmly to the White House.

Mr. Belasco was far from calm. He was as nervous as at an opening-night curtain speech. Going in to see President Coolidge, he had heard, was "like going into an icebox," and he really dreaded it.

His arrival at the Executive Offices was a small sensation, not only with the newspapermen and the photographers who are always outside the door, but with the President's staff as well. Senators and governors are ordinary apparitions at the White House, but the appearance of the cloistered, clerical-collared, white-haired dean of the American theater was something for even Mr. McKenna, past whose desk in the outer hall every conceivable celebrity had passed, to be excited about.

While we were going in, Mr. Belasco begged someone to tell him what he should talk to the President about. We explained that

22

it was usual for the President to begin a conversation, but that if an opportunity came up, it would probably please the President very much to hear Mr. Belasco's opinion of his speech at the opening of Congress a day or two before.

They showed us right into the offices of the Secretary to the President, the courtly C. Bascomb Slemp. By this time shyness had completely overwhelmed Mr. Belasco, and he was coming forward with eyes cast down, as so many first-night audiences have seen him. At the first word of introduction Mr. Belasco, still looking down, and sensing that the crucial moment had come, began, "Mr. President, this the the the greatest honor—" Mr. Slemp was called to the phone just then, and there was time for a hasty whisper to set Mr. Belasco right. He was most upset, but we assured him that no man is annoyed by being mistaken for his chief.

Then we passed into the President's office. Mr. Belasco began again, "Mr. President, this is the greatest honor—" but President Coolidge interrupted him, with real feeling. "No, Mr. Belasco," he said surprisingly, "the honor is mine. There have been many Presidents, but there is only one David Belasco."

Mr. Belasco was simply overcome by such a compliment, after the cold reception he had expected. He could hardly find words to express his appreciation. Then he went on to talk about the President's speech, declaring it the greatest he had ever read.

And then I broke in. I really wasn't trying to be funny, but before I knew it, I had added, "Yes, Mr. President, and it must have been the simplest, too, because even *I* got it!"

For an instant I was petrified lest I might have said the unpardonable thing; and then, to my indescribable relief, the President began to laugh until he couldn't stop laughing, and then leaned back against his desk to laugh some more.

The meeting finished in a glow of good feeling—and with an unlooked-for afterglow preparing. At least I, for one, had no idea that the newspapermen in the background were already planning headlines for the next edition about "The Girl Who Made Coolidge Laugh"!

At the state reception that night at the White House the President held up the line to tell me how much he had enjoyed meeting Mr. Belasco. So I told him what Mr. Belasco had said after we left: that no one had ever impressed him as much as the President. "Did he really!" Calvin Coolidge insisted, as pleased as a boy.

But he was rarely so spontaneously genial. More characteristic is the story involving a woman delegate from Texas who attended a state reception of another night, there to suffer a cold disillusion. She was right in back of us in the line, and during all the long half hour it took to approach the Presidential handshake, she kept bubbling on about what a great hit she had made with the President that morning while her delegation was being photographed with him on the garden steps.

"He gave me the most wonderful smile!" she kept repeating. "I know it was something special, something personal! And when I get up to him tonight I'm going to tell him that I will be waiting in Texas to welcome him whenever he comes!"

She rhapsodized until the sight of the military aide announcing the names to the President subdued her. Meanwhile she had begged me to wait a moment in the East Room so she could divulge what the President said to her in the impending second great encounter. I waited, if a quarter of a second could be called waiting. And then the most downcast, disappointed woman joined me.

"Why, he didn't say a word!" she wailed. "He gave me a handshake like a dead fish and pushed me along! I can't understand it. He gave me the most wonderful smile this morning. Really he did!" My assurances that I believed it were given without tongue-in-cheek, for it was only later in the evening that I happened to learn the real reason for that miraculous smile.

One of the White House photographers, so he told me, had lately extracted the President's promise of a flash of cheer the next time he posed. That morning, with the Texas delegation grouped around him, he had been looking even glummer than usual when the photographer sang out, "Remember, Mr. President!" And straight at the Texas lady went the promised smile. No wonder she lost her head. And no doubt she has managed to retain the enchantment and forget the disillusion, since there remains unmistakable photographic evidence of her wonderful effect upon the most unbeaming of our Presidents.

I remember some rhapsodizing of my own that once brought, not disillusion, but surprise of the kind that devastates.

Since we have been in Washington, I have said two or three things that echoed not only around the country, but apparently around the world; and in each case I had not the least suspicion, and certainly no intention, of causing any front page stir. The first time was when I became "The Girl Who Made Coolidge Laugh"; the next was when I said that "Mrs. Coolidge is worth a million dollars a year to the Republican party."

The occasion was an afternoon meeting at the Carlton Hotel where I had weakly promised to speak on "Women in Washington" to some women in Washington. Two or three watchful good friends came and warned me that this particular club, while quite all right, had a way of getting into sometimes unpleasant situations, and it might be just as well if I gracefully withdrew. I tried to, but they wouldn't let me off. At least, I resolved, my words should be few and innocuous.

There couldn't have been more than fifty women at the meeting, most of them, after all, very nice people whom I knew. So I began my little speech, and getting warmed up by my always uncontrollable enthusiasm for Mrs. Coolidge, I remarked on what an asset to her party were such grace and tact and charm. Then I brought in the Congresswomen, Mrs. Longworth, and Mrs. Mabel Walker Willebrandt, said my thank-yous, and left, not giving the matter another thought, until early the next morning the Associated Press and every other press service began telephoning me for interviews and photographs. It was borne in upon me, with the deliberation of complete confoundment, just how too-brief and far from innocuous my phraseology had been.

It seems a stray reporter had wandered in to the meeting, with the result that both the *New York Times* and the *Washington Post* had front page stories about it the next morning—the beginning of a perfect avalanche of editorials and special articles and even anonymous letters, accusing me, among other things, of "degrading Mrs. Coolidge by putting a money value on her!" And the Democratic papers wanted to know why a Democratic daughter was booming a Republican administration.

The next time I saw Mrs. Coolidge at the White House she said, "Well, Vera, we've certainly had a lot of publicity together!" "Yes," I laughed, "we've had the publicity together, Mrs. Coolidge, but I've had the trouble alone!"

Our contacts with the Coolidges did not end when they left the White House. It occurred to my father, not long after, that perhaps no one else had thought to have the Congressional Record mailed to the former President at Northampton. Mr. Coolidge's letter of thanks would have made a front page story at the time—a recent

25

Chief Executive asserting frankly his complete disinterest in what the national legislature was doing—but of course my father wouldn't make political capital out of any personal letter, least of all one from a Republican President to a Democratic Congressman. But now that Calvin Coolidge is part of history rather than of politics, it can be quoted:

December 9, 1929

Honorable Sol Bloom,
House of Representatives,
Washington, D.C.
Dear Mr. Bloom:

The Congressional Record comes to my office and I wish to thank you for your kindness in sending it to me. I had done nothing about getting it because since I have left Washington I have not cared to know about what was going on in the Congress, but your kindness is none the less greatly appreciated.

With the compliments of the season, I am

Very truly yours,

Calvin Coolidge

The first word we had from Mrs. Coolidge after they had left was this letter to Mother. (The "Congressional breakfast" of which she speaks referred, of course, to one of those famous White House breakfasts to which the early-rising President mischievously enjoyed asking an often very sleepy and reluctant group of Congressional leaders.)

Dear Mrs. Bloom,

Your letter has lain on my desk long unanswered. The days fly by and night comes on long before I have accomplished what I planned in the morning.

Mr. Coolidge has just returned from an afternoon of fishing with fourteen fair sized trout. Please tell Mr. Bloom that I am sure he would like to have a Congressional breakfast with them served up as the chief delicacy.

Best regards to Vera and tell her I am sorry I never heard her sing.

Hoping you are all well,
With cordial greetings,

Sincerely,

May 2, 1929

Grace Coolidge

One day not long afterward we were having some people to dinner, among them Mrs. Rose Gouverneur Hoes, who made the fascinating costume collection of the gowns of all the Presidents' wives from Martha Washington to Mrs. Hoover—including her own great-grandmother, the fifth First Lady, Mrs. James Monroe—which, at least as far as women are concerned, is by far the most popular exhibit at the Smithsonian Institution. Certainly a "must" for feminine sight-seers to Washington, it apparently interests the men, too, for in peacetime it was visited by nearly a million people a year.

Somehow history comes alive, not only in its dignity but in its gaiety and trials, when one sees these models of our First Ladies, gowned as they were in life: Martha Washington, stately and serene in her bouffant brocades, seated, as she alone of all our Presidential hostesses always was, to receive her guests; Dolly Madison, vivacious and imperious, with her high-waisted gowns and one of her famous turbans; or poor, unhappy Mrs. Lincoln in one of her extravagant crinolines. Sometimes I think it is the little things—the gloves, the fans, or the handkerchiefs which accompany each gown—that, more than anything else, make each First Lady so real to us.

The talk that night turned to Mrs. Coolidge's unfortunate choice for her dress at the Smithsonian, which was not only ugly in itself but in no way expressive of her vivid and charming personality.

Several people said, at the very same moment, "Oh, why didn't she give that beautiful American Beauty red velvet dress with the long court train, that she wore at the last State Reception!" It seemed such a spontaneous and general desire, that Mother agreed to write Mrs. Coolidge suggesting it.

Mrs. Hoes warned us that Mrs. Coolidge might not feel she could comply, since her choice had been the result of one of her typically thoughtful promises. The Presidency having devolved on Mr. Coolidge suddenly, Mrs. Coolidge had found that she lacked a dress suitable for the First Lady to wear to an occasion at the Pan-American Union which was to be her first official appearance as the President's wife. Garfinckel's, where she had been buying her clothes in Washington, had rushed through a dress for her on short notice, and Mrs. Coolidge had promised them she would give that dress to the Smithsonian collection. Which, of course, she did.

27

So when Mother had no answer to her letter for nearly a year—and no one could be prompter or kinder about answering letters than Mrs. Coolidge—we all thought that perhaps we had asked too much.

Then one day a plain typewritten envelope arrived which would, I am afraid, have gone in with the monthly bills if we hadn't happened to see "21 Massasoit Street, Northampton, Massachusetts" on the flap. And inside was this letter, that only Mrs. Coolidge could have written:

March 22, 1930

Dear Mrs. Bloom:

Please excuse my using the typewriter. I have become so accustomed to it that my hand has lost most of what small ability it had to use the pen.

Sometime ago, it must be almost a year, you wrote to ask if I would be willing to give another gown to the Smithsonian. I delayed answering because all my reception gowns were packed and in the storage warehouse. Before I went away (to California), I wanted to get one of the simple ones to take with me and in the chest was the velvet one which you mention particularly. I am perfectly willing to send it if you really think it is desirable but hesitate because it seems to me many who are interested to look at the collection will say, "why does Mrs. Coolidge have two and the others but one?" I suppose it would be put in a case somewhere and not conspicuously displayed. I selected the simple white satin brocade gown because of the sentimental feeling which I had for it and because it is inconspicuous.

Will you be my message bearer to Congressman Bloom and tell him how much I appreciate the autographed copy of the marginal Congressional Directory which he sent me while I was away? My old copy was sadly out of date and this later one fills a need which I was beginning to realize. I marvel at his thoughtfulness in the midst of his busy life.

I venture to send my love to Vera. Although I no longer see my friends in Washington, the thought of them gives me happiness.

With cordial greetings.

Sincerely,

Grace Coolidge

There were some intensive conferences with the Smithsonian

directors and Mrs. Hoes before Mother could write back to Mrs. Coolidge that it had been arranged to put the white dress in a side case; that we were all particularly happy that the red dress would be shown in its place, as Howard Chandler Christy had painted her in a red gown for her White House portrait; and that Mrs. Hoes would see to placing the sorority pin on the new gown exactly as she wears it in the painting.

A few days later came a huge box and a smaller one, and another letter, this time on fine cream-colored paper with a GC monogram in gold, and in longhand:

March 29, 1930

Dear Mrs. Bloom:

Two boxes are going out to you by parcel post, insured for special handling, this morning. The larger box contains the velvet dress and train as packed by faithful Maggie over a year ago. My first thought was for her to send it to Mrs. Besson for steaming and pressing, but I finally concluded to do as you said and send it to you. Will you, then, send it over to

Mrs. Josephine L. Besson
1329 Fourteenth St.

and ask her to put it in condition and send the bill to me?

The smaller package carries the slippers and hose. If I have omitted anything please let me know.

This is not the gown of the Christy portrait, but is the one which I wore to the last reception of which you wrote in your previous letter, I think.

March is howling around the corners of the house and Spring fails to give us a foretaste of her delights. When she does come no doubt it will be with a bound.

Just to show you my typing is better than my handwriting and with friendly salutations.

Sincerely,
Grace Coolidge

We took the gown over to Mrs. Besson's little shop, which so many Presidents and First Ladies have patronized, deliberating all the way whether or not it would be presumptuous to charge the steaming to us, and finally deciding that Mrs. Coolidge would prefer to have us follow her instructions and charge it to her.

But when the daughter, Miss Besson, heard whose gown it was, she took all choice right out of our hands by exclaiming, "For Mrs. Coolidge! That angel! Why, we couldn't charge her anything. It will be a labor of love."

So we, and most of the Smithsonian directors, were waiting at the museum a few days later as a reception committee for the dress, which Miss Besson was sending over. There were crowds of people on account of the Easter holidays, and opening the glass case to take Mrs. Coolidge's mannequin out was quite a sensation.

Incidentally, Mr. Ravenel, the curator, whose office was the scene of the dress-changing, told us something about the exhibit that we had never realized. Although all the First Ladies look different, actually the sculptured faces are identical. Foreseeing, when the figures were being made, that the museum would be stormed by indignant descendants of Presidents' wives if one had a prettier nose or lovelier eyes than the others, the directors decided on one classic Greek head for them all. The apparent difference comes from the hair and the headdress, which the sculptor adapted to each period.

The American Beauty gown having been put on the figure with the greatest care to avoid creases and finger marks, we suddenly realized that we had failed to bring along the lovely slippers made of the material of the gown with delicate rhinestone straps and high silver heels. So we had to hold up the proceedings while they were sent for; and then, when they were put on, the whole figure tottered perilously forward because we hadn't figured on the great difference between the comparatively practical heels Mrs. Coolidge had worn when the figure was made and the very high ones now substituted. There was nothing to do but wait again, until the museum sculptor could "operate" on the feet of the model and balance the whole figure on the new heels.

That meant having Mrs. Coolidge absent a whole day from the case she shares with the second Mrs. Wilson and Mrs. Harding (who sent a deathbed request to have her figure wear her beloved black velvet neckband, and an evening cape). It was amazing, and moving, to hear the hundreds of visitors all day impatiently demanding to have Mrs. Coolidge back.

Next day, the orthopedic operation a complete success, we helped drape the train and the dress in the case exactly as we remembered Mrs. Coolidge wearing it, and placed the sorority pin, which had been left her by a dear college friend, just as she wears it in the Christy portrait.

Mrs. Hoes, the directors, the people who crowded around, and we ourselves, all felt that the new gown was a great success. In many ways it is a figure unique in the collection. Mrs. Coolidge's "period" is the only one in which the First Lady does not wear an arm covering of some sort, or shows so much as a glimpse of the feet above the instep. The exaggeratedly low waistline of the gown, the short, nearly knee-length skirt, the flesh-colored stockings— commonplaces of the styles of 1929—already seemed old-fashioned in 1930, when short-waisted, long-skirted evening dresses became the fashion again.

It is an irony that Mrs. Coolidge, whose loveliness had nothing to do with modernity, nor with the old-fashioned, for that matter, should be the one to model flapper-age styles. But even if her gown becomes "curioser and curioser" as a period reminder, I think it will always reflect that vital charm that is so especially hers, and that once impelled her husband to write about her: "For twenty-five years she has borne with my infirmities, while I have rejoiced in her graces."

And here is a letter Mother received from Mrs. Coolidge, in answer to one telling her what happened at the museum, to close the story:

April 21, 1930

Dear Mrs. Bloom:

Feet of flesh and blood must adjust themselves to any sort of slipper. Feet of clay are more fortunate in that they may be pared to fit any shape or tilt.

I am glad that the new gown meets with general favor and I appreciate your interest in the matter.

If at any time Mrs. Hoes wishes to eliminate or make other disposition of the white satin gown, it is all right with me.

I have written to Mrs. Besson.

My respects to Mr. Bloom, and cordial greetings to you and Vera.

Sincerely,
Grace Coolidge

When Calvin Coolidge did not choose to run, Herbert Hoover did. And the Hoovers proved in many ways a surprising contrast to the Coolidges—surprising in that although they had lived all over the world, and for many years in London besides four years in Washington as a Cabinet family in the Coolidge administration, they had actually far less social flair than the Coolidges, who had never known anything but their own New England background.

Mrs. Coolidge's social gifts, were, of course, simply extraordinary; and while you could hardly call President Coolidge's acid manner a social flair, still there is no doubt that he, if not you, was completely at ease, and you always had the feeling that inwardly he was enjoying every minute to the hilt, in his own secret way.

My guess is that although President Hoover had a much more imposing appearance than Mr. Coolidge, and although Mrs. Hoover was a really handsome woman, whose lovely white hair lent her great dignity, their extreme conscientiousness made them acutely self-conscious people.

The story that has been told of how President Hoover refused to bow and smile to crowds waiting for a glimpse of him outside the White House, for fear that they might think that he was making a cheap bid for popularity, seems to bear me out. Even White House guests rarely saw anything but the formal, reserved side of his personality; but intimate friends who shared the Hoovers' week ends in the informal rustic atmosphere of the Rapidan fishing camp in the Virginia mountains, that the President loved so much, told me that he would hold a small trusted group absolutely enthralled for hours on end around a roaring fireplace, with vivid, dramatic tales of his experiences as an engineer all over the world.

But in the White House, life to Mr. Hoover seemed all too real and earnest. The only time I ever knew of his being on the sending end of a good laugh was the day during the George Washington Bicentennial when he played a practical joke on my father, who was busy heart and soul in his job as director of the Bicentennial Commission.

A Swiss sculptor named Durig had come to town with the simple, grandiose idea that George Washington, being the biggest name in American history, should have the biggest statue in his honor. So he proceeded to make a colossal bust weighing about nine tons and standing fully twelve feet high.

Then he telephoned the unsuspecting Swiss Minister, Marc Peter, to request him to petition the White House to do him the honor that he be permitted to present as a gift to President Hoover a bust of Washington.

The poor Minister, unaware what the word "bust" could encompass, and wishing, no doubt, to encourage the appreciation of Swiss art in this country, made an appointment to bring his countryman to the Executive Offices one morning for the presentation. When he approached the scene, the offices themselves could scarcely be sighted behind the huge plaster head that a truck and a derrick had deposited on the lawn a few minutes before.

If any presentation—and goodness knows, our Presidents are used to weird offerings—could have fazed President Hoover, surely the Durig bust would have done it. But he accepted the gift gravely; even posed for a photograph with the embarrassed Minister and the exulting artist; and only after they had left, turned to Theodore Joslin, then the Secretary to the President (who told us the details long after), and said,

"I guess we'll have to turn this over to Sol Bloom!" With a most unusual twinkle in his eye, he instructed: "Just ring Sol up and tell him that I have a bust of Washington for him, and ask him to send over for it, but don't tell him anything more about it!"

Mr. Joslin got Father on the phone and gave him the President's message.

"Thank you!" he said, "I'll have one of my men come over in a taxi right away and bring it over to me."

"That will be splendid," said Mr. Joslin gravely, and reported to the President that the fun was about to begin.

When the messenger drove up to fetch the statuary, his eyes lit on the mountain of plaster on the grass and his mouth fell wide open.

Mr. Joslin came out and inquired pleasantly, "Do you think you can take it in the taxicab?"

"No, sir," said the messenger, feebly.

"Then I think you'd better go back and ask Mr. Bloom to come over himself and see what he can do with it."

The messenger left, and by this time the newspapermen, who are always around the door of the President's office waiting for a good story, knew they had one now.

When my father arrived, knowing already what to expect, of course, I imagine he must have disappointed Mr. Joslin a good deal

33

by looking up at the bust with a perfectly straight face and saying, "What's all the excitement? That isn't so big."

It was only so big that he had to get the biggest truck in Washington to haul it away, and had to telephone every storage company in town until he found one with a large enough space to store the colossus. I can't imagine where Durig found a studio large enough to cast it in.

It stayed in oblivion in the storehouse for several months, except now and then when a newspaperman happened to think of it and put a question in the papers, "What's happened to that Durig bust?" Finally, the Auditorium in Atlantic City put in a bid to exhibit the thing in their enormous lobby, which is probably the only place in the country big enough to take it and still leave room for anyone to get far enough away to view it. The Bicentennial Commission, after deep consideration, finally "consented" to allow the bust to be taken to Atlantic City, and there, for all I know, it still is.

Anyhow, it served at least one good purpose. It gave President Hoover, according to Mr. Joslin, the very best of the few real laughs he had while in the White House.

For Mrs. Hoover, too, White House life was real and earnest; one felt that she could not have been happy if she had left even the merest detail to chance. This impression, for me, dates back to a day soon after the Hoovers had moved from S Street to the White House, when Mrs. Hoover gave a large afternoon reception for Congressional wives and daughters. Mother and I, having taken the rule of arriving at a White House function a few minutes ahead of time a bit too seriously, found ourselves the first of all the hundreds waiting in line in the East Room, and even on down the stairs.

A military aide motioned to us to follow him through the Green Room to the Blue Room, where Mrs. Hoover was ready to receive us. He moved discreetly away while Mrs. Hoover said whatever a First Lady is supposed to say to a Congressman's wife and daughter; and then, while still talking, she called back the aide with a motion of her hand.

"Oh, Captain," she said, with earnestness, "I am sure Mrs. Bloom and her daughter will not mind if we rehearse a bit with them for just what I would like you to do." He bowed, and she continued, "You see, I will chat for a moment or so with two ladies

34

at a time, while you can be moving back to escort the next two. And I would like you to be very careful not to let it *appear* that I am hurrying them, until you see me drop my left hand to my side"—she illustrated with that hand, in which she held a petit-point purse as a sort of flag-signal—"and *then* you can bring up the next group. Have I made myself clear?"

The Captain bowed again, we chatted a moment more, the petit-point semaphore dipped, and on we moved.

The only thing Mrs. Hoover seemed content to leave more or less to another was the question of fashion, for although she was always beautifully groomed and handsomely gowned in a conservative way, she reserved her personal attention for more worth-while matters than the passing mode. This I know firsthand because of a success story whose scene was laid partly in our house.

It was during the Hoover administration that we had an impressive European chauffeur. He and his wife had come to America as part of an American diplomatic household, and stayed on after their employer had left the State Department for another foreign post. Which, as a matter of fact, is how Washington used to get many of its best European servants. The legalities for a longer stay were successfully arranged; he continued chauffeuring, and his wife became a successful "little dressmaker." At first she depended mostly on the diplomatic wives, but soon she had some important American clients too, and before long had even become Mrs. Hoover's dressmaker.

The First Lady left almost everything to her—style, material, and color. All she was told was to "make something for an evening reception" or "something for the Congressional Club luncheon." If she sometime ventured to get a hint of Mrs. Hoover's preference for a certain occasion, the message would usually come back, "Oh, anything. Brown, or something."

It was an ideal arrangement for Mrs. Hoover, and not so bad for the dressmaker, either.

And then suddenly the couple were summoned to appear before the immigration authorities. Perhaps some friend had had to marvel over their success story once too often. At any rate, someone had charged that they were staying here illegally. The possible verdict was deportation.

Of course, they appealed to my father for help. He did everything he possibly could—and he usually succeeds in such cases—

but it still looked as if the decision would go against them. Soon the wife told us, in a flood of tears, that she didn't see how she could possibly finish the "something brown" she was making for Mrs. Hoover for that Congressional Club luncheon.

And that gave Father an idea.

"Listen to me," he told her. "Have you another fitting with Mrs. Hoover?"

"Yes, sir." More tears.

"Then do exactly as I say. First fit the dress, and then say, very respectfully, 'Mrs. Hoover, I am heartbroken, but I am afraid I cannot finish the dress.' Mrs. Hoover will say 'Why?' Then you tell her why, and unless I am very much mistaken, this false accusation against you both will be dismissed, and you will not be deported."

And so it fell out. At least, they stayed in Washington.

3. Under the Sign of the Elephant

It is surprising, I've often thought, that more doctors don't pre-scribe a dose of official life as a cure for some of their problem patients. Washington is quite used to seeing wives who have long been "delicate," if not actually invalids, come to the Capital fear-fully doubting their own ability to stand the social strain; and promptly become so interestedly busy that before long they simply haven't time to remember that they are "not able to do very much."

Especially under the Sign of the Elephant—at least in our expe-rience under two Republican regimes—it took the stamina of a six-day bicycle rider to get through New Year's Day alone.

The festivities generally began at midnight on New Year's Eve with the glittering McLean Ball, where Mrs. McLean, wearing that famous blue bauble, the Hope Diamond, as the central sun of a whole constellation of jewels, and usually in one of her favorite sequin gowns to add to the brilliance of the evening, kept open house until the last guests tore themselves away just in time to catch forty winks and appear at the White House in either formal morning clothes or full dress uniforms in time for the President's official reception at eleven in the morning. To this came the diplo-matic corps and their wives, for a New Year's reception by the chief of state to the diplomats resident in his capital is a tradition the world over; and in Washington our own official families were in-cluded as well, until this part of the list had to be shrunk to "men only" so that the White House could be ready on schedule for the President's public reception in the afternoon, when it was the good old democratic custom from time immemorial for the butcher, the baker, and the candlestick maker to line up for a chance of grasping the Chief Executive's hand and wishing him joy of the season.

One of Washington's pet White House legends goes back to a day when President Taft was the upholder of this custom. A little tailor who had, so to speak, once done some custom upholding for him decided to join in the New Year respects to his exalted patron, even though it entailed hours of standing in line.

As at last he reached the Presidential presence, he said, in an overawed whisper, "Don't you remember me, Mr. President? I made yer pants!"

"Of course, of course!" the President boomed kindly, if vaguely, as he gave him about the two-thousandth handshake of the afternoon. "Delighted to see you, Major Pants!"

Meanwhile (to get back—or forward—to the Republican New Year's Days we remember) official Washington would have dashed away from the White House morning reception just in time to arrive at noon at the Pan-American Union for the breakfast (really a lavish buffet luncheon) which was always given by the Secretary of State and his wife in honor of the diplomatic corps, the Foreign Relations and Foreign Affairs Committees of the Senate and the House, and the State Department higher-ups. How some of the guests who boasted proudly that they hadn't had a wink of sleep managed the Pan-American's monumental marble staircases with no antidote to last night's champagne but a cup of black coffee, is still a mystery.

Then the older and stouter diplomats, who were still trying to wear the expensive gold-braided uniforms they had had made in younger and slimmer days, hurried off as soon as they could to change into more comfortable clothes for the afternoon's social rounds. The day was only beginning.

By three in the afternoon everyone had set forth on "Cabinet calls." All the rest of the Cabinet held open house that day; and with apparently every military and naval officer and his wife out to pay their respects to the Secretary of War or of the Navy, the line of motors at these houses would stretch for blocks, until many callers, in sheer desperation, would beg the bitter-enders to act as proxies, so that often those who did finally get in would leave a fistful of visiting cards at a time. In addition the Chief Justice's was a mecca for all of official Washington during the afternoon. And a very great gentleman and a very great lady—Charles Evans

Hughes and Mrs. Hughes—entertained both as Secretary of State and as Chief Justice within a few years.

By five o'clock, having crisscrossed the town from end to end, everyone headed for Fort Myer, Virginia, to pay respects to the Army's Chief of Staff. After which the die-hards came back to town for the two or three intimate cocktail parties which were sure to be on the schedule.

Yet with all this animated ricocheting—New Year's being just a concentrate of the usual whirl—the Washington of the twenties seems, nevertheless, on looking back, a quiet place: like an island of lighthearted existence one has sailed away from and can recall but not really see again through intervening weather. On the face of things it was the later Washington that grew more quiet, for with the Roosevelt administration one time-honored social occasion after another went by the board. Of the great New Year's observances, only the McLean Ball, being unofficial, lasted until Pearl Harbor. By the inner feel of things, however, the contrast goes the other way around. Perhaps Washington as a whole had nearly its share of the brassy tone and fevered pace we remember as the age of hot mammas, hip flasks, gangster heyday, and Florida boomtime. Probably it had full share of that opposite, equally characteristic strain of the twenties epitomized nowhere more clearly than in two Presidents: one who was everything the name Calvin suggests, and Herbert Hoover, so devout a Quaker that he could not even lend his presence to a patriotic occasion if it included dancing. But the Washington of the parties belonged a little to both worlds and not much to either. It was gay but not hot; decorous but not unbending. It was an island in the sea of prosperity.

During Prohibition it was fairly dry, yet blessed with unique islands within itself. In the beginning of the drouth, those parts of Washington that were legally "foreign soil" (that is, the ambassadorial establishments) loomed as a veritable mirage in the eyes of many Americans. Suddenly even a hitherto unnoticed bush-league-legation attaché found he had hundreds of bosom friends—all thirsty.

The smart embassies and legations—smart both ways—avoided the onslaught of thirsty hordes on the diplomatic hostesses' open days at home by blandly serving nothing stronger than tea or coffee, reserving alcoholic bounty for the invitational parties they gave on other days than the traditional Friday, when they could tell

39

exactly who was coming and know how they would behave. Some of the minor diplomats, however, were taken for the most intoxicated "rides" in Washington history. For one thing, they didn't have the strict and capable social secretaries the other diplomats did; and for another, supposedly disinterested American "friends" probably sold them the idea that Prohibition was their priceless opportunity to cement American friendship for their countries.

Perhaps the climax of the whole thing came when rotund Samy Pasha, the Egyptian Minister at the time, who was as stubborn as he was rich, insisted on giving an "open" tea dance every week (set for Tuesday afternoon instead of the sacred Friday, thus antagonizing both the diplomats and the Congressional set, whose "day" it was) featuring a bar whose flow seemed inexhaustible as the Nile. Naturally word got around town that the Egyptian Legation was the Great Oasis; and poor Samy was hurt and bewildered when the "important" people he had expected to attract were crowded out and repelled by numbers of uncouth and disreputable people no one had known existed in Washington, who utterly overran the Legation, to sweet Mme. Samy's consternation.

The Minister, nevertheless, insisted on keeping up his parties: until it was discovered that they were actually included in "What's Going On in Washington This Week," the throwaway given out at all the cigar stands in town; and then even he had to admit defeat.

This, however, was a Gilbertian exception. Decorous paying of official honor by traditionally prescribed pleasure was the rule of the day.

The Coolidges and the Hoovers, in turn, dined each year with the Vice-President, the Speaker, and every member of the Cabinet and their wives. Some of these dinners were quite small, yet especially engraved invitations were always sent out, even if the guests only numbered a dozen or so. Then, the Vice-President and his lady (first the Daweses, and later that famous trio, "Charley" Curtis and Dolly Gann and Mr. Gann), the Speaker and his wife, and the Secretary of State and his wife were expected to dine once a season at every embassy and legation in town, which meant fifty-two diplomatic dinners times three in honor of those three officials alone. The Longworths accepted only what they considered "amusing" invitations: in other words, to the smart diplomatic houses. The Secretary of State and Mrs. Stimson took it all with great dignity and poise, and rarely dined at home, unless they were entertaining at dinner themselves at Woodley, the beautiful old estate they bought in the heart of Washington. (With the New Deal, also this round robin was to be broken. Neither the Garners, the Bankheads, nor the Hulls have ever dined out except at the White House or on the most extraordinarily important occasions.)

Mrs. Dawes was one of those delicate, self-effacing women who came to Washington with great misgivings, and who went on to the even harder social obligations of the Court of St. James's with health and strength infinitely improved.

When General Dawes filled the Vice-Presidential chair Calvin Coolidge vacated on becoming President, Mrs. Dawes was under strict doctor's orders not to overtax her strength. That was one reason why they chose a house on Belmont Road with a wide covered porch overlooking a terraced garden, so that she could rest out of doors for several hours every afternoon except in the worst weather. Mrs. Dawes told us that she felt her place was by her husband's side, and that she would plan her days so as to be able to go out to dinner with him, no matter what else she might have to forego. And she told us, with surely pardonable pride, just before they left for London, that she had only missed keeping one dinner engagement in those four years, and that had not been for illness but because she wanted to spend the evening with her son who was passing through town.

One day in her long series of rising to occasions Mrs. Dawes landed me in a like spot. It was an afternoon when she and the Vice-President were giving a tea for the delegates to a Pan-American conference then meeting in Washington. I answered her card with an early arrival because I was having some people in for tea myself that day; and was met with an S.O.S. plea to assist her. Knowing that allowances would be made for a "Vice-Presidential command," I accepted Mother's offer to go home and take care of my party, and stayed to reap the harvest of twenty recent Spanish lessons. I had planned my own unorthodox course with an eye to social predicaments rather than classroom custom, determined I should at least be able to get through a dinner party with a "no speak Eenglish" South American partner. So, though quite unable to say, "My aunt's inkstand is on my uncle's table," I had a few sociable and anti-starvational phrases which I hoped would see me through. Señor Recinos, the very nice Minister of Guatemala, turned relentless. Refusing to speak English, which he does very well, he put me through the whole tea ritual in Spanish. Climactically I offered him a cup of tea exactly as ordered. He laughed, declining it. "Just wanted to see if you could really do it!" So did I, I omitted to remark.

Mrs. Dawes was the sweet, mild type of wife you somehow expect the strong, silent, hard-bitten type of military man to have. I'm sure she never tried to make the General over, for when he became our Ambassador to London he took his famous underslung pipe along to dinner parties however formal, just as he had in Washington. Fellow Americans abroad would whisper in shocked dismay to see him unconcernedly light up after the salad, but the English thought it merely showed his independence of character, and rather admired it.

At the Court of St. James's, Mrs. Dawes found herself in an even more exacting role than in Washington, for not only were there the endless social obligations of the most brilliant court in the world, but she also had to take care of a flood-tide stream of Americans touring London in those piping days of peace, as anyone who had ever seen the thousands who came to a Fourth of July open house at the Embassy can testify. But somehow she serenely managed to do it all, by whatever invisible ways she had worked out to save her strength.

It was the Daweses who were to be wand wavers for one of my most thrilling dreams-come-true; and as so often happens, it was a very casual remark that led to a memorable experience. We were in London the summer after the Daweses went there, which meant, for me, among other things, a chance to renew good times with lovable, lackadaisical Countess Rogeri, one of my closest friends during the years when "Dedo" Rogeri was counselor of the Italian Embassy in Washington. She was English, and was now the first lady of the Italian Embassy in London, since their ambassador was a bachelor. Taxiing somewhere one day, we came past Buckingham Palace, and she suddenly said, "Why don't you ask the Daweses to present you at Court? You know you have to *ask* to get there!"

"But Gwenda, how could I?" I said. "They have always been so wonderful to me; it might seem a holdup. And this *is* a Republican administration, and you know the terrific pressure our ambassador is always under from home for Court presentations."

"Oh, don't be so noble!" she, who was quite indifferent to such

The Calvin Coolidges

Sculptor Durig, President Hoover, and Swiss Minister Marc Peter

opportunities for herself, laughed exasperatedly. "After all, you may never know another ambassador of yours so well again, and you must take things when you can get them!"

So it came about that on a warm May evening the next year, I was on my way to Buckingham Palace, with my Court train and three white feathers, and a well-practiced curtsey, for the introduction royal.

The Curtis-Gann Vice-Presidential regime was a very different story.

Mr. Curtis, a perfect contrast to the strong, silent type of General Dawes, was easygoing and, above all, a good mixer. While his figure was no reminder that he had been a jockey in his younger days, his personality otherwise was completely unspoiled by his dramatic rise from the paddock to the Vice-President's rostrum in the Senate. He adored parties, and loved talking to people. Except for his dark complexion, he had almost none of the characteristics we expect to find in someone of Indian blood.

He had lived all the years of his widowerhood with his half sister, the kind but controversial Dolly Gann, and her husband; and he had no intention of leaving his beloved Dolly and Ed back in the suburban Macomb Street house of his Senate years when he moved to the glories of the Vice-Presidential suite at the Mayflower. From here all three would sally forth to a dinner in his honor at eight o'clock every evening.

And then Alice Longworth, who usually didn't care a fig for protocol as such, suddenly issued a call to battle. Never, she declared, would she permit a Vice-President's *half* sister to precede *her,* as the Speaker's wife! The famous feud was on.

It was never really a question of whether or not an unmarried official had the right to choose a member of his family as his hostess. Ailsa Mellon was her father's hostess while he was Secretary of the Treasury; General MacArthur had his mother as his hostess while he was Chief of Staff; farther back our only bachelor President, James Buchanan, chose his niece Harriet Lane to be official hostess of the White House.

No. The crux of the thing, according to Mrs. Longworth and the other embattled official wives, was that Mrs. Gann had a perfectly good *live* husband, whose status she was supposed to share "for better or for worse," and whom she was leaving in social oblivion at the foot of the table while she was seated at the host's right, opposite "Brother Charles," who as Vice-President invariably was the ranking guest. And as long as they could hold out, they refused to admit that she could play the double role of her brother's sister and her husband's wife at the same dinner party.

Ordinarily the rank and file of official wives would have had much more fellow feeling for the defendant than for Alice Longworth, who had consistently ignored them for so long, while Mrs. Gann was always as friendly and approachable as could be. But defense was not in Mrs. Gann's vocabulary. Joy of battle ran strong, and finesse was a weapon she scorned. The redoubtable Dolly was so overeager, and so jubilant whenever she won a round, that, human nature being what it is, feminine officialdom ranged itself more and more determinedly behind Mrs. Longworth the longer the fight went on.

Mrs. Gann, in every sense a robust personality, held her ground, with Brother Charles's complete approval; and when he used all the great influence of his Vice-Presidential position to support his devoted Dolly, Alice Longworth, for the first time in a very charmed life, had to admit defeat.

It had gotten so that everyone in Washington was afraid to ask Dolly to dinner until the matter was settled. The State Department refused even to discuss it. The chief of protocol was "out" whenever anyone called. Finally the British Ambassador, Sir Esmé Howard, who was then the dean of the diplomatic corps, called a meeting of the corps to determine how the crisis should be dealt with. They made the diplomatic decision that they would give Dolly the place the Vice-President demanded for her—and let American officials decide the question for themselves.

So Dolly, tall, florid, resplendent, like a ship in full sail, swept triumphantly with her "two boys" into every diplomatic dining room in town.

At the height of the battle I again found a small remark of mine making a loud noise in the papers, this time, to my relief, anonymously.

It came about this way. A few weeks before the Hoover-Curtis inauguration Mrs. Gann came in unexpectedly to one of our Tuesdays at home to return our call. Now, I liked Mrs. Gann sincerely; and the last thing I wanted in the world was to stir up the tempest in the official teapot more than it was just then. But, as is apt to happen at an official day at home, the people who were there at the moment didn't know each other very well, and, to make general conversation, Mother said to Mrs. Gann, "Aren't they going to name a new color for you, like Alice blue for Alice Roosevelt, and Helen pink for Helen Taft?"

Mrs. Gann turned to me and asked what I would suggest, and I, having a fatal passion for words beginning with the same letter (I think the classic thing to call it is "apt alliteration's artful aid") was just about to say, "How about Gann green?" when it dawned on me how poisonously apt it would seem under the circumstances, and I murmured something—anything—instead.

Soon after, Mrs. Gann left, and I, who had had the sense to keep still that long, was foolish enough to tell the others of my narrow escape. Evidently in some unacknowledged corner of my generally peaceable soul, the battle fever would have its way. The few who were there were hand picked to spread the story in every circle in Washington by dinnertime. And why not, if I couldn't keep it myself? The result was that by the next day the story began coming back to me, and it's a fact that two people out of three I met all that spring told it to me "in absolute confidence, my dear!" It spread through the newspapers, the magazines, the funnies, and even to Europe, as I found when we went abroad that summer.

The best of it was that within a few days it had been tacked on to Mrs. Longworth, to my great and cowardly delight, for I felt that she could afford to have said it much better than I could. To this day I don't know whether Mrs. Gann knows its real source, but if she does, I hope she understands that deliberate aim had exactly nothing to do with that stray shot heard halfway round the world.

Mrs. Gann was really a tremendous help to Brother Charles in many ways. I remember her telling me one day how, during the Vice-Presidential campaign tour, the handshaking got so strenuous that before it was over the candidate simply couldn't shake another hand. Mrs. Gann used to stand behind him and unobtrusively slip her hand through his exhausted arm, offering it cordially to unsuspecting handshakers, who went away pledged by this "personal contact" to vote for Curtis.

And speaking of the Vice-Presidency reminds me of something Mr. Curtis told me one night in the after-coffee session of a dinner at the Japanese Embassy. He mentioned that he was tired, as the

45

President had been receiving no official visitors and everyone had been coming up to the Capitol to see him instead. I asked if he saw everyone who came, even without credentials, and he said he did.

"But do you think that's safe, Mr. Vice-President?" I asked. "There are so many cranks and people like that, you know."

"There's not the slightest danger in the world from them," he assured me matter-of-factly. "Any fanatic is only interested in the chief of state. So far as I know, no one has ever tried to assassinate a Vice-President. Which makes it very safe for me!"

The other principal of the historic Gann-Longworth feud was fighting, of course, from an entrenched position. Not only was Alice Roosevelt Longworth the wife of the Speaker, but from her White House girlhood on she had probably been the most glamorous and original figure on the American social scene.

Her glamour, or charm, or whatever you prefer to call it, is a very baffling one. Sometimes you meet her and it simply isn't there. Then, in a second, she becomes intensely interested in something, and she turns it on like a searchlight which dazzles everyone in sight.

Probably no one was ever less weighted down by official responsibility. The whole time Nick Longworth was Speaker of the House, perhaps not a half dozen Congressional couples—unless they happened to be amusing or smart enough to be eligible for the little Longworth set—ever crossed the threshold of their house on Massachusetts Avenue, which was filled with the priceless wedding gifts that the governments of the world showered on President "Teddy" Roosevelt's daughter when she married the aristocratic young Congressman from Ohio. The one gesture she made religiously every year toward the House as a whole was to send Christmas cards jointly with the Speaker, her signature in one corner and his in the other, which I imagine went to every Congressional family.

Mrs. Longworth's legendary remark to some fledgling Congressmen's wives who somehow met her somewhere, and who innocently asked her when they might leave cards on her, is a Washington classic. "Oh," she is said to have said, "just shove them under the door any old time."

Nevertheless, Mrs. Longworth doesn't impress me as being really snobbish, at least in the usual social sense, though I do think she is an intellectual snob of the first water, to whom the company of the dull or banal is simply torture. What I mean to say is that while both the Longworths belonged by birth to the highest circles, and naturally most of their lifelong friends did too, I think Mrs. Longworth would be much more likely to take up some brilliant or amusing person who didn't "belong" than to put up with some stuffy bore who did.

You might think that anyone they did take up was very lucky. Yet it can sometimes lead to stark tragedy to be suddenly made an intimate of a set to which one has neither the money nor the stamina to belong.

For instance, while Nick Longworth was Speaker, a very attractive young Congressional couple came to Washington from Oregon. The young man played and sang extremely well, and as Nick Longworth was a really good violinist and adored music, they suddenly found themselves very much a part of the little Longworth set.

Had it been only a matter of music, it would have been all right; but also, night after night, they played bridge or poker for stakes which were a mere bagatelle if you happened to be a millionaire but were a crushing problem if you weren't. Besides, the games usually lasted most of the night. These gaieties generally took place at Mrs. James F. Curtis' house on F Street, with a special night shift of servants ministering. Later, when the ebullient Mrs. Curtis could, or would, no longer keep it up "for free," she turned the beautiful, cosy old house into the famous F Street Club, still the holy of holies for the same smart crowd, and run as much as possible in the same casual, informal way.

It was literally a killing pace, at least for the young Oregon Congressman, and for Nick Longworth, too, though miraculously he never once showed the slightest sign of morning-after wear and tear when he arrived at the Capitol. For one thing he had a very real and deep respect for the office of Speaker. For another, he had, it was said, a valet who could out-Jeeves Jeeves at his best, and had some secret formula of setting "the master" up with a massage, a potent potion, and an early morning horseback ride in Rock Creek Park so that he arrived at the Capitol clear-eyed and dignified. Thus he remained until the House adjourned, when he and Cactus Jack Garner, his bosom pal and arch political opponent, then Democratic leader of the House, would go off arm in arm, after a day of furious legislative battles, to join a couple of boon companions in a

47

very private office, in the serious business of imbibing a good time.

Nick Longworth had no financial or other worries that anyone knew of; but the pace killed him, just the same. The poor young Congressman literally worried himself to death, it was said, over all the debts he had incurred in Washington, and jumped off a bridge in Oregon, at the very beginning of a promising career.

The "F Street crowd" have rarely taken up diplomats: probably because they find few who are amusing enough to attract them. Then, too, from the diplomats' side, only those with big estates and large income to draw on, or those who are practically professional bridge experts, can keep up with the financial pace. And I have known quite a few level-headed diplomats who did qualify for the unwritten entrance requirements, yet refused to be drawn into that set because they realized that, once in, they would be expected to ignore everyone else, which seemed an inadequate way of representing their countries, no matter how superior the exclusive friends might be, or with what truth they might murmur, "Oh, my dear, do you really have to go there—they're so dreary!"

The Speaker, however, was one of the best mixers who ever lived, and the members of the House, on both sides of the aisle which separates the two parties, simply adored him. In one way his personality and Franklin D. Roosevelt's had much in common: good looks, charm, and humor, and the background of a great family tradition combined with a truly democratic outlook. The essential difference between them was that to Nick Longworth "a good time" or "a good line" were two things irresistible. Witness this merry motto of his: "I'd rather be tight than President!"

His popularity with the members, and Mrs. Longworth's unpopularity with many of their wives, came to a rather startling climax one night when the wives decided to "strike": the night of the annual reception given by the Congressional Club in honor of the Speaker and his wife. So far as I know, the story has never been told.

That day, a year or so before the Speaker's untimely death, a group of Congressional wives started a crusade against getting all dressed up and going to the club to honor, they feared, an impatient and indifferent Mrs. Longworth. In the end it was only the frantic pleading of their husbands "not to hurt Nick—after all, he's a prince!" that brought out enough people to make a fair showing at the reception. Someone must have given Mrs. Long-

48

worth a hint of what had been going on, for I have never seen her more animated and interested with her dearest friends than she was to the last and latest Congressional lady who passed the receiving line that night. She wore, as she so often does, a picture dress made of one of her priceless wedding-present oriental brocades, but was, as usual, without benefit of either coiffeur or cosmetics.

The one Republican couple except, of course, the Chief Justice and Mrs. Hughes, whose lustre was quite undimmed under the New Deal were Senator and Mrs. William E. Borah. The Lion of Idaho continued to roar at his daily press conferences, and his rare radio speeches carried enormous weight throughout the country.

And Mrs. Borah, blonde, beloved "Little Borah," went on her whimsical way, saying the most startling things in the most inno-cent voice, enjoying her lovely clothes even though "Billy" refused to accept the invitations showered on them so richly, and, although no one would guess it from looking at her or listening to her, doing so much good at Walter Reed and St. Elizabeth's hospitals, even with hopeless mental cases, that the Washington police would im-mediately make for the Borahs' apartment when one of her "boys" was reported missing at the hospital, for they knew they all went instinctively to her.

The Borahs worked out their differing social temperaments in the happiest way. The Senator was always browsing among his books and papers by eight o'clock every evening, so Mrs. Borah, who adored parties as much as he adored solitude, was dressed and ready to sit with him while he had his seven o'clock dinner, and then at eight, when he was already lost to the world in his library, she was off to a dinner party, from which she brought him, I am sure, a wealth of news and amusing stories. Sometimes, when we were picking Mrs. Borah up if we happened to be going to the same dinner, the Senator would bring her down to the car and have a little chat before we went on, but usually he was the most elusive of all Washington's famous figures.

For years Mother and I had a standing date with Mrs. Borah for the night of the White House diplomatic reception to make our stand together in the Green Room right up in the first row by the velvet rope; which often cost the Protocol Division some pointed looks to keep things moving, so many were the handshakes reached and kisses blown there as the Diplomatic Corps went by us in line.

49

We made a solemn promise to keep this yearly date, unless the Senator should become President and Mrs. Borah should take the First Lady's place beside him in the Blue Room. And if she had, I am willing to wager that even Mrs. Coolidge would have had to look to her laurels in a Republican First Ladies' popularity contest.

It was during the Coolidge administration, in December, 1927, to be exact, that my father became a member of the Foreign Affairs Committee. Legend (which the newspapers still dig up now and then) had it that, to satisfy Mother and me, he moved heaven and earth to be put on that committee, which admittedly has the most glamorous possibilities of any in Congress. To call the legend truth might provide a literarily satisfying echo of my first-chapter confession on how I became reconciled to the idea of having a Congressman in the family; but honesty forbids. It was really a case of being kicked upstairs, for his place on the Patents and Copyright Committee was a better political asset from the standpoint of our particular home district, and the change was made entirely without Father's knowledge. I well remember the party at the Canadian Legation when a member of the Foreign Affairs Committee came up and slapped him on the back saying, "Congratulations, Sol, I'm glad you're one of us!"—and the perfectly blank look (probably one of the few blank looks he ever gave anyone in his life) with which he replied before hitting the Legation ceiling.

The Coolidge and Hoover cabinets were both very strong on plutocracy, pulchritude, and pedigree. The two Secretaries of the Treasury—first Andrew Mellon and then Ogden L. Mills—could almost have settled the national debt between them. Pulchritude was very well represented by the beautiful brunette Mrs. Mills; the beautiful blonde Mrs. Pat Hurley, the wife of the Secretary of War; and the lovely, white-haired Mrs. Adams, the wife of the Secretary of the Navy. And as for pedigree, although many in the Cabinet, like Mr. Mills, could trace their descent from some of the proudest family trees in America, surely no name was so historic as that of Charles Francis Adams, one of the most delightful descendants who ever came to Washington, perhaps, for one reason, because he didn't take the family glory too seriously.

I suppose to anyone outside of Washington the elaborate social hierarchy of protocol and precedence, the omnipervasive attention to who-outranks-whom, must seem a most undemocratic phenomenon, especially since it became a national joke through the Dolly Gann problem. But system there must be, and fundamentally it is a democratic system in that it is the office, and not the man, that takes the rank and the place. Family, wealth, and social position simply do not enter into official rank at all.

Take, for instance, a man like Peter Goelet Gerry, who certainly has family, wealth, and social position to equal anyone in America. When he was defeated, to everyone's great regret, for re-election as Senator from Rhode Island in the Hoover landslide, what happened? On the third of March he was still placed at dinner where a Senator with his length of service should sit. But on the fourth of March, at the moment the new administration came in, he automatically went to the foot of the table; for in Washington it's the Congressional Directory, and not the Social Register, that decides. When he returned to the Senate, six years later, then and only then did he reacquire rank, and only in that place which any newly elected Senator would rate.

Because Washington has so many delightful people of tremendous official or diplomatic consequence who unapologetically and cheerfully live on nothing but their salaries (which, though comfortable, surely do not allow for great extravagance), inequalities of money make, on the whole, less social difference here than elsewhere. Of course, people who have great fortunes are equally unapologetic and cheerful about it, but they are apt to use them discreetly, for a flock of Rolls-Royces or a dinner table banked with orchids is much more likely to amuse Washington than to impress it.

Nevertheless, the Capital's own special hierarchy, impersonal though its basis may be, gives scope for social stress and strain as any ladder of distinction must do. After all, offices are filled by people, and surely it is not surprising that some take personal satisfaction not merely in the performance of the office but in its social respects. Nor is it strange that tinges of pride and envy lurk here and there. And there must be few of us, really, who cannot recall some characteristic triviality, at least, over which we have laughed and ruefully realized that "Pride goeth before a fall": as I did one day at an embassy tea where I met Mrs. Everett Sanders, who offered me a ride home.

It came to my mind that because Mr. Sanders was Secretary to the President, the proffered ride involved a White House car, no less, with a big gold crest on the door. So I laughingly told Mrs. Sanders it would be a special pleasure to make such a grand exit with her.

As she said to the carriage man, "Please call the White House car," I looked for him to be deeply impressed with our Presidential standing.

He, however, stolidly picked up his megaphone and called out, "Mrs. Whitehouse's car! Mrs. Whitehouse's car!" And amid our anticlimactic giggles, I foreswore all enjoyment of pomp and circumstance—at least temporarily.

4. There Was a Man Named Mussolini

This will be a chapter of incredibilities, to me, perhaps, as much as to you.

Tyrant, clown, and villain—you may never have thought of Mussolini in any other way. And now that he is just a crumpled, grotesque figure, whose deeds must still be paid for not only by the sufferings of the Italian people, whom even their enemies could not bring themselves to hate, but by our own sacrifices on Italian soil, it may even seem wrong to recall the now almost unbelievable past when he was acclaimed both as a man and as a leader.

"So you know Mussolini!" people used to exclaim, when nobody, least of all Mussolini, had even heard of a little man in Munich with a funny mustache who was to become his evil genius. And then how gradually came those changes ("And what do you think of your friend Mussolini *now?*") whose shocking signposts read: Ethiopia . . . Rome-Berlin Axis . . . Spain . . . Albania . . . Greece . . . Egypt . . . Libya . . . and surrender without peace.

Well, foresight is still a rarity, and hindsight no great compensation. Of one thing I am sure. It does no good to pretend a wisdom we lacked, retouching our pictures of the past to fit the unforeseen present. I once knew Mussolini as a friend, charming and human, tolerant, with a sense of humor. How I came to know him is at least a good adventure story, whether or not one may find in it food for other reflections.

To start at the beginning is to start with our first trip to Italy, when Mussolini was not even a name to America, and when d'Annunzio had just electrified the world and confounded the governments of Europe, including Italy's, by seizing the Adriatic port of Fiume, where he was entrenched literally as monarch of all he surveyed, having put every foreign consul out of town on the heels of the obstructing local officials.

I was still in school, and being in what William Gillette used to call "the zone of absolute certainty," I went down to Mr. Clinton Brainerd, president of the McClure Newspaper Syndicate and of Harper's, the publishers, with a list of exalted European victims for interviews and articles that would have staggered all the veteran foreign correspondents put together. There was only one proviso: *If* my father really would give me the European trip he had promised me that year.

Naturally, Mr. Brainerd agreed to publish such a series of articles as I guaranteed blithely to get, about Queen Mary, the Empress Eugénie, Pope Pius XI, Lloyd George, Clemenceau, Puccini, and more besides. For good measure, I also undertook to get Paderewski's memoirs signed up! From start to finish, even when the percentage of rash promises fulfilled proved really quite high, the whole venture remained for me at least half unbelievable.

When I came home with this glittering program *and* a publisher, Mother and Father could hardly refuse to go as soon as school was over. And just before we sailed, Mr. Brainerd decreed that if I really wanted to do something worth while which would startle the world, we would make straight for Fiume and get past the triple blockade to d'Annunzio. Since I had arranged to do a weekly article from abroad for the *New York Telegram*—looking back, I don't see how I ever did it—all the response I could make was to promise to "do" d'Annunzio as soon as I had stayed in Paris long enough to write enough sprightly stories for the *Telegram* to carry me over the weeks we might be in Italy.

In Paris we met Lady Luck, who made a fourth to our party from there on. For while we were planning how to get to Poland and Paderewski, we noticed across the restaurant some officers in a uniform we didn't know. Father went over to ask them which it was, and learned what you've already guessed. After a bit, when the conversation turned to Paderewski, as all Polish conversations in those days invariably did, one of the officers mentioned that the Prime Minister was in Paris at that very moment, just around the corner at the Ritz.

The next morning *we* were just around the corner at the Ritz, and in negotiation with his secretary—the French "*chef de cabinet*" sounds so much more important—Jan Ciechanowki, who later came as Polish Minister to Washington, and returned again as the Ambassador of the Polish government in exile. I offered Mr. Brainerd's offer, and without much trouble the premier-pianist agreed. I could send my first jubilant cable to New York, untroubled by any thought that the long drawn out negotiations would eventually fall through.

So we were off to Italy, with our Parisian friends' gloomy forebodings of murder and starvation in our ears, and what proved to be the most unnecessary luggage ever loaded: hampers of provisions in the baggage car. We had nothing to count on but my Italian, which had never been tried out in real life, and a card of introduction to d'Annunzio from Percy Mitchell, editor-in-chief of the Paris *Herald,* which even I didn't expect could be passed off as a *laissez passer* at those triple frontiers. We arrived at the Swiss-Italian border without a plan in our heads, except that we had to get off at Milan.

Some homesick Italian soldiers were lounging on the platform on the Swiss side, and while the customs inspectors did their interminable worst, we leaned out of the window and offered them some cigarettes—in those days, when the First World War was still a vivid memory, the universal open-sesame for establishing any contact in Europe.

I cautiously led the talk around to d'Annunzio and how to get to Fiume, but they had no ideas to offer. Finally, while the train was already moving and we were almost out of earshot, one of the boys called after us,

"Try the *Popolo d'Italia!*"

We had no idea what or where the *Popolo d'Italia* might be, except that it meant literally "the people of Italy," so there was still nothing left for us to do but to get off at Milan, and see if there was a *Popolo d'Italia* there.

We had been told to go to the Hotel Cavour, where all the great Italians, including d'Annunzio between his fantastic exploits, always stopped. And there, it seemed by a convenient magic, the next step was shown. The concierge promptly informed us that the *Popolo d'Italia* was not, as I had vaguely imagined, a department store, but a newspaper, and in Milan!

We set out at once for the address he gave us, came to a dingy and depressing building, through a courtyard, and up a dark stairway to the office of what appeared to be a thoroughly third-rate newspaper. I asked for the editor. A charming young man responded, explaining that he was the sub-editor; the editor was out but would surely be back after midnight, as they would be waiting for the returns on the primary elections being held that day. Would we come back?

We went out into the Milanese morning not at all sure whether we would or not. A dingy little Milanese office, and Fiume: what possible connection? Lady Luck must have leaned again on the affirmative scale; otherwise I might never have met Mussolini, for he was the absent editor of the *Popolo d'Italia!*

After midnight, the place looked more disreputable than ever. But when we were ushered into a tiny, smoke-filled room, heavy with the scent of strong Italian coffee and crowded with newspapermen, I suddenly forgot everything but the pair of electric eyes on me—the eyes of Mussolini.

It was an impression there is no need to retouch. Totally unknown, and in the most unawesome background, he still had the most powerful personality I have ever met. So powerful, that the next day I *had* to send a cable to the *New York Telegram,* saying that somehow, someday, this man was bound to dominate all Italy. That is what I thought of him then. What he thought of me, an absurdly inexperienced American girl, solidly chaperoned by a mother and father, appearing in the wee hours of the morning on election night and asking to go to Fiume, I cannot even vaguely imagine.

Mussolini wasn't then, and never has been, melodramatic in private life. His words were clipped, and he gestured very rarely. He was like a leashed lion.

And now, probably to see if I was really serious, he began hurling questions at me in Italian. Why had I come? What were my motives in wanting to go to Fiume? Did I know anything about the Italian situation? Then he switched abruptly to American politics, and of course asked that inevitable European question: "What is the difference between a Republican and a Democrat?" My answers must have satisfied him, for on dismissing us he promised to get in touch with me at the Cavour during the day.

Before the morning was out, the usually imperturbable concierge knocked at my door, to say in a very awed voice that "Signor Mussolini himself" would like to speak to me. Would the *signorina* be good enough to come down to the telephone booth in the lobby, as there were no phones in the rooms.

Mussolini merely wanted to ask if we would come over at once. Leaving the booth, I found a curious crowd of hotel guests had been watching, even if they couldn't hear. Something more than mere interest in his personality must account for this, I thought.

Guarded replies to persistent questions told me that Mussolini was coming to be considered the power behind d'Annunzio's Fiume throne; all the money and provisions that enabled the poet-dictator to hold his seized city were collected and delivered, it was believed, through that little office of the *Popolo d'Italia*. Well, then! our soldier boy at the frontier had certainly put us on the right road.

As we arrived for the morning-after visit, I saw the charming side of Mussolini for the first time. He smiled that surprisingly likable smile, and chatted quite humanly; we even found we had mutual friends at the Metropolitan Opera in New York. Finally, mentioning he had yet to prepare for his speech against the Socialists in the Cathedral Square that night, he said we had better get down to business. He pulled some sheets of writing paper toward him and began a series of longhand letters to his agents at Venice, Trieste, Abbazia (the last town this side of Fiume), in Fiume, and to d'Annunzio himself, asking them to give us every aid and attention, and signed, with a lordly flourish, simply "Mussolini."

"Good luck," he said, giving them to me with a few instructions. "Come in to see me when you get back and tell me what you found."

I tried to thank him for this unstinted help, and then remarked as we were leaving that we would hear him speak in the square that night.

"No!" he said, like a clap of thunder, all the geniality gone in an instant. "I do not wish you to. It may be dangerous. There may be clashes between my men and the Socialists."

"Oh, please!" I protested. "Surely we can listen a few minutes after we have dinner in the Galleria?"

"Where will you dine?" he demanded, as there were many restaurants in Milan's great glass-roofed arcade.

"At the Grand' Italia."

"You can dine there if you are home by eight," he said, with finality.

I think we would have sneaked into the forbidden Piazza del Duomo anyway to see what was going on, if two *carabinieri*—the Italian police—had not come up to our table at the Grand' Italia just as we were finishing some of their superlative pears in wine, and asked politely if I were *"la signorina* Bloom?"

When I answered an astonished yes, they went on, still politely but firmly, that they had orders to escort us immediately to our hotel, and to wait until they saw us safely upstairs.

There was no doubt where the orders originated, or how hopeless it was for us to try to hear that speech, so we gave in and followed them home to the hotel, where they delivered us into the elevator and saw us out of sight. The next day the papers reported serious clashes in the square, and we really felt grateful for Mussolini's care of us, though a bit disappointed that we missed the excitement.

But we had plenty of that ahead, on the way and in Fiume itself. How fantastic it seems, now, that we deliberately walked into all that danger, when we never take the slightest chances at home! It must be that taking risks abroad is very much like being a spendthrift with foreign money—it simply doesn't seem real.

Neither does it seem real that we were finally stranded, in the car we had hired in Trieste, at the last Italian outpost; or that we somehow, with Mussolini's letters and our own persuasions, rode into Fiume through the three barriers serpentined across the road so that a car could only crawl corkscrew-wise between them: rode into the forbidden city huddled on the mail sacks in the back of the car, in a driving rain. Or that we found the only good hotel in Fiume, the Europa, had been commandeered by d'Annunzio's officers, whose gallantry in giving up the two best rooms to us we appreciated, though with a shade of wondering if they hadn't left a dictaphone in a locked wardrobe. Or how we woke up in the morning to look out on a beautiful harbor threateningly inhabited by a double row of warships, the inner ones those d'Annunzio had seized, and the outer ones the Allied squadron, with their guns trained on our windows. No, it was not a nervous fancy. The guns pointed exactly in our direction, for the hotel, located on the waterfront, stood at the foot of the hill crowned by the white marble Governor's Palace, where d'Annunzio now made his headquarters. It was the first real danger any of our usually timid trio had ever faced.

I sent my letter at once to the Commandante, as everyone called d'Annunzio, and his first recognition of it was to send his own aide, with a nice young Fiuman soldier who was to be *my* aide during our whole stay, and who had instructions to show me anything I wanted to see and let me speak to anyone, high or low, from whom I wanted to get impressions or information. Soon Mother and I found ourselves bewilderingly popular with the smart and charming officers, many of them of the best families in Italy, who had followed d'Annunzio into Fiume to claim for the Italian nation, and in spite of Italy itself, what they considered, and I was beginning to understand, was a truly Italian population.

The reason for our popularity was very simple. We had no competition. Aside from the wives and daughters of the simple townspeople, every lady had left the city long before. So while we waited for d'Annunzio's dramatically postponed interview, we found ourselves flooded with invitations for luncheon, tea, dinner, or anything else we would accept.

One day, as we were returning to meet one of the naval officers for tea at the hotel, whom should we see hurrying along—with one half of his magnificent Italian hair shaved off to the scalp!— but that same officer. We had not yet had sight of d'Annunzio, so we couldn't understand that, with true Italian hero worship, every young officer, no matter how good-looking he might be, considered it the greatest possible honor to be permitted by the Commandante to shave off his hair completely, in proud imitation of d'Annunzio's utterly hairless head, and so become one of the envied *Teste di Ferro,* or Iron Heads. Those who were not naturally as unnaturally thin as their hero starved themselves almost to death to copy him in figure as well as in face. But our young naval aristocrat was hurrying back only half glorified, because he had discovered when the barber was half through that he was late for our engagement.

Frivolities in plenty; yet one was constantly aware that they were merely surface gloss on a very serious situation: an issue of war and peace important to all Europe, and directly involving the happiness and prosperity of a whole city. We became deeply imbued with the spirit and the courage of all these people, protectors and protected, before we ever met the man who was the brain and heart of the whole thing.

The commander we finally met in his luxurious quarters in the palace was the new d'Annunzio. Almost every trace of the great lover, the great sophisticate, was gone, and in their place was a very serious soldier, impressive in spite of his slenderness, his baldness, and his total lack of ordinary good looks. It was hard to imagine him in his earlier character of the *charmeur,* who in his Parisian days would earn fortunes on occasion to pay for a fabulous jewel that had caught his passing fancy in a shop window. Seeing him so sincere in an utterly different role, one had difficulty to credit the old d'Annunzio as anything but legend. Nor would one easily have believed a true prophecy of the third d'Annunzio, who was to live a lonely but magnificent life at the villa on Lake Garda as Prince di Montenevoso, who could only be reached through his own "ambassador" at Brescia, seventy-five miles away; who had his letters delivered all over Italy by his own private messenger, and burned all his mail unopened. His last home was the beautiful Villa Vittoriale, gift of the Italian government (after Mussolini had come into power) with a princely pension to keep it up. There he led an almost monastic life, with strange rules and regulations which he imposed on the few guests he agreed to receive, whom he always sped on their way with gifts of fabulous value.

But the d'Annunzio we knew in Fiume was a very practical and soldierly one, burning with the one desire to have the world realize that this was not a romantic exploit but a crusade for freedom.

He received us often in the ten days we were there, and finally, when we had to go, he had three of his most daring officers drive us in his own car on a wild night ride back over the mountains to Trieste.

When we came to say good-by, he gave me the Gold Star of Fiume, "for valor." Then, before we left, he took from the sleeve of his uniform his own gold-embroidered insigne, made by the women of Fiume, and pronounced me a captain of the Arditi, the intrepid shock troops of the Italian army! I thought of those guns in the harbor, and accepted it proudly. (And sometimes reminded myself of it later, when trying hard to retain composure in flash-bulb surroundings.) Next, he gave me some of his books, inscribed with dedications that only he could think of, and as the climax, a photograph inscribed "To Vera Bloom, Citizen of Fiume—from the First Citizen of Fiume, Gabriele d'Annunzio." Finally, he entrusted me with some letters and cablegrams, which I promised to send off from Venice, never dreaming what a story *that* would be.

When we reached Venice, all dire predictions of our murder or starvation having proved untrue, we went straight to the general post office to send those letters and cables. One letter was to his wife, born the Duchessa di Gallese, with whom, although they had been separated for years, he was still on excellent terms. There was a cable to the United States Senate, and another to Samuel Gompers, the president of the American Federation of Labor, setting forth d'Annunzio's side of the Fiume question. Mr. Gompers was an old friend of ours, so we included a personal cable of our own and, all commissions accomplished, thought no more about it.

As soon as we were back in Milan, we went to thank Mussolini; but he had very little time or patience for thanks.

"Can you write what you have seen?" he demanded.

"Yes."

"Then I will give you my own column on the front page of the paper tomorrow. Whatever you may write, for or against, not one word will be changed."

I went home to do it, and the next morning, under an introduction signed by Mussolini, in the first column of the first page of the *Popolo d'Italia,* that article appeared, word for word.

When we went to thank him again and say good-by, we found him stamping up and down, brandishing a newspaper, and in the only real rage I have ever seen him in.

Naturally, I thought he was brandishing the *Popolo d'Italia,* and anxiously began trying to remember what I might have said to cause such fury. Then I saw it was not the *Popolo d'Italia* he was holding but the *Avanti,* the ultra-Socialist paper. The cause of his anger? Those telegrams we had sent and forgotten about in Venice! Some Socialist working in the post office had given copies to the *Avanti,* which forthwith printed a horrible article—the one Mussolini was brandishing—linking a nefarious Signorina Bloom with d'Annunzio, Mussolini, and Gompers, whom they called the "plaything of the plutocrats." It was unrestrained scurrility, and Mussolini insisted that the minute we got to Rome we should go to our Ambassador and demand through him an open apology from the *Avanti.*

In the train, I felt as if accusing strange eyes were recognizing me; but long before we got to Rome, we all cooled down and concluded that to make an issue of it would only result in amplifying a small blast in a little Italian Socialist sheet to a loud noise in the

American press. We let it drop, much, I am sure, to Mussolini's displeasure.

In Naples we heard that he had run for parliament in the recent election, had been defeated, and then imprisoned. Back in America, we heard that he was forming a new party of the youth of Italy, who were utterly disgusted at the way the old-school statesmen were letting the Socialists drive the country to the very brink of bolshevism, with the daily general strikes we could remember so well paralyzing the country more and more. We thought of the day in November when we had gone to see Puccini, who was working on a new opera at his hunting lodge near Viareggio—a fashionable summer resort left entirely to the townspeople during the winter months—and had seen men marching down the main street carrying Red banners and shouting over and over again, *"A basso la borghesia! A basso la borghesia!"* ("Down with the bourgeoisie!") It made us feel a much greater chill of fear than all the warships in Fiume.

Then, two years later, out of a blue sky came the March on Rome. Mussolini became world-famous in a night, the only man in history who had ever staged a revolution for his king.

No one in America knew anything about him, and an article I had in the papers the next Sunday was the only one that could give a first-hand picture of the man who had fulfilled my intuitive prophecy about him so soon. Naturally, I had offers on every hand to go back to Italy and get the interview from him which he refused to give to anyone. That spring, Father having been elected to Congress meanwhile, and the House being in session, only Mother and I sailed for Naples. Would Il Duce, the dictator, remember those whom Mussolini, the obscure editor, had known?

We planned a motor trip through Sicily to precede our own march on Rome. But first, a day in Naples—already orderly and miraculously free from beggars under the new regime. Mussolini had gotten rid of the beggars by giving them a month to make up their minds whether they preferred to go to a hospital (if they were really helpless), to one of the African colonies, or to work!

Naples to us meant the terrace of Bertolini's Hotel; there we made our headquarters until it was time for the Palermo boat to sail that evening. And at luncheon on the terrace, drinking in the blue beauty of the Bay, we were surprised to see some friends from

New York, who had started months ago on their honeymoon without hinting their destination. They had just arrived from Sicily, and when we said we were on our way there, they observed, "Oh, of course; you must be going over to see Mussolini!"

We must have looked utterly blank, for they went on, "Don't you *know* that he has left for Sicily on an official tour on a battleship? He has taken most of his cabinet along, and the Sicilians are in a great state, because no plans have been announced, and he is likely to appear anywhere at any time."

"Then," we answered, "we shall just go ahead with our unambitious motor trip and not try to bombard any battleships."

We arrived in Palermo after an overnight trip on an awful old boat called the *Italia,* which I devoutly hope has been scrapped long ago, and were greeted by a bad sirocco, a sandstorm straight from Africa, through which we could faintly see the outlines of Mussolini's man o' war in the harbor from our windows at the beautiful Villa Igea.

Siroccos always last for three days, which gives one a fine feeling of finality, and when it let up a bit, we went down to the American Express to rent a car, a chauffeur, and a guide who could speak both Italian and Sicilian—two quite different languages—so that we should have two strong men, with two serious-looking revolvers, to protect us through Sicily. In spite of the sirocco we had the optimism to take an open car, so that we could "see all the scenery." Well, we not only saw it all but absorbed it. Particles clung so cruelly to our complexions that by the time we got to Rome we had to go into seclusion for a few days until we were presentable again.

Our honeymooning friends had been right: nothing could be learned about Mussolini's movements. So we started off on the route we had planned, wondering if our paths might cross, alternating between "Why not?" and "Nonsense, most unlikely." Our first stop was to be Girgenti, to see the marvelous Grecian temples that are one of the great glories of Sicily. (One may hope they have survived; at least the fighting around Girgenti when the liberating armies in 1943 began their hard Italian victories, was not so heavy as elsewhere on the island.)

Driving into the town late in the afternoon, much the worse for wear since we had had a sample of every possible climate during the day, we saw that the streets had been cleared and were being carefully patrolled; there was a great feeling of excitement in the air. Ah ha! Could it be? Yes, it was quite true. Il Duce was to be guest of honor at a tea at the Temple of Hercules within an hour!

We went to the hotel and hurriedly repaired ourselves as well as we could. In the car again, hastily making for the temple, we were stopped every moment by Fascisti guards and soldiers. Fitful progress having brought us to the officer in charge, we produced our passports, and letters from the Secretary of State and from Governor Al Smith of New York, and all the other identifications we had. They *looked* impressive enough, he admitted; but not being able to read English, how could he tell that they really said what we said they said?

Luckily there was an Englishman within fetching distance, a Captain Hardcastle who was spending his own fortune restoring the temples. On his vouching for our letters, we might pass, but only as far as a little hill opposite the temple, where waiters and caterers in a state of frantic excitement, well guarded by Fascisti, had erected booths where they were preparing tea and cakes, and ices, for it was a broiling afternoon. Chaperoning the buffet was a privilege for which we had at that moment no taste; but no matter how I pleaded, we were not to move an inch until the Mayor arrived.

At length that gentleman and his staff, in full afternoon dress, top hats and all, appeared, and I was allowed to approach. After eloquent persuasion, and probably to forestall more of the same, he agreed to let us stand where Mussolini would pass, on my word of honor that I would not speak to Il Duce.

It sounded like a very cramping compromise, but what could one do? I gave my word, and we crossed over into the shadow of the temple.

I had promised not to speak to Mussolini, but no mention had been made of his executive secretary, Marquis Paulucci. So when I heard that the Marchese was standing near by, I went over and introduced myself, explaining that I had come all the way from America to see the Prime Minister, and that I had known him before.

The Marchese was very suave. Also quite clear. It would be impossible for the Prime Minister to see me now, and he very greatly doubted whether it would be worth our while to go on to Rome, as His Excellency had made inflexible rules . . .

At this most discouraging moment His Excellency himself, fol-

Dolly and Edward Gann

H. H. Ras Destu Demtu of Ethiopia and
Jefferson Patterson at the White House

Mussolini (*in rear seat*) in Sicily, 1924

lowed by a cortége of dignitaries, all equally high-hatted and spatted, turned the corner of the great, tawny, time-stained temple where we were standing.

He gave me one hard look and exclaimed, all friendliness and astonishment, *"Ma, Vera Bloom, che cosa fa qui!"* ("Vera Bloom! What are you doing here?") I hesitated a moment, thinking of my word of honor to the Mayor. But I was *not* speaking to him, I was *answering* him; an entirely different thing!

So, clear of conscience, I explained that Mother and I had come all the way to Italy to see him, and told him what an injustice I had done him in worrying whether he would have forgotten us.

We had a long, happy chat, and at last, promising to see me as soon as we got to Rome, and to give me any kind of an article I wanted, he turned to Marchese Paulucci and, commissioning him to stay with us for the rest of the afternoon, bade him hurry to get us some ices. The Marchese became our devoted cavalier, until he had to join Mussolini in the car to drive back to the warship, and they both turned and bowed and smiled at us until they were out of sight.

Our guide and chauffeur, having watched all this from our old vantage point with the caterers, were so overcome that they simply lost their heads, and spread the news all over the hotel, where Mother and I found ourselves suddenly treated like royalty, and even offered the royal suite. Next day we started off again, seeing no reason why luck shouldn't strike twice or even thrice on the same touring car; but in all the rest of our ten days in Sicily, we heard no hint that Mussolini was anywhere near.

We still trailed clouds of glory, however, thanks to our two protectors. Once, along a lonely road, a peasant came up and stopped us to speak to our guide. Surely a bandit, we thought. A word or two, and he let us go on. A moment later we heard a shot behind us, and were sure all was over.

Nothing had hit us but fright, we soon realized; no confederates leaped out to surround the car; and we went on to the next town to find the whole population in the streets, all the church bells clanging, and everyone shouting and waving. I asked Vincenzo, our courier, what it was all about, and he said proudly that it was all for us.

It was! The peasant we had met had been the town's lookout for Mussolini, and when he had stopped us, Vincenzo had told him that we were Mussolini's party; the shot had been the signal to ring the bells and call the people. They were almost as wild with excitement as if it had been Mussolini himself. Vincenzo really believed that we were Mussolini's party—hadn't he seen it with his own eyes? So there was nothing for us to do but to bow and smile at the crowds as if we really were.

We arrived in Rome, our minds a mosaic of the Greek and Roman and Saracen and Bourbon impressions one takes away from Sicily, and our faces so weatherbeaten that we hid in the Excelsior Hotel for days, not thinking it auspicious to remind Il Duce at once of his promise to see me.

A great state occasion was preparing just then: the opening of parliament by the King. The galleries of the Senate in Rome, which is a converted Renaissance palace, are quite small, and it is very difficult to get a ticket for them on any day, but almost impossible for the opening of parliament unless you have either court or political connections; and so I hardly hoped to witness Mussolini's glory on this occasion. The unlooked-for chance to do so came along with one of the most singular gifts ever tendered to me.

The first person to find us in our retreat at the Excelsior, as it happened, was an Italian senator whom we had known in New York. He had come with a letter of introduction from dear friends of ours in Italy, and when I say we had taken care of him for a month, the accent is on care, and the tone is strained. He didn't speak a word of English, and I had to interpret for him hours at a time when we were with him, although we had arranged that others would help him at his hotel. A mere hour of conversational translating can be more exhausting than a whole week of expressing one's own thoughts in a foreign language, unless one has the very rare natural gift of a born interpreter, which I definitely have not.

Italian senators were impressive dignitaries, appointed by the king for life. This one, we knew, was one of the richest men in Italy. Considering all the circumstances, we were not surprised to see him come bearing a gift.

The surprise came when we unwrapped it. Behold: a large paper Easter egg in which a few stale chocolate candies rattled lonesomely. It was now the end of May, and Easter had been early that year.

By and by the Senator rashly disclosed that he had one ticket for the opening of parliament, and asked if I would like to go. I

66

promptly accepted, supposing he had realized, himself, that the Easter egg was a rather "minus" reciprocation, if he really wanted to reciprocate to us.

But the next day he was back, saying that he felt it his duty to warn me against using the ticket, as I would probably be trampled to death if I tried to get to the Senate that morning! I thanked him for his consideration, but remarked that if all the ladies of the Court and of the diplomatic corps thought it safe to go, I, too, could summon confidence in Fascist discipline.

So the Senator departed, reluctantly leaving the precious ticket behind him, and I will give him the benefit of a doubt: perhaps he really didn't know that the arrangements at the Senate were as perfect as they could possibly be. Every section of the gallery had its own entrance from the street and its own staircase to the gallery, with ushers in black and silver uniforms at every few paces, so that you practically stepped from your motor to your seat.

Nearly everyone had opera glasses, which amused me, as the moment you produce opera glasses in the Senate Gallery in Washington you are firmly told by an attendant to put them away.

Parliament and onlookers assembled, the principals made their entrances: first, the premier, Mussolini, in full ceremonial uniform and wearing Italy's highest decoration, the Collar of the Annunziata, which made him a cousin of the King. Could there have been a greater contrast from the Mussolini of that little smoke-filled office in Milan?

The Queen, strikingly tall and dark, entered her box, curtseying low again and again to the applause that greeted her, and closely followed by Crown Prince Umberto, who was quite as good-looking in his dark, slim Italian way as the Prince of Wales was in his blond British one. The Prince was then not quite twenty-one, which accounted for his being with the Queen, and not near his father at the throne. The upbringing of a prince of the House of Savoy has been rigidly prescribed for centuries; friends of mine in the Prince's household assured me that he was never once allowed to go out alone until he came of age.

And then at last the King, so short, in spite of the exaggeratedly tall military cap he wore, and, probably, the built-up heels, that he had to sit on the very edge of the throne and stretch his toes to be able to touch the floor. And grouped all around him was the six-foot magnificence of the Duke of Aosta, the Duke of Spoleto, the

Duke of Apulia, and his other cousins, all as tall as his son. Nevertheless *he* was king; his word calling the parliament into session was the *raison d'être* and climax of all this splendid formality. Mother had watched the beginning of it, the state procession from the royal palace through the golden-sanded streets, from a friend's balcony; so between us we had seen the whole colorful ceremony.

Soon after, I left a letter for Mussolini at the Chigi Palace, the Ministry of Foreign Affairs, which housed his office. And then began that self-inflicted imprisonment that everyone who is waiting for an important interview knows. You are afraid to leave the hotel for more than a few minutes at a time, lest the summons come—and the opportunity vanish—while you are out.

To make things even more difficult, I had already made contacts at the Vatican so that I could carry out my hopeful promise to write an article about Pope Pius XI, with whom we had had the honor of being received in semiprivate audience, and whose saintliness and goodness made an impression on me that has never been dimmed. This was before the Concordat with Mussolini, and I was in constant dread that I would receive a summons from some high Vatican dignitary at the same time that Mussolini might wish to see me.

That, indeed, happened; but fortunately in connection with a later appointment than the first one we were awaiting so nervously. In the eventual dilemma, I relied on a very wise old Roman friend of ours, who counseled that since the appointment at the Vatican was with an archbishop and not a cardinal, and since, after all, Mussolini held the rank of chief of state, I could only request the archbishop to change the time. When the Archbishop received us in the awe-inspiring magnificence of his Vatican apartment in the last of a long row of superb reception rooms, he asked some rather coldly pointed questions about my appointment with the Prime Minister. But apparently he could see how sincerely concerned I was about the difficulty, because during several later visits he supplied interesting material for the article on His Holiness; and to my deeply grateful surprise he was even instrumental in the conferring of a photograph of the Pope personally inscribed to me with a special Papal absolution for a non-Catholic, which has always been one of my greatest treasures.

On that first occasion of anxious waiting for the Duce's summons, we were prepared to undergo a long uncertainty, for I knew of influential callers who had cooled their heels in Roman hotels for weeks awaiting word from Mussolini. But long before the day I had set for beginning to hope in earnest, the telephone rang about four-thirty in the afternoon. It was a voice from the Chigi Palace saying that His Excellency would receive me at five! Only half an hour to dress and make it by slow, horse-drawn *carozza* past the Queen Mother's Palace and down the Via Trittoni to the Chigi Palace; not to speak of finding the questionnaire I had been given with a handsome contract from the International News Service if I could get Mussolini to answer a dozen ticklish questions which he had been refusing to discuss ever since his coming into power.

Just before five, nevertheless, Mother and I, having presented credentials at the little office at the entrance, were on our way up the grand marble staircase, with an usher waiting for us at the top to lead us into the first of a seemingly endless series of reception rooms, all of that surpassing magnificence that becomes so commonplace in Rome. Generals, clerics, diplomats, and simple people all were waiting patiently for their turn to see the Premier. The only difference was that the more important they were, the more salons they passed through before they were asked to be seated, and the less literally was that invitation accepted. The farther one progressed, the more one was surrounded by impatient pacings up and down.

Although we attained to one of the more jittery rooms, sober survey convinced us that our turn could hardly come that evening. However, a young secretary brought the hope-renewing message that His Excellency asked our patience and would see us soon. About every fifteen minutes another secretary would repeat the performance. It must have been nearly seven o'clock when we were beckoned to, and led through some last magnificent anterooms to the door of Mussolini's famous office—that huge square room, dim and gorgeous, with the big flat desk, always so uncluttered, at the farthest corner from the door, so that there was an endless, awesome walk under those X-ray eyes, which surely gave him time to take the measure of anyone who came to see him.

There were two great armchairs placed facing his across the desk, which, although we didn't know it then, were the barometer of a very cordial reception. Most visitors found no chairs in sight.

His first question was, "Tell me, have I changed?"

"Not with me, *Excellenza!*" I assured him, "but after seeing you at Girgenti, at the Senate, and here, how could I say you haven't?"

Just then a servant brought him a huge thick white cup full of steaming coffee, so I added, "No, I take it back. That is surely the same unbreakable crockery you had at the *Popolo d'Italia,* which *proves* you haven't changed!"

That put him in excellent humor, and we spent at least an hour and a half laughing and gossiping, for he loved to hear the fantastic tales the American papers wrote about him. His favorite posture was to put a great pile of books on the corner of the desk near my chair, and stand leaning his elbows on them, looking at me very directly.

Finally I showed him my questionnaire, which he was able to read in English, although he had not yet begun to speak it at that time. He promised to answer everything in writing, and to see us soon. Not knowing how it was his custom to conclude an interview, I had asked him beforehand to let us know when we were to go. So at last we said a grateful good night, and, starting for the grand staircase, which looked rather dizzying after all the excitement we had had, we were relieved and surprised to be led instead to a special private elevator; which was, the usher told us as it went slowly down, the greatest compliment of all His Excellency had paid us.

Of course, at home Mother wouldn't have thought of going with me for an interview; but in Italy, where it was unheard of for a young girl so much as to take a walk unchaperoned, and where, indeed, it is extremely rare to see any Italian lady on the street alone, we always did at the Romans do.

I heard no more from the Chigi Palace for some days, although we hovered faithfully around the hotel. Now came the day of that most popular Roman holiday, the *Festa di Divin' Amore,* the Feast of Divine Love, for which every Roman cab driver and little shopkeeper saves all the year long, lira by lira, so that he can enjoy one great festive progress through the Campagna in a fantastically decorated carriage in which he sits with his wife, proud in calico dress and rented diamonds, and all the bambinos. The ritual refreshment is yard-long loaves of bread, down which flows one long sandwich of meat and cheese, from which the entire party in each carriage, including the horse, each takes a democratic bite. The winner of the best-decorated carriage has to treat everyone he knows and everyone who knows him to wine at every *trattoria* on the road back to Rome, so there is a Roman pun that, instead of the Feast of Divine Love it is really the *Festa di Amor di Vino:* the Feast of the Love of Wine.

We couldn't resist a drive into the Campagna to see all this, and it was late in the evening, about ten o'clock, when we regained the Excelsior, to find—of course!—a message to telephone the Chigi Palace at once. Even the most dandified diplomats there had to work until nine or nine-thirty at night (fortunately for them, the smart dinner hour in Rome was almost after-theater supper time in America); but even so, our call was too late. Not a soul answered, and we went restlessly to bed wondering what wonderful thing we had missed for our fancy to enjoy a Roman holiday.

In the morning, after endless relays, I was connected with a voice that described itself as "a functionary of the Foreign Office" who would like to call upon me immediately. It was a very correct and cold young man who materialized into our sitting room a little later. He announced curtly that it would be utterly impossible for His Excellency the Prime Minister to answer any of the questions I had left him.

I was dumbfounded. I simply couldn't believe it, for Mussolini had read them over while we were there and had promised whole-heartedly to answer every one. It was bad enough to see my article fading out of possibility, but much worse to lose faith in his sincerity, which I had seen no reason to doubt.

The young man was so authoritative, that for a moment I could think of nothing to say. Then, finally, I asked him if this word came from Mussolini himself.

The young man hesitated, then replied that he had not conferred personally with His Excellency on what, he gave the impression, was a very trivial subject indeed.

"Then," I said, "will you please go back to the *palazzo* and find out more definitely before you bring me such a message?"

He left, and shortly after was on the phone begging me to come over at once. Mother and I found him waiting for us, almost embarrassingly fawning and apologetic. Mussolini, it seemed, had turned the questions over to this particular functionary to have certain statistics supplied, which instruction must have been lost or overlooked. Finding the questionnaire on his desk when he returned from Geneva, the young man had hastily concluded to give it Treatment No. 1 for questionnaires, on his own initiative. Evidently he had had a bad time of it when he went back after seeing us, for his good-by was a most earnest plea that I put in a good word for him with the Duce. Later, he came to the Embassy in Washington, but we never became very good friends. The beginning had been too acutely uncomfortable on both sides.

Mussolini sent for us unexpectedly several times during the weeks we stayed on in Rome, for it seemed to refresh him to have an hour's talk now and then. One day I asked for his photograph, and he said, "Of course, but what shall I write?"

He held his pen over the photograph, considering; then he said suddenly, "Well, d'Annunzio made you a citizen of Fiume, but *I* can make you a citizen of Rome!" And so he did, then and there, for he wrote, in Italian, "To Vera Bloom, Citizen of Fiume, and Citizen of Rome, with cordiality, Mussolini." Another picture he gave me later was inscribed simply, "To Vera Bloom, devotedly, Mussolini." Naturally, at the time, I was terribly proud of those pictures, for Mussolini had won admiration the world over for what he had done for Italy. If anyone had told me then that the day would come when it would be a front page issue whether or not I had destroyed them as a gesture of protest, I should have thought it utterly fantastic.

I didn't meet him again, except at his office, until one night our hotel was plunged into the same tense preparations as a Washington hotel is on a day when the President is expected to dine there. Mussolini, who rarely went out anywhere, was expected that evening to attend a great banquet the Italian government was giving for the delegates to an international conference then meeting in Rome. All day long, just as in Washington, secret service men supervised the cooks in the kitchens, tested the elevators, prowled through the foyers, and watched the entrances and the ground floor windows.

At banquets in Rome the reception takes places after the dinner, when they think people have had more chance to get acquainted, and as we always came down late to dinner ourselves, we didn't see the arrival. But Mr. Gelardi, the manager of the hotel, later the presiding genius at Claridge's in London, asked us if we would like a glimpse of the banquet while it was in progress. As we dared a quick look, Mussolini spied us in the doorway, and smiling and lifting his glass of champagne, he gave us a silent toast. Then we slipped back into the rose-marble lounge, where one could watch the glittering company come back to the private reception room, since the connecting doors were open.

By and by a staff of ushers and footmen came marching solemnly toward the crowd of onlookers saying, *"Fa via Sua Eccellenza!"* ("Make way for His Excellency!") as the Prime Minister, followed by high government and military dignitaries in full uniform, blazing with orders and decorations, started to leave, while everyone else stood at attention. Mother and I, finding ourselves right in the line of march, stepped back behind one of the French doors, lest he feel he was being waylaid. But he had seen us already, and he gave me one of the most exciting moments of my life when he reached the crowded lounge, for instead of going on through the lobby he stopped short, the gorgeous retinue necessarily stopping stock still behind him, and came around to greet us and stay for a good long chat.

Mother said, "Tell him he's an angel!" and, as he never missed anything, he demanded to know what she had said, and I told him in Italian.

"Un angelo!" he laughed delightedly. "Well, I've been called everything. But never an angel!"

We laughed and joked for some time, until finally he and his suite moved on, leaving, of course, something of an aura in our neighborhood.

The next moment I felt someone grip my arm and heard a nice Southern voice cry, "I know you! I know you!" And there was Mrs. Hugh Cumming, the wife of Surgeon-General Cumming, both dear friends from Washington, who were in Rome for the conference, although we hadn't known it. That was really the crowning touch to a perfect moment; for what's the good of a triumph if there's no one from home to see it? Mrs. Cumming was the ideal witness, too. Thereafter she appointed herself chief hornblower for me in Washington whenever Mussolini was mentioned.

For days afterward Mother and I were covertly pointed out wherever we went, until I began to feel like what the Italians call a *donna fatale,* or one of "the glamorous ladies at whose beckoning History shook." Even the elevator boys would look at me big-eyed and say *"Lei é la signorina che conosce Mussolini!"* ("You are the young lady who knows Mussolini!")

It was hard to make up our minds to leave Rome; but Congress was preparing to adjourn, and we wanted to make some visits in northern Italy before we met Father in Paris.

Mussolini had asked us to come in to say good-by the evening before our departure for Florence, and when we came, I thought I had never seen him in such a charming and carefree mood.

The first thing he asked was whether I had noticed anything special about the Via Trittoni, the street leading to the Chigi Palace. I answered that I couldn't help noticing that it was all torn up, because we had had to ride all around town to get to the palace.

"But don't you see how wonderful that is?" he demanded, drawing us to the window where we could see the torn-up street. "Yesterday I told the Governor of Rome that I wanted those street-car tracks taken up, and this morning when I came to the office, they were gone! I don't think you could have done any better in America!"

He drew us back to the great armchairs at his desk, and taking up some typewritten sheets, he stuffed them laughingly into my hands, one by one, saying, "There! There! There! There! There!" It was my list of ticklish questions, answered in full.

I tried to thank him, but he waved that aside, and taking up his favorite posture, leaning on a pile of books at my corner of the desk, he began to put me through a kindly third degree. Why didn't we stay in Rome? Was there anyone else I would like to meet? Or anything I would like to do? Say the word and he would arrange it all, if only we would change our minds and stay.

I assured him we had had a wonderful time, everyone had been more than kind to us, and if it had been possible to stay on, we would have needed no other inducement than the hope that he might see us now and then.

We talked of one thing and another for about an hour and a half, and when we finally left, he came all across the room with us to the door, where he kissed Mother's hand and then, surprisingly, mine; for in Europe, where it is the custom only to kiss the hand of a married woman, it means a special tribute to kiss a girl's. He stood in the doorway looking after us as we made our way to the elevator, turning to wave good-by again several times, and I walked out into the golden Roman twilight feeling very glamorous and very sad: sentiments renewed next day by the many Roman friends who came to see us off, laden in the generous Italian way with bouquets and boxes of bonbons, and waved until the train was out of sight.

We still had Joseph with us, the mild, middle-aged, scholarly-looking courier who had been guiding our sight-seeing and running errands for us all those weeks in Rome. And in spite of his presence in the compartment, I confess, I shed regretful tears most of the way to Florence.

But before we were out of the Florence station in the wake of the porters he had corralled, all preoccupations were swept aside by Joseph himself, who came back flourishing a newspaper extra which he read by the station arc lights with astounding fierce joy.

The news was that a prominent anti-Fascist deputy, Matteotti, had been murdered the night before, not far from Rome; and the anti-Fascist press was declaring that the murder had been instigated and directed by Mussolini himself, and that his ruin and the fall of Fascism were a matter of days, if not of hours. The murder had taken place about half past seven—at the very moment, then, of our carefree farewell visit with Mussolini! Joseph's quiet exterior, we soon realized, covered an interior seething with political passion. That he was a bitter anti-Fascist he had carefully concealed all the time in Rome; but now his joy was as lightning.

Naturally, our whole North Italian trip was clouded. Our anxiety about Mussolini, and our complete inability to believe that the serene well-being of his mood at the time could have been pretense, were sufficient for that. Besides, Joseph made our lives one harrowing succession of newspaper extras, what with English and American editions coming in from Paris, adding to the sensational reports. He had a new one to flaunt even in a rowboat in the middle of Lake Como.

It was a relief when the time came for him to leave us in Milan, his last duty seeing us to the Genoa Express on our way to visit the Mackenzie family (who after six generations in Italy were still British subjects) at their Castle San Bartolemeo, which dominates all Genoa, and houses the finest private collection of Dante in the world. (The present tense is only hope, not certainty; for as I write, we cannot yet know how San Bartolomeo will have fared in the war.)

We found we were to share our compartment with an old Italian gentleman of most distinguished presence, who looked as if he had had a proud Moor as one of his ancestors. He came escorted by a long and respectful suite of secretaries and servants, all of whom, however, departed, except for one young man, who was evidently to travel in another car.

The old gentleman paid no attention whatever to us for hours. Then, to Mother, in excellent English: "I beg your pardon, Madame, but were you a Miss Patterson of Baltimore?"

Mother said she was not, and wondered why he had thought so.

"On account of that ring," he said, pointing to a Napoleon ring that she wore: a diamond crown and an N on deep blue enamel, surrounded by a wreath of rose-diamonds. "I know Jerome Bonaparte married a Miss Patterson of Baltimore, and I wondered if that might be how you came to own such an interesting piece."

Mother explained that the ring had come from a ne'er-do-well descendant of one of Napoleon's generals who had migrated to South America, and that my father had bought the ring from him years before, offering to sell it back if ever he regretted parting with it; but he had never come back.

We kept on talking until, when we were actually in sight of the tower of the Mackenzie castle, the old gentleman said suddenly and with certitude:

"You are American ladies traveling in Italy alone, and you naturally feel rather unsafe at this unsettled moment. So I feel it my duty to tell you confidentially that I have just come from Rome, from a conference with His Majesty the King, and all his counselors, generals, and admirals, and I can assure you positively that the crisis is over, that there is no further danger, and that Mussolini will not fall!"

We never found out who he was, for the train pulled into Genoa and we lost sight of him in the excitement of greeting Mrs. Mackenzie and her sister-in-law, Baroness de Thierry, who had come down to meet us.

As I look back now and think what "Innocents Abroad" we were, I realize that the distinguished old gentleman could quite possibly have been planted in our compartment. Who knows?

Later that day I slipped away from everyone and wrote to Mussolini that we were on our way to Paris, where I hoped to be able to tell the press what he had actually been doing at the time of the Matteotti affair, and to declare my conviction that he would be entirely exonerated and that his government would be secure.

In Paris, I found that every newspaper, French and foreign, was predicting his fall from moment to moment. But confident in Mussolini and the old gentleman on the train, I gave out a statement to all the papers asserting that in spite of all signs to the contrary, Mussolini would continue with power stronger than ever. And sure enough, by the time a Sunday or so later when my cabled question-and-answer article was published in America, Mussolini was once more firmly established and the Matteotti affair had apparently become past history.

Looking back, I can see that we may have been too naïve and trustful; and yet at the time it was simply impossible for us to believe that things were not exactly as they had seemed in Rome. Anyway, at least my prophecy, if not my judgment, proved right. For several years more we could continue to know Mussolini by memory, brief correspondences, and many other eventful visits to Rome as the rational, responsible, friendly person he was before his pro-Nazi betrayals; and we enjoyed, both in Washington and abroad, friendships with Italian people, and a delight in Italy itself, which one man's perfidy could darken, but never destroy.

Inevitably, in the circumstances, I was constantly being approached by people who knew I knew Mussolini, and wanted me to intercede with him in their behalf. If they were Italians, they wanted anything from a new cow to a new road past their estate. If they were Americans, they wanted a contract with the Italian government, an interview for the press, or, often, only a smile from him on their way through Rome. But Mussolini's kindness to me, I felt, gave me no license to impose upon him by asking favors. So, however much in sympathy with some of the requests, I invariably had to answer, "I'm sorry, I can't."

But there is always an exception, and a reason for it, and this time it was Will Rogers.

He came to Washington especially to see Nick Longworth, the fun-loving Speaker of the House, for he was already heading for Europe to write those hilarious *Letters of a Self-Made Diplomat to His President* (which President Coolidge probably enjoyed more than anyone else), and he hoped Nick Longworth could get him to Mussolini.

The Speaker said there was nothing he could do, and suggested that he try my father. Will Rogers and Father were old friends, so that was easy; but Father told him it would be up to me whether I would help him out and risk the justified bad feelings of all the people I had refused. But it seemed to me as well as to Father that it would be doing Mussolini quite as much of a favor as Will Rogers; for Rogers' homely witticisms on current events, appearing daily in papers throughout the country, probably did more to color American opinion than all the editorial pages.

It happened we were giving a dinner party that night, and that Count Rogeri, who was Italian chargé d'affaires at the time, and General Villa, the military attaché, were both going to be there. We invited Will Rogers too, but he had promised already to dine at the Longworths. However, he would come to us just as soon as "Nick and Alice" let him off.

Seated next to Rogeri at dinner, I had a good chance to tell him about our modern Mark Twain who was coming to petition him. We were all having coffee when Will Rogers made his entrance, in evening clothes, to be sure, but still unmistakably the lounging, lovable Oklahoma cowboy he always was, even though the chewing gum and the lariat were temporarily missing.

He has described that dinner himself in the first of those rollicking *Letters of a Self-Made Diplomat;* but even he might well have wished, on occasion, that some power would "the giftie gie us to see ourselves as ithers see us." I doubt that he realized what a sensation he was at that party.

It was a large and very formal one; and Will Rogers, dutifully following Mother around the room to be introduced, looked for all the world like a suffering little boy being dragged into the parlor when the folks had company. He said something so outrageous and still so good-natured to each of forty people, they just stood around him in a spellbound circle. I remember that when he got to the Minister of Lithuania, he said, "Where are *you* from?" and when the Minister told him, he said, "Well, I'll go there, too— if I can *find* it!" The joke was on him, though, in the end. He did go to Lithuania, and without any effort on his part, as he fell into the country from an airplane en route from Soviet Russia.

He had some quip for each one, and finally, when he had done the whole line, he heaved a great sigh of relief and demanded right out loud, "Now, who's the guy who's going to fix me up with Mussolini?"

I pushed forward the always retiring Rogeri, and before I could repeat the introduction, Rogers had Rogeri by the arm and with a hearty "You come with me, kid!" hustled him off to another room.

When they came back, Will Rogers was beaming with satisfac-faction, and Dedo Rogeri, like everyone else, had fallen completely under his spell.

"Well," said the master of roping, "now that it's fixed that I'm going to see Mussolini, I think I'd like to get a look at the King, too, if the Duce leaves him around loose!"

General Villa, who hadn't been in Washington long, evidently caught the lese majesty of this, even through the haze of his unfamiliarity with English. We saw him feel for his sword: which fortunately wasn't there, or Will Rogers might have had to make a rendezvous for a sword-and-lariat duel in the morning. Of course we explained to Villa that the Rogers disrespect was universal and friendly, whereupon he joined in the fun as heartily as all of us.

Rogeri arranged everything splendidly in Rome; Villa, on his own account, sent the self-made diplomat to the Italian Military Academy, thinking he would enjoy comparing Italian daredevil horsemanship with ours; Will Rogers' articles on Mussolini and Italy were the most enthusiastic he sent from Europe. So everyone was satisfied.

A decade further on, and satisfaction was an impossibility for an American lover of Italy. First, the cruel conquest of Ethiopia; then the Axis pacts, dragging Italy into the maelstrom of Hitler's aggressions. Yet in a world racked by sufferings and fears, there was a capital where two photographs could become a brief issue.

Congress having been in session almost the whole summer of 1938, we were to spend that fall in New York; and on September 13 we left the Virginia mountains, where we had taken a house for the summer, to come back to Washington just long enough to exchange country clothes for city ones. Father was to reach Washington early in the morning and go on to New York the same afternoon. Mother and I were to follow a few hours behind.

The night before, after checking up on everything, Father said, "There's one more thing. Try not to give anything to the papers about your being back in Washington. After all, we're leaving right away. If they phone, ask them to say as little as possible." We said we would; but no detail of moving loomed large in our thoughts, strained as we were by the tension felt everywhere at that time.

Hitler was forcing the Sudeten crisis to his own conclusion. The 'decision for peace or war could fall at any moment; the democracies' capitulation at Munich was less than two weeks away. Everyone's nerves were near the breaking point, and it was almost impossible to keep away from the news broadcasts that, bulletin by bulletin, built up their incredible import. We had no radio in the car, and it was torture to drive the hour and a half into town that day without knowing what was happening.

As we came in the door in Washington, the telephone was ringing. Thinking it must be Father calling to say good-by from the station, I ran to answer.

A strange man's voice asked, "Miss Vera Bloom?"

"Yes."

"This is Harold Phillips of the Scripps-Howard papers and the Washington *News*."

"Yes?" I felt something startling coming, and remembered Father's caution against getting into the papers.

"Will you answer a question?" he went on. "I have heard that you have two photographs of Mussolini in your drawing room—one inscribed to you as a Citizen of Rome, the other signed '*Devotamente*.' Now, since Mussolini has become so completely allied with Hitler, are you going to destroy them or not?"

I had to think quickly. If I followed instructions and didn't say anything, the result might be a much more startling story than if I did. After all, I couldn't deny I had the pictures. It seemed best to try answering in terms that wouldn't make news.

So I said, "Of course I shan't destroy them. That would be as stupid as the things they are doing in Germany and Italy today. After all, Mussolini belongs to history. It would be the same as if someone had had a signed photograph of Napoleon, if there had been photography then, and destroyed it as a protest.

"But of course I will not put them on view. They are in storage now, and there they will stay until Mussolini is himself again. So, you see, it really isn't much of a story, is it? I'd appreciate it so much if you would just let it drop."

He thanked me and said he would see what he could do, and the episode completely left my mind while I listened to Hitler screaming insults over the radio at the President of Czechoslovakia.

Next day, about noon, Father's secretary, Mr. Crawford, rang me up.

"Have you seen the *News*?" he asked.

"The *News?* They haven't used that story about me, have they?"

"Used it? Why, it's all over the front page. I thought you would like to know!"

Well, I didn't altogether like to know, but I sent out for the paper and there it was, right under the latest bulletin, with Mussolini's picture and mine. I phoned Father to explain, fearing that the story would scream out at him from the Scripps-Howard paper in New York. It did. And that was how we sneaked quietly through Washington!

The photographs are still in storage. And needless to say, I have no heart now to imagine a future for them, with so much suffering paid and yet to be paid on account of the most despicable alliance the world has ever known.

5. The Roosevelts and the New Deal

If I had been trying, after the first few years of the New Deal, to say what effect the Roosevelt administration had had on the sacred social structure of Washington, I might have needed only two themes: the Great Disappointment, and Whirlwinds in the White House. It took a while for it to happen, and for us to see, that Washington had changed character completely. It just isn't what it was. But then, neither is the nation, and neither is the world. Franklin Roosevelt's administration, from the very first day when he closed the banks, has eaten crisis for breakfast, lunch, tea, and dinner. After bank failures, price collapse, the deepening Depression, dust storms, unemployment, and floods, came the constantly encroaching shadow of the Axis with its pacts, aggressions, and brutalities. And then, the Second World War. Yet Washington changed so gradually . . .

The Great Disappointment came at the very beginning of the New Deal, when Washington had to accept the fact that several of its highest positions were filled by men who avoided formal festivities whenever possible. For instance, unless you were asked to dinner at the White House, there was very little chance of your dining with President Roosevelt—about eleven times less than you would have had of meeting an earlier President at dinner. One of the first social reforms of the New Deal was to do away entirely with the annual dinners given in honor of the President and the First Lady by the Vice-President, the Speaker, and each member of the Cabinet, and their wives.

The reason, of course, was not lack of sociability on the Roosevelts' part, but the practical difficulties posed by the President's physical handicap, which he surmounts so gallantly that I have

82

always thought his buoyant example must have meant almost as much to other sufferers as the millions of dollars raised every year for the infantile paralysis fund by the birthday balls throughout the country, so worthy a tribute to him.

About the only occasions when the President dined out, before the war (aside from the stag gatherings of the Gridiron Club, the Alfalfa Club, or the White House correspondents), were the dinner given each year by the Vice-President and Mrs. Garner, and, usually, a joint dinner given by the whole Cabinet at one of the hotels each fourth of March, to celebrate the birthday of the New Deal. When it was decided to cancel other custom-prescribed dinners, it was also decided to do away with the two New Year's Day receptions at the White House; and when the Cabinet naturally followed suit, one of the most strenuous of typical Washington traditions passed out of the picture, at least for this administration.

Washington, which accepted the White House decisions with a sigh of regret, was in for more social tradition-breaking.

The Garners proceeded to change completely the time-honored Vice-Presidential role of official diners-out for the administration. Mr. Garner had never made any bones about it that he looked on a white tie as a social noose around his neck; and becoming Vice-President didn't change his opinion a bit. He even took gleeful joy in persuading the President and Mrs. Roosevelt to abandon the annual Vice-President's dinner at the White House, whenever he could think of a good excuse. However, the Garners would spread themselves magnificently at their hotel for their dinner in honor of the President and Mrs. Roosevelt every year, when they usually asked Gene Buck, then the president of the American Society of Composers, Authors, and Publishers, to bring glittering professional talent from New York to appear after dinner.

Ordinarily, the Secretary of State and his wife dine out as constantly as the Vice-President and the Speaker and their wives, but the story goes that when Senator Cordell Hull rather reluctantly accepted President Roosevelt's appeal to head the Cabinet, it was understood between them that to assure him strength and time for the heavy work before him, he must be allowed to decline all dinner invitations (except for inevitable concessions to visiting royalty or high foreign dignitaries), the only way to avoid hard feelings on the ground of favoritism. Which meant, of course, that during the New Deal the three ranking families, after the First Family itself, would be hors de combat in the Capital's social melée.

The Speaker and Mrs. Bankhead were so congenial and so happy just to be together, that I'm sure neither of them considered it a sacrifice when, after quite a serious illness, he was advised by his doctors not to accept evening engagements except on very special occasions; but Washington felt the loss of two more exalted and delightful diners-out.

Probably there has never been a First Family who so completely personified an administration as the Franklin D. Roosevelts.

The odd part of it is that, although Mrs. Roosevelt has become about the best source of anecdote material in the country, there are strangely few good stories to tell about the President, certainly nothing like the fund of Coolidge stories that used to keep the country chuckling. The only explanation I can think of is that President Roosevelt is so handsome, so charming, and so spellbinding, one cannot think of him as a "type." If he were a character in fiction or in a play, I imagine any author would cast him in the leading man's role rather than in a character part. And I think that's why, despite his inexhaustible wit and humor, he has provided the country with so few amusing stories.

Seldom has an extraordinary charm been more energetically countered with attempts to disenchant. But when he goes on the radio to explain to the country, in that warm, beautiful voice of his, just how he feels about something and why, as if he were sitting down with you in a quiet room, talking friend to friend, I imagine it must be hard for anyone but the most rock-ribbed Republican to resist him. He never insults his audience by talking down to it. He is always just what he really is—an aristocratic gentleman—with no needless inhibitions or apologies about it. Or, in other words, Harvard-with-a-heart.

When you stop to think of it, it isn't very often that a First Family can qualify on the score of aristocratic background. For since the early days before Andrew Jackson, before aristocracy became a political curse, most of our Presidents have been elected mainly because they were "plain folks," who kept any proud ancestors they might possess discreetly in the background. But not the Roosevelts—on whichever side of the political fence various ones have belonged. They are all frankly and casually aristocratic, and, as with anything that's done casually enough, everyone seems to accept it as something to be taken for granted.

I even have an idea that Mrs. Roosevelt's extraordinary success in establishing the right of a First Lady to be a whirlwind sprang partly from this inherited Roosevelt characteristic. Many people probably felt subconsciously that a double Roosevelt, both by birth and marriage, "could do no wrong," to use the customary exaggeration, and easily became used to the idea that she would go serenely on her tirelessly active way, as she had done in New York even long before she became the Governor's lady.

So even the Old Guard in Washington society ran completely out of gasps, as she started one Whirlwind in the White House after another. Where no First Lady had so much as given an interview, Mrs. Roosevelt calmly proceeded to write a daily newspaper column, appear on commercial radio programs for charity, go on speaking tours, travel incessantly, and hold regular press conferences for the newspaperwomen, long before she started her globe-circling flights.

Where no First Lady had permitted anything to interfere with the White House social schedule, Mrs. Roosevelt made it a practice to accept two or three luncheon or dinner engagements for the same meal: she would speak and take the first course at an early banquet in a Washington hotel, then dash back to the White House just in time to receive the guests at a state dinner. The Old Guard gave one last gasp when it saw her, in traveling clothes, calmly carrying her own suitcase down the stairs from the private Presidential apartments, past the guests who still lingered at a state reception from which she had escaped in time to catch a midnight plane for a speaking engagement.

And no one laughed louder than the First Lady herself when the Women's National Press Club put on a skit that showed the Byrd expedition at the South Pole when someone spied a tall figure approaching across the trackless snows, and "Admiral Byrd," taking up his spyglass, exclaimed in a stunned voice, "Good Lord, it's Mrs. Roosevelt!"

Even after years of it, one is still surprised how closely she keeps in touch with things in every part of the country, and proceeds to do something about them.

At one time the First Lady was intensely interested in a plan to hold an international convention of the Farm Women of the

World, in Washington. She felt very keenly what an opportunity it would be for the American women belonging to the association to exchange views with women from all over the world who face the same problems they do. Of course, this being an international affair, the legislation to appropriate the necessary money—a mere ten thousand dollars—came before the House Foreign Affairs Committee, or rather, into a cubbyhole of bills that might or might not get its attention; and there it languished. At a time when my father was temporarily acting chairman, Mrs. Roosevelt brought it to his attention, and he immediately called a hearing.

Strangely enough, some of the committee members showed opposition. After some rather puzzled questioning, Father finally led one member to confess that the witnesses looked so well dressed and up to date, he couldn't believe they were really farm women and entitled to the appropriation. Father thought a second, then said to the lady who happened to be testifying,

"Madam, would you mind taking off your gloves a moment?"

The surprised rural lady did as he asked, and revealed the unmistakable signs of years of hard work on a farm. Objections were quickly withdrawn, and the bill soon became law.

And when the convention met in the Capital that June, Mrs. Roosevelt, who is one of the most appreciative people imaginable, asked Mother to stand with the ladies of the Cabinet and a few others while she and the President addressed the hundreds of lady farmers from the ends of the earth, whom they honored with a White House garden party.

How Mrs. Roosevelt with her interest on a thousand things, and while apparently being in several places at the same time, could manage to follow through in a detailed way projects of special concern to her, is illustrated by a story in connection with the New York World's Fair. Her interest in the plans for the Fair, especially for the Federal Building, was prompt and consistent.

One day, several months before its opening, Mother and I arrived at the White House for one of those triple teas Mrs. Roosevelt had inaugurated so that she would be able to receive everyone who left cards at the White House during the season: one group of a hundred or so would be asked for four o'clock, another for five, and still another for six, the White House aides politely but firmly seeing to it that one group departed before the next was received. At this one, Mother was surprised by Mrs. Roosevelt's wanting to talk to her privately, though it meant holding up the line, as it turned out, for a good ten miutes.

Most of what Mrs. Roosevelt said was confidential, but Mother did tell me that Mrs. Roosevelt began by saying she had been wondering why Mother had not appeared in the White House box to hear the speeches at Grover Whalen's banquet at the Mayflower a week before, in honor of the foreign governments who would be represented at the Fair. Invitations, apparently, were supposed to have been issued to certain ladies suggested at the White House, and it must have seemed very strange indeed when Mother did not appear, as even an indirect White House invitation is regarded as a command.

For a moment Mother was taken aback. What had actually happened was that a Washington woman we know, who was doing social contact work with the diplomats on behalf of the Fair, had telephoned asking for me, not Mother, and saying casually, "Vera, I was wondering if you'd like to bring a beau down to the Mayflower after the World's Fair dinner this week, about ten o'clock. I'm asking some people to use the boxes then, to hear the speeches, and perhaps have a glass of champagne." I explained that I had a dinner on for that night and couldn't possibly get away by ten o'clock; and gave the matter no more thought, except to mention it to Mother at the time. That was a lucky stroke, for now, after recovering her breath, she could explain to Mrs. Roosevelt just how casually the invitation had been extended.

When Mrs. Roosevelt realized how it had been done, she naturally wanted to hear anything else Mother could tell her about the workings of the Fair, to compare with what she knew already. What they told each other, I don't know, but from the length of the conversation it must have been a lot.

It was inevitable that having a superwoman as First Lady should give feminine Washington a terrific jolt.

Mrs. Borah used to say that she would read Mrs. Roosevelt's schedule for the day in the morning paper and promptly go back to bed, exhausted! Someone else proposed to get reams of publicity for a charity affair by announcing, "Mrs. Roosevelt positively will *not* open this bazaar!"

No one thought of trying to emulate her. Who could? She must be possessed of the most perfect health and stamina any woman ever had. I can't remember hearing once in all these years that she was even laid up with a cold, and apparently she never rests, except possibly during those few weeks in the summer when she is "off the record."

Perhaps the simple fact that Mrs. Roosevelt has frankly never considered herself a beauty has had a lot to do with her extraordinary career. The average woman with just the average amount of vanity will try to "save" herself for an important occasion. She will want to look rested and refreshed even if she can't be beautiful; but I don't think Mrs. Roosevelt has any such vanity at all. I think she is quite as unconcerned over her looks as she apparently has been about all the storms over her enthusiastic championship of certain people and causes during her years in the White House. One thing, though, I'm sure is true: that in every case, fortunate or unfortunate, she has been completely sincere; in fact her very sincerity, it seems to me, has often blinded her.

There can be little doubt that Eleanor Roosevelt will go down in history as one of our most famous First Ladies—but what effect she will have on American women as a whole, I don't know. Perhaps if she were not quite so extraordinary, if she didn't have quite such boundless energy, she would actually have had more effect— but I'm afraid the rest of us just consider her something unique in women, murmur, "How on earth does she *do* it all!" and go on our own usual, average way.

That the President inherited much of his charm and good looks from his mother, anyone who met her must be convinced. For if there ever was a great lady, it was Mrs. James Roosevelt—not the overbearing imitation *"grande dame"* of the movies, but a warm, human, fun-loving person, so sure of herself and her position that it would never occur to her to assert herself.

How we came to know the senior Mrs. Roosevelt is quite a roundabout story. Some years ago my father had helped a brave White Russian lady, whom we didn't even know, to enter this country and eventually become a citizen, after an almost incredible escape from the revolutionary terror. She was Mme. Lydia Kniagevitch, whose husband had been a high official at the court of the czar. Fortunately for her, she had had the almost professional musical training of so many aristocratic Russian amateurs, and she was making her living now by giving lectures, with her own piano accompaniment, on that group of immortal amateurs who became the great genuises of Russian music, especially Borodin, Moussorgsky, Rimsky-Korsakov, and Tchaikowsky, some of whom she had known personally.

She wrote Mother that, to show her appreciation for Father's help, she would be delighted to play for some of our friends if Mother would like to arrange a musicale. Mother and I were then on the entertainment committee of the Congressional Club, and we felt it would be a welcome experience to the members, as well as a chance for Mme. Kniagevitch to become known to people from the country over, if she were to play at the club rather than for a few friends at our house. So a date was arranged.

When we called for her, we found a frail, pale, white-haired little woman, whose tragic adventures had left their stamp on her fine face. She was dressed then, as always, in simple black, which seemed never to change with the changing fashions.

The audience, like any which hasn't come primarily because of a real musical urge, was rather a difficult one, in spite of the inspiration Mme. Kniagevitch brought to her subject, and the great charm which shone through her frail physique like a light in an alabaster vase. But at the end of the program she did something which must have thrilled even the most phlegmatic.

This happened in the time before the United States recognized the Soviet Union, when we had no diplomatic relations with Russia at all. At the end of her talk Mme. Kniagevitch rose from the piano, and facing the audience, said in a voice trembling with emotion, "I am going to ask you to rise with me while I play the old Imperial Russian Anthem—not to condone the mistakes of Old Russia, but in memory of the good we tried to do, and of the dream we dreamed which failed! Will you?"

In a flash we were all on our feet, while she turned to the piano and, still standing, crashed out with unbelievable power the great chords of the Imperial Anthem. It was one of the most magnificent and touching moments I had ever experienced. One felt that she was a really great soul.

It is the usual thing in Washington, of course, to stand whenever a foreign national anthem is played. What was unusual was the honoring of a country which, at least politically, no longer existed.

We were not in touch with Mme. Kniagevitch very often, after that, for quite some time, but one day we had a letter from her mentioning that she had met the President's mother at the Colony

Club in New York and they had struck up a friendship at once. She had just made a several weeks' visit at Hyde Park. Soon they were the closest of friends.

Several times her letters mentioned that Mrs. Roosevelt wanted to meet us and to express her own appreciation for what Father had done. We answered in kind, of course, but hardly thought of the suggestion as more than a long-distance kindliness. Then one day there was a letter saying that she was to give a musicale in Washington, and that Mrs. Roosevelt was coming down with her to be patroness of the affair, and was hoping to meet us on this trip.

We were in a quandary. If Mme. Kniagevitch out of gratitude, was merely *hoping* to arrange for us to know Mrs. Roosevelt, our calling on her at the White House might seem forward. On the other hand, not to call on the President's mother first might appear unpardonable, no matter how good the motive.

We finally decided to leave cards at the White House; and later that afternoon, at the musicale, found the quandary altogether passé. Mrs. Roosevelt's greeting was direct and warm, and almost at once she was saying, "And, by the way, Mrs. Bloom, what time tomorrow would it be convenient for you to have us come and see you?" Of course, she *would* put it that way!

The next day was Tuesday and our day at home, which Mother mentioned, adding, of course, that any time Mrs. Roosevelt chose would be a happy time for us.

"Then let's have a real visit by ourselves," she said. "Would eleven in the morning do?"

So it was arranged, and with a merry "Until tomorrow!" she turned to other friends.

We departed already musing on what to serve at eleven in the morning. For aside from the question of hospitality, there is no doubt that any visit lacks half its spontaneity until something appears on a tray. But what? Tea or coffee seemed rather foolish at that hour, so at last we decided on the choice of tomato-juice cocktails and sherry, with some amusing biscuits made out of sea-weed, that tasted almost like nuts, which Mrs. Hull had sent us shortly before. And we decided that Mrs. Roosevelt might prefer a New York sherry, put up quite near Hyde Park, to our best Spanish Amontillado from Jerez itself.

The morning broke cold and rainy, and we wondered for a while if they would come, after all. But when eleven o'clock drew

90

near with no message, our colored butler stationed himself proudly outside the front door, with a huge umbrella, on the lookout. Which proved an unnecessary precaution, because at the stroke of eleven, a White House car drove up to the door, and a footman sprang off the box, umbrella in hand, to help the enterprising callers from the car.

They came in bubbling over like two school chums, saying all at once how successful the musicale had been, how lovely the house was, and how dreadful the weather, as we walked back to the drawing room (for we had followed Presidential protocol and greeted them at the front door).

We were all talking along at that infectious rate, when the tomato-juice cocktails and the sherry appeared. Which would they have? That took a lot of thinking. Tomato juice first, they decided, and the sherry after.

What fun! And did that really good sherry actually come from New York State? Mrs. Roosevelt declared she must have some at Hyde Park, and of course, we asked her to let us send her some; there was both a tawny and a golden kind, and she could see which she preferred. Would we, really? But how lovely!

The conversation simply flew, interspersed every now and then with "my son,"—never "the President"—and "my daughter-in-law." As with all good talk, one topic melted into another so quickly and easily that it is hard to recapture them.

One moment I have smiled over many times was when Mme. Kniagevitch and Mother were engrossed and Mrs. Roosevelt whispered to me, "You know the real reason why I came down this time with Mme. Kniagevitch? Well, a famous fortuneteller told her that she would die suddenly in her seventieth year—and as she's past sixty-eight now, I felt I really should come along to take care of her!"

To take care of her—although Mrs. Roosevelt was eighty-two herself! (Fortunately, Mme. Kniagevitch has since passed that seventieth milestone; the fortuneteller didn't know so much after all.)

A good long time flown swiftly by, they declared they had to be going. But first, Mrs. Roosevelt must see every room downstairs, and hear about every piece of furniture that especially caught her eye. Naturally we went with them right out to the front steps, and as they went on after the good-bys, Mrs. Roosevelt called back with a joyous chuckle, "Thank you again for the *cocktail party!*"

Only a night or so later Mother and Father were dining at the White House, and because all the men who outranked Father happened to be unmarried, Mother found herself in the thrilling but difficult position of going in to dinner with the President.

Some Chief Executives have been so difficult to talk to that to neighbor them at dinner could be a rather mixed blessing. But President Roosevelt is so witty, so jolly and so brilliant that no matter what his position in life might be, he would keep any dinner partner on her mental toes trying to keep up with him.

Mother, of course, mentioned his mother's visit, when an opportunity offered. It turned out that the President knew all about the "wicked cocktail party" and had been vastly amused by it.

From there, the talk naturally turned to the New York sherry and American wines in general, so Mother suggested that perhaps the President might do something to help our own winegrowers with the financial aid they need to keep our perfectly good grapes long enough after they are barreled to produce really good wine. She asked if he knew the New York wines which we had found the best among the domestic brands, and he said no, and called across the table to Father to ask laughingly if he would send him some.

"Certainly, Mr. President," he replied, "I shall send you a bottle tomorrow!"

"A *bottle!*" said the President, "How about a case!" Of course the holdup victim was delighted.

It would be stupid to pretend that the President, charming as he was to most people who came under his spell, was not "That Man" to a very sizable section of the country—if you can call the upper financial brackets a sizable section. For undoubtedly the most bitter anti-New-Dealers were the highly solvent: and why not, as they were the ones who were expected to pay and pay to make the Roosevelt utopia come true?

But as far as Washington was concerned, though there were many who felt as bitter about the New Deal as the most martyred millionaire, they never allowed their feelings to reach the pitch where they would give up a lifelong friendship—or a dinner invitation—over the fate of a few million (or was it a few thousand?) little pigs. Capital dinner tables might buzz over the "idiotic idealism" of paying the farmers for not planting anything, and Washington matrons might moan about the rank ingratitude of long-time dusky handmaidens walking out the day of a party to sit home doing nothing on W.P.A. funds—but no one ever dreamed of refusing a White House invitation because of it. For no matter how distasteful were "That Man" and "Eleanor" politically, they were still "the Roosevelts" socially, and even the old Washington-ian cave-dweller set, who have often blandly ignored occupants of the White House who did not fit their social standards, could not bring themselves to snub a Roosevelt.

Not until the heyday of America First was there to be a question that split social Washington into two camps so deeply opposed that they were simply unmixable. After all, little pigs, the Blue Eagle, and all the deep-dyed devices of the whole roster of alphabet agencies could be reduced to absurdity, and really cried out for the satirical touch of Gilbert and Sullivan; and while the smug, snug group who were the most vocally anti-New-Deal felt primarily a pain in the pocketbook, America First and isolationism involved the stark realities of life and death, and tensions far more crucial than any in the days when the Brain Trusters were providing the mystery element in the Washington show.

You might think that the Brain Trust, which was so close to the President, would have made its imprint on the social scene. But the truth is that your authentic Brain Truster fancied himself as a modern Delphic Oracle, a sort of disembodied spirit of the New Deal, not to be seen by the profane eye of the unbeliever. They were mad about the invisibility which Tommy Corcoran made so fashionable among the New Deal elect, whose idea of relaxation was said to be to gather a few cronies together in one of their Georgetown houses and sit drinking coffee all night while they argued what to do about the world.

General Hugh Johnson, Raymond Moley, Rexford Tugwell, Louis Howe, and Harry Hopkins, although they were the big "news names" of the day, were to all intents and purposes as much legendary figures to Washington as they were to the rest of the country. In most cases no one even knew whether they were married or not; at any rate, so far as I know, their wives did not come into the Washington picture at all; and of course, except in some cases like that of a socially self-sufficient bachelor diplomat, it is the wife who does the social spade work.

93

And that, perhaps, is why Washington seemed to change so gradually from what it was under the Sign of the Elephant to what it became under the Sign of the Donkey; and although for the country at large the spotlight seemed to have shifted from the old-time stars like the Vice-President, the Speaker, and the Cabinet to the new characters in the Capital cast, it was the traditional head-liners who still held the center of the stage for us who made up the rest of the company.

Vice-President Garner, with his cheerful ruddy face, and famous bristling eyebrows under his ten-gallon hat, was a political "character" if there ever was one. Since Calvin Coolidge, I don't suppose there has been anyone in politics to fit so well into that particular frame. His pungent cowboy sayings were legion, and the men on the Hill, at both ends of the Capitol, simply adored him.

When Father first came to Congress, and had to face the contest over his seat in the House, he made a bet with Mr. Garner that if he won he would give Mr. Garner a really good cigar every time their paths crossed, regardless of whether "Cactus Jack" saw him or not. The bet turned out to be pretty costly—but a duty that he was naturally delighted to pay and pay; and whenever he lunched in the Senate restaurant, he sent a waiter over to the Vice-President's table with instructions to offer him the cigar without a word. He invariably chuckled, and sent the waiter straight back with his thanks, unless his table happened to be so near that he could call across.

Slight, energetic Mrs. Garner was and always had been her husband's secretary. Rain or shine, she was at her desk at the Capitol bright and early every morning.

There was a rumor that they both infinitely preferred the streetcar to the limousine which the government provided for them, as it does for the Speaker and the Cabinet. Mrs. Garner cared as little for the *beau monde* as the Vice-President did. Even the Wednesday at-homes, which most of her predecessors kept so religiously, were so rare that when once or twice she really was at home on her day, practically everyone simply left their cards and drove off, not dreaming that she was in.

She was totally unspoiled by the climb from a little Texas town to Vice-Presidential eminence. She just went along in her own friendly, unpretentious way, apparently quite indifferent to the more glamorous side of Washington life.

94

One day while I was under the dryer at the beauty shop, the girl who was "doing" me relayed the message that a lady "two booths down across the aisle" would like to see me when I was through. As she was a usually unfailing Who's Who on feminine Washington, I asked her if she knew who it was, but she had no idea. I investigated, and who should it be but Mrs. Garner. Not another soul in the shop seemed aware of who she was, and I doubt that any other Second Lady of the Land could have gone about Washington so completely unrecognized.

When Mr. Garner gave up the Speakership to become Vice-President, Henry T. Rainey, of Illinois, became Speaker.

He would have made a wonderful department store Santa Claus, with his white hair, rosy cheeks, comfortably upholstered figure, and benevolent but slightly sleepy look. I always felt that tall, plain Mrs. Rainey, who, like Mrs. Garner, continued being her husband's secretary as she had been for nearly thirty years, really supplied most of the enthusiasm and ambition for them both.

No one ever enjoyed a high position more than the Raineys. They had kept very much to the Congressional side lines in Washington for all those years, but when the turn of the political Ferris wheel brought them almost to the very top (for only the President, the Vice-President, and the Chief Justice outrank the Speaker in the American official scale), they threw themselves into their new life with the greatest gusto, and somehow rather touchingly ignored the fact that all those who were so persistent now in their invitations had been completely oblivious of them for years—a thing that often embitters people when high position comes to them at last.

But not the Raineys. Every afternoon, as soon as the House adjourned, the Speaker and Mrs. Rainey, although her secretarial duties for her husband usually found her at her desk at the Capitol at eight-thirty every morning, would appear, as surely as the sun went down, at the reception, or tea, or cocktail party of the afternoon, with almost always a diplomatic dinner in their honor to follow. Naturally, the Raineys had a much heavier round of official dinners than the Speaker and his wife would ordinarily have had, since they were the only high-ranking official figures for whom the embassies and legations were able to entertain during the season, except the Chief Justice and Mrs. Hughes, who would dine out only on Saturday nights. How the Raineys kept it up was a marvel, because they must have both been well over seventy. But somehow

95

she managed, along with everything else, to keep her at-homes every Wednesday, to which Washington flocked the more multitudinously because in all the years Nick Longworth was Speaker, Mrs. Longworth had never opened her doors to anyone but intimate friends.

And Mrs. Rainey wasn't satisfied just to take pot luck on who would come. One day she rang Mother up to tell her about a grand idea she had had: would Mother see that Mme. Troyanovsky, the newly arrived Soviet ambassadress, would surely come to her next Wednesday, and would she ask the other wives of the Foreign Affairs Committee to come too? As an afterthought, she asked me to invite some "amusing" young people, so I collected some from the State Department and diplomatic sectors, and she was as thrilled with them as if she were a young girl at her first party.

I am so glad they had all the fun of their day in the sun. Some people think that a man in a high position has more prestige, when he is never, or very rarely, seen—like Senator Borah. But the great prizes come to so few people, I like to see each one enjoy his while it lasts, in his own way, not missing a moment; because the political wheel may turn again before he knows it.

This was brought home to me strongly in the case of an official family who are now out of the Washington scene. The father was highly placed in a former administration: so highly that it seemed quite possible the next election would see him either Speaker or Vice-President. He and his wife had a college-senior son, and a daughter of debutante age, who rarely were brought to Washington. That winter would have been just the time to let them both experience the delightful delirium of Christmas holidays in the official whirl.

But no. The parents decided to wait until the next Christmas; for after all, why should they bring the young people here in a second-rate position, when grander things were sure to come? So? Before that next Christmas the father, because of a really despicable example of unbridled ambition by a colleague who felt that he stood in his way, had been so politically humiliated that the only dignified thing left for him to do was to retire from public life. The son and daughter never had the memory of a Capital Christmas to carry through life; and it has always been a vivid lesson to me to enjoy what I have, just where I am in the scheme of things. Evidently the Raineys felt that way, too.

The last time Mrs. Rainey entertained officially in the "Speaker's pew" in the front row of the members' gallery of the House, was at the joint session of Congress commemorating the hundredth anniversary of Lafayette's death, when President Roosevelt made the principal address and French Ambassador de Laboulaye delivered a message from the President of France: the first time a foreign envoy had ever taken part in a Congressional session. My father, because of his experience with the Washington Bicentennial, had been made director of arrangements for the occasion.

As always, when there is to be a historic joint session of Congress, the pressure to secure one of the few hundred seats in the gallery was almost unbelievable. Mrs. Rainey had telephoned Mother a day or so before, inviting her to be a guest in the Speaker's pew, and that morning, after Mother and Father had left for the Capitol, with a string of last-minute ticket-requesters trailing him hopefully all the way up to the Hill, the widow of a former Speaker, for whom Father had secured a seat in the gallery, telephoned saying that Mrs. Rainey had "simply insisted" on her coming to the Speaker's pew, and she didn't know what to do with the other ticket. It was too late, of course, to do anything but to stop by for it at her house and let Father find a last-minute alternate at the Capitol.

On arriving, I glanced over to see who else was with Mrs. Rainey, and simply couldn't believe my eyes, for the pew was already full and Mrs. Rainey herself was absent.

Hearing a rumor later in the morning that Mrs. Rainey was ill, we left a message "to inquire" at their hotel, and when I met her a day or two later at a Danish Legation tea, where she seemed to be having a healthy and wonderful time as usual, I told her how very sorry we were that she had been too ill to come to the Lafayette ceremonies, which were still the talk of Washington.

"But I wasn't ill at all, my dear," she protested. "It was only that Mrs. So-and-So telephoned me *at the last minute* that she didn't have a seat, so I gave up my own and stayed home. And frankly," she added, "the Speaker wasn't at all pleased that I wasn't there; and I was looking forward so much to being with your mother."

"But Mrs. Rainey," I blurted out, "she had a seat the day before. I *know* Daddy gave her one."

Just then, who should come up to us but the lady herself.

"Dear Mrs. Rainey," she purred. "I do want to thank you for the other day at the Capitol, and tell you how terribly sorry I am that you were ill."

There was an awful pause while Mrs. Rainey, tall and gaunt, looked at Mrs. So-and-So, pretty and patrician as a Dresden figurine. And then Mrs. Rainey said distinctly, with a dignified displeasure that any queen might have envied, "I was *not* ill. But I understood you had no other possible way of being there. I stayed home so that you might go."

Naturally, there was nothing much for the other lady to say, since I was right there. Perhaps her act had been sheer thoughtlessness. Or perhaps it was the rare instance of a person momentarily determined to come back: an exception to that avoidance of scenes of former glory which generally characterizes former stars of official life, often to the extent that they will not even revisit the Capital. Be that as it may, the moment was unquestionably Mrs. Rainey's.

When Speaker Rainey died suddenly during the Congressional recess that year, Joseph W. Byrns, of Tennessee, became Speaker. Of course, it's quite possible for a Vice-President's inauguration to bring a new figure to Washington; but a Speaker has always reached his office only after a long Congressional climb. The Byrnses had been part of the Washington scene for nearly thirty years. Mr. Byrns's tall, spare frame, strong bony features, and courtly Southern dignity (in all of which he was so strikingly similar to William B. Bankhead, of Alabama, who was to succeed him) and Mrs. Byrns's queenly figure and pretty face crowned with snow-white hair, had not been seen very frequently against the Capital's more brilliant backgrounds, however; and Mr. Byrns's tenure as Speaker was not long enough for them to leave a strong imprint on social Washington, although they were both well qualified to do it.

Mrs. Byrns was always forthright and outspoken, and suddenly finding herself on the dizzy heights didn't faze her at all. One day Mother asked her if she found it difficult to do all the thousand and one new things that were expected of her. She laughed and said, "Oh, they don't bother me a bit. I don't have to '*must*' anything!" Which gave us a fine phrase to bring out whenever we felt like slipping the traces.

Mrs. Bryns usually dressed in very soft colors, but one spring

Sunday made a red-letter occasion when she arrived at a formal luncheon we were giving for them, in fire-red from hat to hem— even to the ribbon on her lorgnette.

Mrs. Bankhead, who succeeded her as Speaker's wife, adored sophisticated black with pearls, or else the warm beige and browns that went with her auburn hair. She looks astonishingly like her star-stepdaughter, Tallulah, and there is a very strong bond between them.

Speaker Bankhead was a born raconteur, and on the summer Sunday they spent with us at the house we had taken in the near-by Blue Ridge Mountains that year when Congress was in session all summer, he kept everyone fascinated for hours on end. But he was essentially very reserved, and I imagine it was hard for him to show his feelings unless he was with close friends.

That same Sunday, Mrs. Bankhead told us the story of how she suddenly discovered (to the Speaker's great pride, one could see) that she had a latent talent for art. When she was watching Howard Chandler Christy do his lovely portrait of her, she had suddenly felt the urge to try her hand at painting, an impulse quite new to her. After painting a while, she decided to try sculpture—and found she had discovered a medium for which she had real talent. So, besides politics and the stage, a third field was added for Bankhead accomplishments.

We hadn't seen any of her work until the day the Neutrality Act passed the House. And then, while the Speaker, Majority Leader Rayburn (the future Speaker), and Father, with various members of the Foreign Affairs Committee, were posing for photographs in the Speaker's rooms at the Capitol—their faces reflecting the joy and relief over the outcome of months of threats and strain—Mrs. Bankhead motioned to Mother and me to follow her, and we tiptoed off to the Speaker's private office, which, like all the offices in the Capitol, is a thing of beauty, from the marble floors to the crystal chandeliers.

We forgot everything else when we saw Mrs. Bankhead's astonishing likeness of the Speaker on the mantelpiece. It was a head in greenish bronze on a square black base, and, as we could see in the mirror over the mantel, it was perfect from every angle. Mrs. Bankhead seemed a little amazed, herself, at her new-found talent.

She mentioned, that day, how she had seen a picture in the

papers of a Polish woman refugee (this was just after Hitler's march into Poland) whose tragic, helpless defiance still haunted her, although she had mislaid the clipping. We had seen it, too, and Mother said she would try to trace it for her and have a photostat made. Fortunately, she could, and sent the picture down to Mrs. Bankhead late one Saturday afternoon.

Sunday morning the telephone rang, and after thanking her, Mrs. Bankhead said, "Well, that's off my mind, at last!" Mother imagined she must mean that on seeing the picture again she had realized that she didn't want to do it, after all. But Mrs. Bankhead went on, surprisingly, "I worked on it until all hours last night—won't you all come down and see it this afternoon?" When we arrived at their apartment, there on the mantelpiece was a heartbreaking little masterpiece in still-moist clay. The whole tragedy of Poland was in that poor woman's face.

Having mentioned the Neutrality Act, this is probably the place to tell the true story of how President Roosevelt signed that bill, at the cost, to my father, of a very good fountain pen—which gave the newspapermen a good laugh.

It is a custom for the President to present the author of a historic bill with the pen he used in signing it, as a souvenir. Since most bills have two sponsors—one in the House and one in the Senate—the President uses two identical pens, doing half the signature with each.

The Bloom-Pittman Bill, otherwise known as the Neutrality Act of 1939, was first introduced in the House, by my father; and Senator Pittman, as chairman of the Foreign Relations Committee, carried through the famous fight in the Senate, before it came back for the dramatic debate and final vote in the House.

For years, Father had had a secret picture in his mind of the magnificent fountain pen he would buy for the Presidential signature on the first important legislation to bear his name. So now he went out and bought the pen of his dreams, which was sent up ahead of time to Stephen Early, the Secretary to the President, to be ready on the President's desk before the signing ceremony, which took place at noon the day after the bill passed the House.

Not until the very moment for signing, apparently, did Senator Pittman realize that he had forgotten to get his special pen. So the President held up the ceremonies while he laughingly sent out to Rudolph Forster, the Executive Clerk at the White House for so many years, for two identical pens.

Those they brought him were identical, but it might be too much to say that they fitted the bill: two five-cent wooden pen-holders with ordinary pen points! The President signed half his name with each one, and presented one to the Senator and the other to Father, with his congratulations.

In the meantime, Father's magnificent fountain pen had completely disappeared, and has never been seen since—to the unfeigned delight of the newsmen, who had almost given up hope of a human interest story that morning.

Of the little group gathered around the President's desk that Saturday noon, I imagine none saw him sign the neutrality revision with deeper satisfaction than Secretary of State Cordell Hull, for the State Department had been in almost as great a ferment over it for months as the Capitol.

The Secretary and Mrs. Hull, for all their very great social graces and very good looks, have always lived an extremely quiet life. We knew them when he was in the House, and of course when he was Senator from Tennessee, and they had proved warm friends, even though we saw them rather seldom. We always appreciated it when, in the time before his becoming Secretary of State, they would make an exception to their usual rule and come to us for dinner.

Mrs. Hull herself always attends to every minute detail of their official entertaining, although there is always someone from the Protocol Division of the State Department to take care of seating arrangements and present the guests. She has no social secretary, and even answers the telephone herself, if she happens to be there when it rings. Some other State Department wives, far below her in rank, have been known to insist that all incoming calls be routed through the department, where one of the operators would have to relay the message over a private wire to find out whether the call could be put through.

The Hulls, like the Bankheads, are so entirely congenial that they share every interest together. There are even two identical desks in the cozy office they have made in their apartment, and when the Secretary developed a great enthusiasm for croquet, Mrs. Hull, whose every thought is for her husband, learned to play such a good game than she could beat the State Department champions, who join the Secretary nearly every fine warm day on the croquet grounds at Woodley, former Secretary of State Stimson's Washington estate.

I love to remember one Sunday the Secretary and Mrs. Hull spent with us, quite alone, at our summer house. It was the only day he was able to escape the Washington heat through a whole stifling summer. Mrs. Hull told us she had expected up to the last second that he would have to stay in town, after all, and she was happy that he did manage to get away at least for that day— which he enjoyed particularly because being in the Blue Ridge Mountains reminded him so strongly of his boyhood home in Tennessee.

I can still see the Secretary, with his fine, scholarly face, forgetting for a moment the imminent war problems of the present in reviewing the Civil War campaigns, which he has learned by heart, and which he could almost make us see as if they were then being fought on the Virginia valley which spread out like a great map far below us.

We have never made any secret of what a wonderful President and First Lady we think the Hulls would make.

If I've somehow given the idea that because the New Deal's ranking families have done so little socially, protocol has lost any of its hold on Washington, I have given a very wrong impression.

No indeed. For instance, as I came in one day to a tea given by a new Congressman's wife, the hostess dashed up to me saying anxiously, "Please help me out! I hear you're good at protocol—"

I couldn't imagine what protocol there could be at a tea, until she went on earnestly, "You see, I have a Senator's wife and a Congressman's wife in the dining room right now, who are both supposed to pour for me at five-thirty—but they won't sit down until it's decided whether tea outranks coffee, or coffee outranks tea!"

That one was too much for me. Later I succeeded in finding out that tea does "outrank" coffee, with chocolate, if there is any, only a poor third. Now, really!

Among New Deal Cabinet ladies, the one who rebelled the most against protocol was plump little Mrs. Cummings, wife of the tall Homer S. Cummings, first Attorney-General of the administration, who was famous for her informal parties, her wit, her amusing hair-do, and her dread of candid cameras.

The one time she had to submit to photographers was when she appeared so brilliantly gowned in red for her presentation at the Court of St. James's. I'll never forget seeing that famous dress a night or so before Mrs. Cummings sailed for London. She and the Attorney-General had gone with us to hear the Philadelphia Orchestra, and then asked us to come home with them for a bit of supper afterward. Mrs. Cummings asked Mother and me if we'd like to see her court costume before it was packed up, so off we went.

There it was, flame red, with bamboo boughs appliqued on the skirt and the court train in silver, all carefully spread out on one of the guest room beds. It took my breath away in more ways than one! Should I tell her that it was going to burst on pastel-minded London court circles like a bombshell? After all, there wasn't much time to do anything about it. But I did ask her if she didn't think it a bit "unusual," and added that I didn't remember having seen any red dresses at Court. She said I must be wrong, as she had had it made by a dressmaker who was born in London; surely it would be all right.

So off she went blithely to astound the British—and I'm glad now that she had so much fun; for who could have foreseen that anyone so full of life and laughter would so soon be gone?

Thinking of Mrs. Cummings reminds me of a story Senator McAdoo of California told about his marriage to President Wilson's daughter, Eleanor, when I sat next to him at dinner at the Cummings' one night not long before he was to be married for the third time.

At the time of his second marriage he was, of course, the Secretary of the Treasury, and a widower, and much older than his young fiancée—so much, in fact, that he said his chief worry was to keep the fact of his fast-approaching grandfatherhood out of the papers!

"I felt," he confessed frankly, "that nothing could possibly make the situation so ridiculous. And then, what do you think happened? The Cabinet held a meeting to decide what wedding present they would give us, and Mr. Bryan, the Secretary of State, in all innocence, I am sure, suggested a grandfather's clock!— Fortunately, I got word of it before it was given out to the press; and the Cabinet compromised on a noncommittal piece of silver!"

One warm June night, in the first summer of the New Deal,

I came home from a party to find that Mother and Father had been entertaining a Cabinet member unawares. An old friend of ours from New York had telephoned to say that he was in town, and Mother had asked him to come to dinner. Then he had wondered if he might bring a friend.

The friend of the friend turned out to be a kindly, unassuming, very young-looking man named Wallace, who, after an informal dinner in the garden, proceeded to stretch out on the grass and regale the others with stories of the summer stars overhead.

When they were about to leave, Mother said innocently to our New York friend, "Mr. Wallace is so nice. What does he do?"

"What does he *do?* Why, he's the new Secretary of Agriculture!"

We still laugh over it often, when we are with the Vice-President and pretty Mrs. Wallace.

There may be other New Deal Washingtonians we have known of whom I should tell; but I am restrained by the realization that it isn't always easy to know who will interest someone else.

I learned that lesson one day when Mrs. Edmund Starling, whose husband, Colonel Starling, was the head of the White House Secret Service through five administrations, asked me to go with her to one of Mrs. Lawrence Townsend's morning musicales at the Mayflower. We got there quite early, while the parade of mink coats and silver fox jackets was at its peak; and we were hardly seated before a rather shy little woman in the next seat leaned over and said in a soft Southern voice, "Excuse me, but is one of you ladies Mrs. Starling? You see, I am from Colonel Starling's home town in Kentucky, and the friend who gave me the ticket this morning told me that Mrs. Starling sits right next to her."

Of course they proceeded to have a grand talk about Kentucky in general and Colonel Starling in particular. Then Mrs. Starling said, "Wouldn't you like us to point out some of the celebrities here this morning? The place is full of them."

"Oh, thank you ever so much!"

So we started off, taking turns as we spied people, and the conversation went something like this:

"You see that lovely-looking lady in the mink coat in the front row of the White House box? That's Mrs. Cordell Hull, the wife of the Secretary of State!"

"Oh, yes." (Not much enthusiasm.)

"And see that sweet-looking lady with curly gray hair in the first box at the left, in black with Persian lamb? That's Mme. de Laboulaye, the wife of the French Ambassador!"

"Oh, yes." (Still not much enthusiasm.)

"Well, look over there in the third box at the right—the little blonde lady in the beige coat with brown fur. That's Mrs. William E. Borah!"

"Oh, yes . . ." (Even Mrs. Borah didn't go over as well as usual.)

So finally I said, "Do you see the white-haired lady in the sable coat and the hat with purple feathers, in the fourth box at the left? That's Mrs. Jacob Leander Loose, of the Loose-Wiles Sunshine Biscuits."

"Not really! *Where?*"

There was no doubt, as I told Mrs. Loose later, that Sunshine Biscuits came much nearer home than all the official glamour of Washington.

Time came, as world conditions grew more and more ominous and complex, when even the Brain Trusters suddenly found themselves "back numbers" to the public eye, and a whole new batch of alphabet soup was poured into the Capital cauldron. The Donald Nelsons, the Knudsens, the Leon Hendersons, the swiftly changing chiefs of the WPB, the OPA, the NLRB, and all the others, became the *real* big shots, who were pointed out wherever they appeared, to whose smiles and frowns not even powerful Senators were indifferent. True, in many cases the Protocol Division hadn't even heard of them yet. They had no rank, and to this day no one quite knows where to seat them at dinner; but it doesn't matter much, as they rarely have time to go out, anyhow.

Times and tempo, it was strikingly plain at last, had changed remarkably in two terms of Roosevelt administration. The old Washington, that carefree island, was gone: or at least past. If something of it survived, it was part of a character much altered. One could realize what a metamorphosis had begun on that first day when a hand in Washington shut the door of your bank on Main Street and later reopened it with a guarantee. Main Street's population soon rubbed shoulders with government. New agencies opened there and here. The Capital experienced that long parade of men from your town and your county who came to inform, request, complain, and aid. The nation's business—recovery—was your business and Washington's, a common agitation such as had not been felt since World War I. And now world catastrophe was beginning to test the sinews of government and citizenry together.

Can you remember the days when foreign relations were for traders and diplomats only?

6. "So I Said to the Ambassador—"

Washington dotes on diplomats and diplomats dote on Washington—and no wonder, for it is one place in the world where the last attaché of the least influential legation is treated with almost as much awe and deference as only ambassadors might expect in London or Paris.

There are several reasons for this Washington diplomat-worship. One is that in most countries the capital and the metropolis are one; you would have to imagine Washington transplanted to New York and lost in the mazes of the financial, commercial, and artistic interests of a great city, to get an other-country perspective on diplomats as seen against the more varied background of most other capitals.

And then, we welcome the diplomats' bringing into our democratic atmosphere some of the aura of courtlier ways. You need only glance through the State Department's little monthly bluebook, the Diplomatic List, to conjure up a world's worth of pageantry and panoply as you turn from page to page and country to country listed in the order of their chief of missions' length of service in Washington.

The diplomat's life seems a charmed one: just a round of glamorous parties sprinkled generously with intrigue. Pleasure, however, is his business; and when one *must* do something, no matter how pleasant, it easily ceases to be "pleasure." Rare champagne to a wine taster is just part of the day's work. I wonder how many times a diplomat would have given anything to stay home by the fireside with his slippers, a book, and his pipe, rather than go to a dinner he had had "the honor to accept" five or six weeks before, where he would probably have to sit next to some dull dowager and look properly entranced while she told him to the last deadly detail about the marvelous Cook's tour she had taken through his country "thirty-two—let me see—no, thirty-*three* years ago."

Surely there is no career in which the wife is such an important factor—asset or liability—as in diplomacy. Before the war, Italy and, I believe, certain other countries recognized this by granting their ambassadresses personal clothes allowances. In domestic politics, a man whose wife is no asset can make her one by proudly declaring that the little woman is "just a home body" who leaves public affairs to him; but in diplomatic life the wife is called on, really, to make more contacts than her husband, and I've never known an envoy's wife who kept in the background, except one or two Mohammedan ladies, who did stay in harem-like seclusion the whole time they were in Washington.

To be sure, there have been diplomats' wives blandly listed as "absent" in the Diplomatic List month after month and year after year—a polite way of noting separation without divorce. One ambassador told me that before he and his wife agreed to disagree, the only way they could keep up some semblance of domestic harmony at their dinner parties was to have the florist make such high centerpieces that they couldn't glare at each other across the table!

Only one capital group is quite unimpressed by any diplomat, as such, no matter how important his country or how noble his family-tree, unless he fits into their own classification of "smart" or "amusing": that is Washington's supersmart set, whose idea of seventh heaven is the F Street Club.

Only two capital groups refuse to dabble in diplomatic circles at all: one, those official families who come from districts so unsophisticated or narrow-minded that they seriously object to their "mixing with foreigners"; the other, those few sentimental souls, in and out of politics, who say they cannot bear to make diplomatic friends because it would break their hearts to have to say good-by and see them go off to the ends of the earth a few years later.

At that point they usually sigh and quote, *"Partir, c'est mourir un peu!"* And you can only agree that the old French proverb speaks truth, and to say good-by is indeed "to die a little." That is the sad part of all diplomatic friendships. But to refuse therefore to make them is rather like saying that you can't bear to enjoy the loveliness of spring because you know the flowers will fade.

Eventually you have to come to the point where you take the constant comings and goings of official life more or less for granted; but it takes time.

I remember one day when, feeling very blue after seeing some diplomatic friends off at the station, I ran into Mme. Simopoulos, the blunt British wife of the Greek Minister, who was so popular in Washington.

She asked why on earth I looked so sad, and when I told her, she exclaimed, "Good heavens, don't you know yet that you only miss people *before* they go!"

Another pearl of wisdom from Mme. Simopoulos, which I remembered and used, was: When you introduce people, always mention their country or state—"This is Señor Marimba of the Chilean Embassy," or "May I present Congressman Corncob of Iowa" —if you want to nip faux-pas jokes before they bud.

So far I have spoken of the diplomatic corps *in toto,* as distinguished from other groups. It is an entity in some respects, but by no means one happy family. Within the diplomatic circle itself there are countless smaller circles, which even in peacetime only meet in the most formal way at some function large enough to take them all in, like the Diplomatic Reception at the White House or a huge party at some embassy or legation to celebrate a national holiday.

The smallest and smartest of these circles, until Hitler ground Europe under the Nazi heel, was made up of the "big" embassies: the British, the French, the Polish, the Belgian, and the Spanish. ("Big" in this case doesn't necessarily mean a Great Power, for some countries not among the powers were outstanding socially because they were usually represented by members of famous families such as the de Lignes, the Potockis, or the Szechenyis.) In former days the German and the Italian embassies were always high on the list, until Hitler and Mussolini brought them to complete social eclipse, the natural reaction to Nazi and Fascist aggressions. And then, suddenly and unbelievably, the French Embassy too was taboo, because everyone knew that it was in practical fact an annex of the German Embassy. And the Polish and the Belgian embassies, although they represent their governments-in-exile in London, are, of course, socially speaking, mere shadows of what they were before the war. The British Embassy has always been almost a hard little circle in itself in the very center of everything.

Next to these would come the circle of the other embassies, and (except in wartime) they all entertain beautifully and constantly. Yet some of them were outshone socially by certain legations, for instance, the Netherlands, the Canadian, and the Hungarian.

Since the war the legations of all the occupied countries of the United Nations, except little Luxembourg, have been raised to embassies as a gesture of respect for their peoples, and all the South American legations, down to the smallest Caribbean country, have been made embassies as part of the Good Neighbor policy. Thus the Canadian Minister, Leighton McCarthy, attained the distinction, as he said, of being the only minister in the Western Hemisphere, but before long he suddenly found himself raised to the rank of ambassador, too.

I suppose it is only natural that we should find more social magic in the great European countries than in the rest of the world, for their traditions lie behind our own, even though the United States was born in rebellion. When Washington heard that the young Earl of Chichester had arrived as attaché at the British Embassy, or a son of the Duc de Gramont at the French, those were names threading history still real to us. Yet friends of mine who had been stationed in Tokyo used to tell me that the Japanese considered anyone with a family background of a mere five hundred years practically an upstart, and that the proud patricians of Japan can often produce a written family tree going back at least five thousand years. What a pity that five thousand years of "civilization" couldn't produce something better than, the Japan of today!

The largest single diplomatic circle in Washington is made up of the Latin Americans, who usually include some of the most cultured and charming people in town, with their fine Spanish heritage. American officialdom fully realizes this, but many European diplomats, unfortunately for themselves, do not, and even many distinguished Latin American ambassadors never come within their range of vision.

Smaller and smaller circles on the diplomatic pond crowd each other. Often through the charm of one diplomat's personality a legation that has previously enjoyed but little social distinction becomes a real factor for a time.

Aside from these purely social groupings there are always diplomatic coteries which form inside the corps as echoes of treaties, ententes, axises, or royal matrimonial alliances abroad. At the same time there are groups coldly avoiding each other because of strife, moderate or acute, between their home countries. Obviously, the only thing to do is to follow the news always, and up to the latest broadcast before a party, if you expect to steer a safe course among diplomatic shoals. Besides those charted daily in the papers or over the radio, you must know, or at least sense, all the undeclared and hidden tensions which make it social suicide not to know how to mix your diplomatic guests. Since in peacetime most Washington dinner invitations were sent out four or five weeks in advance, you had to be a political prophet into the bargain. Once your invitations have been accepted, there is nothing you can do to change the rules of protocol; you might find to your horror that you must seat mortal enemies side by side, if you missed your guess about what plays would be made on the international checkerboard in the meantime.

One of Washington's pet stories is about the American wife of a European diplomat who found herself seated beside a diplomat from a nation which was almost at the point of war with her adopted country. She was very fond of her hapless hostess, and not wishing to be conspicuous by refusing to talk to her dinner partner at all, she gravely recited the multiplication table to him whenever she had to turn his way.

You would think, with all this social merry-go-rounding, that all of official Washington would be pretty well acquainted. The truth is that almost any diplomat can count on the fingers of his two hands the Senators he has so much as heard of, not to say met, and that one hand is usually enough to count the Congressmen whom he knows. We have proved this, for fun, to many a well-informed diplomat's surprise, as an after-dinner game, and have watched him rack his brain for half an hour trying to name an eleventh Senator.

The group of those they know in Congress is almost invariably the same. While some of these Americans make their diplomatic contacts through inherited social connections, others, like Senator Borah, for example, who detested "going out," do it through their own personalities and their importance on the Congressional committees which deal with foreign affairs. But as far as I can see, being on those committees, while it means invitations for the large formal receptions, does not in itself bring intimate contact with the diplomatic crowd. What is more likely to give it is a genuine liking for many nationalities, granted, of course, real opportunity to get to know them.

If you imagine the official gaieties as going far around the clock, you are due for disillusion. In reality Washington lives on a Cinderella schedule, and most official dinners are over in time for guests to be home long before midnight. The truth is that the men in Washington really work hard, and the only way they could possibly stand the strain of their long office hours and still have a little relaxation afterwards has been to reverse the reversal of an old saying and make it, "Early to bed and early to rise, and you'll meet all the interesting people."

The exact time when an official dinner party breaks up depends on the social conscience of the ranking lady. It is up to her to make the first move to leave, and it is almost unthinkable for anyone to depart before this. Only for some rare, genuinely urgent reason, duly and formally explained to her, can it be done.

Most official dinners go along almost as smoothly scheduled as a battleship drill. If the invitations are for 8:15, as they usually are, you are expected to be exactly on time. It is conspicuous bad taste to come in after the guests of honor have arrived. The rule is to wait five minutes for a man, ten minutes for a woman, and fifteen minutes for a couple. If cocktails are finished by that time, in you go to dinner no matter who is still missing, except—unthinkable!—the guests of honor.

Each man has found his escort card in the hall and has discovered, inside the tiny white envelope bearing his name, the name of the lady he is to take in to dinner. If the dinner is large and very formal, there is probably a chart of the seating arrangements in the hall as well, which makes it easy for him to pilot his partner to the right place at the table, and spares all the confusion of a criss-crossing search. After cocktails in the drawing room each man finds the lady he is to escort and offers her his arm for the march to the dining room. The host leads the way with the ranking lady as the procession forms two by two, the hostess and the guest of honor coming last. When the procession forms again after dinner, the host goes last and the hostess first. Why, nobody knows.

The hostess has had no choice at all in arranging the seating unless the dinner is entirely unofficial. For protocol decrees exactly where everyone is to sit, and all she can do is to guard in advance against the fatal blunder of including officials who must never be invited to the same dinner because their relative rank has never been finally decided—such as the Chief Justice and an ambassador, or an associate justice of the Supreme Court and a foreign minister. There is but one change a hostess can make in the rigidly prescribed rules: if she finds that a husband and wife would be seated together, she may ask the wife of a higher official if she would be willing to change places.

It has always been an unwritten Washington law that there *must* be an even number of men and women at a dinner, or at least only an odd man; which in case of a late withdrawal may mean frantic telephoning for someone to "fill in" on the day of a dinner, with consequent reseating of the entire party, perhaps at the very last second. The escort cards are written after the seating plan is charted, each man escorting the lady who will be at his right, except for one—usually whoever sits at the hostess' left—who has to "drop" his lady and then take his own place. Men in Washington, through long practice, achieve the art of falling into the procession to the dining room at exactly the place where they belong. Only official rank counts. A mere "Mr." invariably precedes the most resounding foreign title, if his official position is higher.

The escort cards and procession, of course, go with a white-tie dinner. If it is black-tie, the hostess usually starts off to the dining room informally with the other ladies and the men just trail along behind. Before the war, one always took it for granted that a dinner was white-tie, unless black-tie was written on the invitation or mentioned over the telephone. In wartime every dinner, even at the White House, has been black-tie.

Once at the table, of course, everything goes along on the usual lines. All that is expected of you is to be as amusing as possible, and always to switch the conversation to the right or the left when your hostess does, with each course. After the procession back to the drawing room the men usually disappear to have their coffee and liqueurs in another room, leaving the ladies to talk of temperamental cooks, wonderful little dressmakers, and the current social feud, if there is one.

When the men come back after coffee, the women break up the little groups they have been in, with the ranking ladies on the "sacred sofa" with the hostess, and there is usually general conversation for about another twenty minutes while the hostess moves from group to group for a few minutes' chat with each, until the ranking lady takes a surreptitious glance at her wrist watch, or her husband gives her a prearranged signal that it's time to go.

And right here, I suppose I will have to take away someone's last illusion by admitting that table talk at Washington dinner parties is all too seldom brilliant or scintillating. There are a lot of reasons why. For one thing, the people who really have something to say are scared to death of being "quoted." For another, consider how much attention must go for avoidance: how many are the controversial subjects, any one of which, if touched on, would blow up a party in two minutes. Everyone in official life has to learn the art of talking on and on for hours and saying nothing, for even Dale Carnegie hasn't figured out yet how you can make friends and influence people—and their votes—and say what's really on your mind at the same time. And how can you have really good talk when most people are more interested in sharpening up the axe they have to grind than polishing up their repartee?

Then, too, good general conversation is impossible with more than eight, or at the most ten, people at the table. Any larger dinner automatically becomes just a polite buzz-buzz of twosomes; and most formal dinners in Washington usually have from twenty to forty guests, or more. When you add to all these conversational handicaps the inescapable protocol law that seats people according to rank, with no regard for congeniality at all, you can see what you have. Besides, there seems to be some perverse imp who hovers around Capital dinner tables to see that the same people have to sit next to each other night after night all winter long. No matter how much you like someone, you are likely to run short of sprightly topics if that keeps up too long. And if you *don't* like him—!

You can find good talk in Washington, but nine chances out of ten it will be at a very small dinner of trusted, intimate friends, with probably at least one blunt, argumentative newspaperman to get things started. Even then it isn't likely to put Noel Coward's dialogue to shame.

To make up for the dearth of conversational brilliance, occasionally there is a little music after dinner by one of the guests, who may be either a concert-artist countryman of the host's or even one of us amateurs who really work at our music. But I have never known bridge to follow an official dinner. Usually a hostess makes up a bridge dinner as such, so that people will know in advance that they are expected to stay and play. Otherwise they rather resent being let in for a late evening without warning. Bridge I have always avoided, being wonderfully unadept mathematically; but I love poker, where you're responsible to no one for your blunders, and am always glad when someone suggests it after an informal dinner.

Fortunately you *are* on your own, for a partner would surely have murdered me the night I had a royal straight flush and didn't bet on it!

It was at the Chalkleys', who were giving an informal supper to celebrate the completion of the Anglo-American Trade Agreement, which Harry Chalkley, as commercial counselor of the British Embassy, had worked on so hard and so long. When the game started, I found myself between Harry and Sir Willmott Lewis, of the London *Times,* who for years has been known as the unofficial British ambassador to Washington. He is a great character: as British as crumpets, but through long association, and by marriage, he probably understands America and Americans better than any Englishman who has ever come here.

He's a terrific kidder, and with half my mind on his persiflage and half on the game, I looked at my hand and saw the impossible—a royal straight flush. I simply couldn't believe it. Obviously, the cards couldn't have been shuffled! The pot grew and grew; I weakly passed, convinced that in the circumstances they would never pay me anyhow. Hands were laid down. They gave a sort of strangled gurgle in unison—and asked me what on earth I had been thinking of while the betting was going on.

When I told them, they nearly had hysterics. And to cap it all, I had to borrow sixty cents from Sir Willmott when it came time to settle up! To this day he solemnly warns newcomers in that Big Ben voice of his, "Beware of playing poker with Vera—she's the slickest poker player in Washington!"

Unexpected and charming epilogues can happen at even the most formal dinners. I remember especially one that we gave for the former Polish Ambassador, Filipowicz.

It went well from the first moment, for there was not one person "out of key"—either sharp or flat—to upset the developing harmony. The table bore the enchantment of the set of very beautiful three-colored Polish glass whose wine glasses and finger bowls the Ambassador had overwhelmed me by sending after I had admired them at the exposition in Poznan; and there were the antique silver service plates we had discovered in Warsaw.

After dinner, when we were all together again after coffee, the Italian military attaché, Colonel Pennaroli, asked me to make good my promise to sing the little Italian song "Cara Piccina" for him with my guitar. Not wishing to hold up the whole party for something that might not suit their mood, I led Pennaroli, Bob Kelley of the State Department, and one or two others off to my sitting room, where we wouldn't be heard, and sang the song for them. I finished to a rather startling burst of applause from behind me, and turning, found that the whole party had tiptoed in. Soon I was doing my whole rather meager guitar repertoire, and when that was ended, doing it over again.

Mother had mentioned to Mrs. James Carroll Frazer that I was going on to a costume party later with Bob and a few of the others, and that I had worn a black picture-dress so that by the quick addition of a white wig and some paste jewelry I would be ready to go. Immediately Mrs. Frazer, who adores everything French, suggested that we should have a "levée de la reine," with true Versailles ceremony in the decking of the queen. I knew nothing of the plot until I suddenly found myself urged by my "courtiers" that it was time to prepare for the ball. They played their parts handsomely; and by the time they had seen to my "diamonds," snowy headdress, and properly brilliant make-up, it was nearly midnight, and nobody remembered that we had started out as a formal official dinner.

But to get back to the diplomatic groupings: Besides all the political and social cliques, the diplomatic corps, like any other group, falls naturally into clusters drawn together by mutual tastes. The horsey set, led by the Polish Ambassador, Count Po-

116

tocki, was as much at home in the Virginia hunting country as in Washington. The bridge players fell into several groups ranging from little afternoon games at various embassies for a quarter of a cent a point to a famous evening group which practically made bridge a career, where it was quite possible to win or lose up to eighteen hundred dollars at one session.

In addition to the horsey and the bridge sets (for which I could never qualify) there was a musical group whose meeting place, until war activities left us too little time for music, was the Yugoslav Legation, where not only the Minister and Mme. Fotitch but the current counselor, Dr. Rybar, were all exceptionally gifted pianists. Mme. Fotitch had installed two grand pianos in the legation drawing-room, and gathered a little group of amateurs from the diplomatic and official sets who were prepared not only to do consistent practicing but also to sing or play for some of her small informal teas. Mme. Fotitch and Anita Burke (Mrs. Tom Burke of the State Department) usually gave the two-piano part of the program—and no simple "salon" pieces, either. My most ambitious contribution was to join them in some of the Brahms Liebeslieder Waltzes for four hands and voice: difficult, but well worth plenty of practice and a dash of recklessness.

One of the most enjoyable things about being asked to sing after a diplomatic dinner is that it can lead to unexpected new repertory. Often someone has come up afterwards to say, "You *must* sing my favorite folk song!" And, sometimes months later, there would arrive from Mexico or Norway or Poland, or some other part of the globe, an enchanting bit of music one would probably never have discovered otherwise. When you explore the music of many different countries, you learn, I find, to sing the French songs with the mind, the classic Lieder with the heart, Italian and Spanish with the emotions, and Russian and Polish with the soul.

Speaking of music reminds me of a little wraith of a lady who came to Washington as a refugee from the Russian Revolution. She was not only the daughter-in-law of one great Russian composer but the niece of an even greater one, Tchaikowsky. Which did not save her and her son, who both spoke the incredible number of languages that only a cultured Russian can, from becoming practically penniless in Washington.

In their darkest days a friend had left a standing order at one of the Russian restaurants in town for them to be his guests for one meal a week. Then they were inexpressibly grateful because a young Washington man who owned an apartment house, and who wanted to learn Russian, offered her the position of superintendent, with a tiny apartment but no salary, in exchange for the Russian lessons. No one knows how they existed this way, grateful for a roof over their heads and that one good meal a week, until a friend of mine who happened to live in that building discovered it accidentally and persuaded the linguistic landlord to give them at least sufficient salary so that they could be sure of enough to eat. Through my father the son found work as a translator, which helped from time to time, though poor health prevented his keeping it up.

And yet, during all that time, you would meet Mme. Rimsky-Korsakoff at the most distinguished houses in Washington, a very great lady in spite of everything, and one more shining example of Russian character.

The younger diplomatic set, to get back on the subject, is a little world within a world where, according to the papers, each ambassador's daughter is "beautiful," each attaché's wife "glamorous," and every bachelor "dashing." Besides the young-marrieds, daughters, and extra men of the embassies, legations, and State Department, it includes some past and present local debutantes, and a few daughters of American official families. The young-marrieds have always supplied a lot of the Capital's amusing and informal "little dinners," with the latest game fad or bridge to follow; and the younger married diplomats were in peacetime always expected to give a tea or cocktail party or two during the winter, to help their chief foster cordial relations among those who in the course of time would inherit the seats of the mighty in their own countries.

For men do appear at Washington cocktail parties, and in droves. Not always just for fun, by any means. One thing every diplomat knows is that there is no better place to put over an idea casually or get a little information, which he would be doing much too obviously if he were to go to someone's office for that especially.

Almost all Washington afternoon parties are from five to seven; it is considered dreadfully provincial to show up a minute before a quarter to six, even if it means only being able to stay a second or so in case you have four or five things to go to that afternoon, which in peacetime wasn't at all unusual. (Once, for fun, we put "4:30 to 7" on some cocktail invitations to see if anyone would appear earlier. They did not.)

The bachelors, especially those under ministerial rank, led a charmed life in every way. Not only were most of them able to choose from two or three dinner invitations every night, but no one expected them to do anything about entertaining, and very few did. They were considered to have quite an exceptional social conscience if they occasionally threw a cocktail party. The more attractive ones were in such demand that they rarely had to take a girl out just for the sake of passing an amusing evening, for they were booked solid, weeks in advance, with dinners and dances.

In Washington, at least among the girls I know, the only taboo about going to a bachelor's house is that there must be a "crowd," which means at least another couple. There is no "Third Act: His Rooms" atmosphere just because your host is "a dashing bachelor diplomat." Everyone acts and talks as they would anywhere else, and in Washington people are really very well behaved. Of course, some may give a different sort of parties for a different sort of people, but I only speak whereof I know.

Naturally, the younger the attaché, the more seriously he is likely to take himself. I remember a few years ago a young secretary at one of the Scandinavian legations had been persuaded to appear in some tableaux for charity; and when the news photographers came, they kept begging him, "Please smile! Come now, smile, please!"

"I am very sorry," he answered solemnly, "but I cannot smile. You see, I represent my country!"

I hope to be here long enough to see the beaming smile he will probably have found useful by the time he comes back as minister.

Fortunately, not all diplomats take themselves so seriously, as witness the Zilches.

It all started because Bee Sokolowska, who was my closest friend through all the time she was the American first lady of the Polish Embassy while "Peter" Sokolowski was the able and popular Polish chargé d'affaires and counselor, had been quarantined for weeks while their eldest boy had scarlet fever, and several of us got the idea at the same moment that she ought to have a coming-out party.

Unable to decide where to have it, we agreed on all places: a different course in each house. And here it comes again. As well as we all knew each other we were seated at each house differently, and exactly according to protocol; and it would have been so even if Jefferson Patterson, one of the State Department's protocol experts, hadn't been along. For a while it was just a nice little progressive dinner. It became inspired because of a story nobody would believe.

At that time the whole country was laughing over the antics of a mythical family named Zilch in *Ballyhoo* magazine. But no one dreamed there was a Zilch in real life, until one was discovered in, of all places, the State Department, when Secretary Hull asked one of his assistants to locate a confidential stenographer on a Sunday. After trying the whole list in vain, he could hardly believe his eyes when he saw that his last hope was Miss Helen J. Zilch.

She was quite real, and did the afternoon's work. The only trouble was that no one would believe the story, which I had direct from Miss Zilch's proud discoverer.

Anyhow, we saw in the Zilches possibilities for a society on the pattern of The Souls, that fun-full London group of which Margot Asquith had been the center; and suddenly we felt called. Bee Sokolowska became Zenobia Zilch. Peter—with a bow to Poland —became Mazurka Zilch; and John Franklin Carter, better known as Jay Franklin, with true literary flair had to have different names for different times to the day. I forget most of them, but I do remember we liked his evening name, Zipper Zilch, the best.

John finally immortalized us in his detective story *The Corpse on the White House Lawn,* using of course, a good dose of poetic license in describing our progressive party. In *Death in the Senate* several of us emerged again: "the beautiful Bee Bokanowska of the Polish Embassy"; "Pat Jefferson of the Pomp and Circumstance Division of the State Department"; and a character for me to emulate, "the witty Veronica Flower."

If I had to name the most popular diplomatic couples in Washington, of all we have seen come and go, at the top of the list would come the Howards, Sir Esmé and Lady Isabella.

The Howards were born to grace a British embassy, in every sense of the word. It is easy enough for anyone at a British embassy to inspire awe; a lot of them do inspire real admiration; but no Britishers since the Howards, except those two dear people,

Harry and Marjorie Chalkley—the Commercial Counselor and Lady Chalkley—have inspired affection wherever they went, although Lord Lothian, with his spontaneous kindliness, would very likely have done it had he been spared longer. And Lord and Lady Halifax, both such sincerely kind and good people, have more nearly taken the Howards' place than anyone else.

I have always thought of the Howards, to myself, as Sir Darby and Lady Joan, for they proved that

> Hearts as pure and fair
> May beat in Belgrave Square
> As in the poorer air
> of Seven Dials.

They were that rare kind of people, democratic aristocrats; handsome, kind, good, and beautifully happy together. I remember especially how they looked one night at the musicale after the Diplomatic Dinner at the White House: Lady Isabella so lovely in a soft gold lamé, with her Renaissance tiara of delicate diamond roses trembling on their golden stems on her silvery hair, and Sir Esmé so distinguished, with all his decorations, and both looking exactly as if two Van Dyke portraits had stepped down from their frames.

Lady Isabella was born a Princess Giustiniani of Rome, with an English title in her own right besides, as her family was originally one of the English Catholic families that went to Italy during the Protestant persecutions centuries ago.

She met Sir Esmé when he came to Rome as a young secretary at the British Embassy there. He belonged to the great Catholic Howard family of England, of which the Duke of Norfolk is head, but evidently he belonged to a Protestant branch: Lady Isabella told me once that when he wanted to marry her, her mother had told him that she knew "Isa" would never be happy married to someone who was not of her own faith, and that he must wait six months to decide whether he would be happier changing his religion to marry her, or keeping it without her. Of course he chose the first, and there can never have been a shadow of doubt in his mind about the rightness of his choice, for they appeared to be about the most congenial couple I have ever seen in any walk of life; and every morning in Washington found Sir Esmé a devout attendant at early morning Mass.

How Lady Isabella managed to be doyenne of the diplomatic corps (for Sir Esmé became its dean) as well as British ambassadress, and still do all the unknown good works she did, I shall never understand. Her idea was to give not merely money, but her time and herself.

Gwenda Rogeri told me once about having offered her services, one time, to a Catholic mission in Washington, the Little Sisters of the Poor. On her first morning there, she was taken into a big room where a long table of unfortunates were being served by a woman in a gingham apron, who waited on them as if her very life depended on it.

Suddenly she looked up and greeted Gwenda, who to her amazement saw that it was Lady Isabella coming over to her and beginning to take off her apron, apologizing for leaving, but explaining that they were giving a big luncheon at the Embassy that day and she must hurry to be back in time. And she was off to sit at the head of a brilliant table just as wholeheartedly as she had been serving those poor souls half an hour before.

The sweetest sight in Washington used to be Sir Esmé and Lady Isabella out walking, arm in arm, when they found a few moments for themselves between engagements, perfectly happy in each other and so essentially simple and unspoiled by the formal, glittering world they lived in.

One night at dinner at the old Embassy on Connecticut Avenue, Mother was looking around regretfully at the lovely rooms which so soon would be torn down, and she told Sir Esmé how sad it seemed that their old-fashioned, high-ceilinged charm had to go.

"Yes, but then, you know," he—who could fit so perfectly into any background—answered wistfully, "those high ceilings are so awfully hard to live up to!"

Typical of Lady Isabella's kindnesses is one I remember from the time of Prime Minister Ramsay MacDonald's first visit to Washington. There was to be a very exclusive reception at the Embassy, and Mother and Father had been invited but I had not, although of course I would have given anything to go. The day before, I happened to meet Lady Isabella at a tea, and as she was saying good-by, she added, "I'll see you tomorrow night."

Not knowing what to say, I just murmured, "Thank you." I didn't want to hold her up by saying I had not had an invitation;

and since none of the other official daughters were to be there, I realized how much it might embarrass her if I took advantage of what might be merely a casual kind remark. Feeling noble indeed, I decided not to go.

But when I came home at dinnertime the next night, there was a telephone message to say that she *had* meant what she said, and was expecting me. When I arrived at the Embassy, I found that besides Ishbel MacDonald, the Prime Minister's daughter, the only other girls at the reception were Gytha Stourton, Lady Isabella's cousin and her social secretary, and Eleanor Hard, the daughter of William and Anne Hard, the writers. Lady Isabella had told Gytha that she could invite two of her friends, and only two, to keep her company, and she had known when she spoke to me that I was to be one of the two.

We had an amusing experience with the Howards one night when the Egyptian Legation gave a dinner in their honor.

It happened to be the night before we were to sail—on two days' notice—for the International Copyright Conference in Rome, and we had to pack, close the house, and go to all kinds of parties in between. Father was to leave for New York on the midnight train to arrange his letter of credit and all the details, and Mother and I were to meet him on board the *Duilio* the next night.

We thought the Howards would surely leave the dinner by about ten-thirty, as the ranking guests usually do, but either they were having an especially good time or else they wanted to show Egypt special honor, for they stayed on and on; Sir Esmé kept on chatting in the drawing room with Mother—and of course, as I have mentioned, in Washington it is almost unheard of to precede a guest of honor of such rank in departing.

At last, about eleven-thirty, Sir Esmé said casually to Mother, "And when are you leaving Washington?"

"Tonight!" Mother had to answer, so the Ambassador, realizing the situation, grabbed an astonished Lady Isabella by the arm, barely said good night to the Minister and Mme. Samy, and rushed downstairs with us literally at their heels, so Father could catch his train.

After the Howards returned to England, when Sir Esmé retired from the diplomatic service, the King raised him to the peerage as Baron Howard of Penrith. That changed Lady Isabella, as she was called in her own right as the daughter of a British peer, to

Lady Howard, as a peer's wife; and Sir Esmé to Lord Howard, as I never succeeded in remembering. We saw them again in London the next summer, and invariably I would get as far as "Sir Es—" and stop short.

"Don't worry," he laughed. "No one is ever going to get used to calling me anything else!"

They had several happy, quiet years together before he passed on, and the last word we had from Lady Howard was in answer to Mother's heartfelt letter of condolence. She seemed to be, understandably, almost happy that he had not had to see England at war again, and their five sons called to the colors. And she added, after telling us of her life in wartime, that she had accepted King George's offer of an apartment for life at Hampton Court Palace (where, you remember, Henry VIII paid court to Anne Boleyn), where several other distinguished widows live as the guests of the royal family. It seems fitting and lovely to think of her living there.

My second choice in an ambassadorial popularity contest would have to be between the French Ambassador and Mme. de Laboulaye, who stood for the finest French traditions, in every way, and Ambassador and Mme. Sze, of China.

In the end, I suppose I should decide on the Szes: they were here so long, knew such shoals of people in every Capital circle, and were adored wherever they went.

The Ambassador had come to Washington first as a small boy, to stay with his uncle, a very great Chinese gentleman who was then the Chinese envoy and, I've been told, the most picturesque and distinguished figure in Washington, in his Chinese robes. Unfortunately, since then, only the wives of Chinese diplomats wear their lovely Chinese clothes.

Little Sao-Ke Alfred Sze went to the Washington public schools and later graduated from Cornell University as the most popular man in his class. So quite aside from his lovable personality, it was natural that he should have won extraordinary popularity when he came here as minister and then as ambassador, for he was as American as it is possible for a good Chinese to be, and when he wasn't busy at diplomacy, he was usually absorbed in a game of bridge.

Lovely little Mme. Sze spoke excellent English, too, with only a fascinating lisp of an accent. She told us that Chinese girls who marry into distant parts of China have to speak some European language to their in-laws, since the various Chinese dialects are so completely different.

The Szes had trained a wonderful colored cook they had for years to make all the most intricate Chinese dishes, and they sometimes gave real Chinese dinners of a leisurely twenty-seven courses for intimate friends, when at least a try at chopsticks would be in order. I was surprised to learn from them that spaghetti is really a Chinese dish, brought back to Italy by Marco Polo centuries ago, as you may have seen in the picture about his adventures in which Gary Cooper appeared. But of course at the Szes' formal dinners the menu was quite as classically French as at the French Embassy.

Of many dinners at the Szes', I remember one particularly. They were expecting a friend, Mme. Wu, to arrive from China, and arranged a dinner for her on quite short notice. My father was in New York, but due back on the Congressional that night, so Mme. Sze said it would be all right if he came in late.

When he arrived we were, of course, already at the table, and he found his place beside an enchanting little Chinese creature who didn't look a day over sixteen. To start the conversation, he said to her, "Are you here to go to school in Washington?"

"Oh, no!" she laughed, in perfect English, "I'm Mme. Wu, and I've come over to see my eldest son get his medical degree at Johns Hopkins!"

We were able to satisfy a lifelong curiosity of Dr. Sze's when we rented the house we now live in on Columbia Road, for he had watched that house go up, stone by stone, when he played as a small boy in the open fields which were all that then lay between it and the old Chinese Legation a block or so away. To his surprise, instead of the Georgian red brick and white Colonial columns which were the expected things in Washington in those days, the house turned out to be of Spanish architecture, with tawny stucco walls and a roof of terra-cotta tiles. There was even a Spanish patio with an antique fountain, which he had tried to peek at through the iron grilles.

But in all those years Dr. Sze had never been inside the house, and when he told us how anxious he was to see it, we had a little private housewarming just for them one afternoon.

They had given us some almost priceless China tea sometime before, which we had been saving and saving for a great occasion;

and this was it, we decided. Time came, but not the steaming tea. The delay lengthened, and at last Mother sent out asking why—and learned that the puzzled cook had already used a half pound of that priceless tea in vain, trying to make it "look right"! We had forgotten to explain that fine China tea never gets a dark color, no matter how long you brew it. After that, of course, we got a teacaddy and made it at the table, as we should have in the first place.

When Dr. Sze retired, they and most of their seven children returned home to China (some were still studying abroad). Dr. Sze became one of the heads of the Chinese Red Cross; and we heard that they were miraculously safe, although bombs dropped into their Shanghai garden during the siege of the city, in the course of what Japan for so long preferred to call "the China incident." Then one day to our great delight we had an unexpected visitor. It was Mme. Sze, come to tell us that they were again in Washington, where Dr. Sze was to serve as China's delegate to the International Red Cross.

The two diplomats, of any I know, who would have fitted the most perfectly the Hollywood idea of what an ambassadress or a minister should be were Donna Antoinetta de Martino, for so long the horribly haughty Italian ambassadress, and Charles A. Davila, long the unbearably glamorous Rumanian Minister.

To start with the lady. (*Donna* is the Italian equivalent of the English title of Lady in one's own right, like Lady Diana or Lady Mary, which, in Italy, is also given by courtesy to the wives of ambassadors and high government officials.)

Donna Antoinetta was thin, blonde, and of that dated brand of elegance which only feels well dressed in a ball gown and tiara, with a cloud of tulle around the shoulders. She wielded the deadliest lorgnette in captivity, and though her parties at the Embassy were famously lavish, even many sophisticated diplomats hated to go, so great a trial was it to face her freezing hauteur, that only melted a little if a resoundingly titled guest appeared.

One day I happened to be present at a discussion between several diplomats as to whether or not it was worth going to a forthcoming party at the de Martinos. One shy British diplomat confessed that whenever he was invited to the Italian Embassy for dinner, he always came with his invitation in his pocket, so that he could touch it to assure himself he was a rightful guest as he ap-

Mrs. Sol Bloom Pouring Tea for the Chinese Ambassador and Mme. Sze

The Czech Minister and Mme. Hurban Listening to the News
of Hitler's Invasion of Czechoslovakia

Veiled Women Picketing the Bloom House in Protest Against
the Revision of the Neutrality Act of 1941

proached the ordeal of Donna Antonietta's icy greeting. A realistic Spanish grandee—a distant relative of King Alfonso's—who was then at the Spanish Embassy reasoned with him this way: "But, really, my boy, don't you think one bad moment is worth several hours at a beautiful party, with the best chef in town? I don't let her get *me* down!"

One night we were at a dinner given for the Ambassador and Donna Antonietta by a high official in the Hoover administration. It was perfectly obvious that the Ambassadress had only accepted because she had been told that it was political wisdom to go, for she never turned even a cold shoulder to the host all through dinner!

She was, for her, exceptionally kind to us, and we were at the Embassy a great deal in those days. As she fortunately visited Italy a lot, we were often there when the Ambassador entertained alone. He was a kind, mild little man, and, incidentally, an excellent and disarming diplomat.

One day during the court mourning for Queen Mother Margherita of Italy he was lunching with us quietly in our apartment at the Mayflower. It happened that Sabatini, the hotel's head chef, was a Neapolitan like the Ambassador, and he had turned out in his honor the most marvelous Italian meal imaginable, in appearance as well as in taste, for everything was in the Italian colors, red, white, and green.

After luncheon the Ambassador said how much he had enjoyed everything, but that he must confess some disappointment that we had had nothing distinctly American. Mother asked what distinctly American dish he craved, and he answered immediately, "Hot dogs!" (This was, of course, long before Mrs. Roosevelt put the hot dog in society by serving it to King George and Queen Elizabeth at Hyde Park.) We confidently promised the Ambassador some of the best hot dogs procurable, as Father's secretary knew a little delicatessen shop somewhere in town where they made them to order.

He sent her there the next day bearing a request to make them superlatively good, with mention of whom they were for. And a square box duly arrived at the Mayflower, looking so much like a bomb that I labeled it SAUSAGES all over to forestall a panic when it reached the Embassy. Fortunately, Donna Antonietta was in Italy or I'm sure they would never have reached the table.

The Ambassador glowingly acknowledged the hot dogs, and we gave the matter no further thought until my father's secretary went back to the shop to order some for herself a few days later, to be faced with a beautiful sign on the door of the delicatessen, which read: *By appointment—To the Royal Italian Embassy.*

It's almost impossible to find mere words to describe Charles A. Davila. Tall, slim, silver-haired, supercilious, and straight out of E. Phillips Oppenheim, he certainly made the Rumanian Legation by far the most "exclusive" diplomatic house in town while he was here.

One night, at an embassy dinner, I found myself seated next to Davila. His expression left no doubt that he felt himself martyrized to a wasted evening. It was very bleak: the lady on his right was someone he didn't know at all; and though he knew I at least knew what and whom he was talking about, nevertheless I quite failed of being either Alice Longworth or Virginia Bacon— Mrs. Robert Low Bacon—the Congressional crème de la crème.

Finally, with the dessert, as I remember, he drawled wearily and very pointedly, "Isn't it amazing how one can go around Washington for weeks without seeing someone?"

By this time I had had just about enough.

"That's quite true, Mr. Minister," I answered; "and the amazing part of it is that no one ever misses anyone else!"

Amusingly enough, Davila had to decorate my father, when the King of Rumania conferred the Order of Carol on him for his "encouragement of good will and cultural relations between the two countries."

By law, incidentally, an American official may not keep or wear a foreign decoration except through a special act of Congress. Otherwise it lies in a safe at the Protocol Division of the State Department, as long as he remains in public office. More than one official decoration holder has been known to come up to the department every so often just to hold the prize long and lovingly in his hand. Really! But Father has been spared the temptation. After the Washington Bicentennial—when every country in the world had united to honor George Washington, some with special stamps, some with statues, and some with streets named in his honor— several of the countries wished to recognize his work in the only way they could, with a decoration. His great interest in international expositions, dating all the way from early days at the Chicago World's Fair in 1893, has often made foreign countries ask his advice on their own expositions; again, they could only thank him with a decoration. And, I suppose, because his colleagues wanted to thank him too, a bill was passed permitting him to keep and wear them; but he seldom if ever does.

Speaking of decorations reminds me of the time when Italy decorated Colonel John Q. Tilson, who was then the Republican majority leader of the House, with the Order of Grand Officer of the Crown of Italy. I have mentioned our long Montague-and-Capulet friendship with the Tilsons, which made it natural that when the large Italian colony in his New Haven district gave him a testimonial dinner so that Count Marchetti, then the counselor of the Italian Embassy in Washington, could repeat the decoration ceremony in the Ambassador's absence, he asked us to come along. On our arrival, the Colonel explained apologetically that he was afraid that I would be in for a very dull time at the speakers' table: the way the seating arrangements worked out, my dinner partner would be the ogre of Connecticut politics, J. Henry Rorabach, then still extant as boss of the state, whom some people generously called a rough diamond, though others insisted he wasn't even a rough rhinestone.

When the dinner got under way, I found Marchetti at my left; he was obviously not the redoubtable Mr. Rorabach. I summoned all my courage and turned to my right—to find a distinguished gray-haired gentleman with twinkling eyes, who turned out to be about the most charming and cultured man I had ever met.

I couldn't imagine why everyone had described Rorabach so unjustly, and later, when we were talking everything over with the Tilsons, I told the Colonel that I couldn't understand his misleading me that way.

He burst into a roar of laughter and explained, "Good heavens, Vera! I completely forgot to tell you that the seating had to be changed at the very last moment, and instead of Mr. Rorabach we gave you the pride of Yale, Professor William Lyon Phelps!"

Perhaps the greatest hullaballoo which ever greeted a new diplomat was reserved for the day when Washington saw Red and the first Soviet Ambassador arrived in this country following President Roosevelt's sensational recognition of Soviet Russia.

The President's totally unexpected invitation to roly-poly, astute

Maxim Litvinov, the Soviet Commissar for Foreign Affairs, to come and discuss restoring diplomatic relations; Litvinov's triumphant visit here; the appointment of Alexander Troyanovsky as the first Soviet Ambassador to Washington; the immediate departure of William Bullitt as our Ambassador to Moscow, and the turning over of the long-closed Imperial Russian Embassy here to Boris Skvirsky, the Soviet chargé d'affaires, who had quietly and unofficially represented the Soviet here for many years, all happened so rapidly that we were still gasping for breath.

Catching it, we realized that in some mysterious way the Red menace had ceased to be a bugaboo overnight, and that we were simply following most of the rest of the world in opening our eyes to the fact that the Soviet regime in Russia was a pretty permanent affair. And incidentally, facilitating U.S.–Soviet trade.

Ever since the Kerensky regime the huge, white Russian Embassy on Sixteenth Street—built originally as the background for the social triumphs of Mrs. Pullman of Pullman Car fame—had been kept "in trust for the Russian people" by the State Department. The windows were boarded up, and there was barbed wire across the driveway. A White Russian couple of the old regime still lived in makeshift style as caretakers, in the office of the Chancery that juts out at the side of the Embassy building; but they lived very quietly and had no diplomatic connections. We had lived almost directly across the street for several years, and every time I passed, I gave a little mental sigh, half for the departed glories of Russia and the old Embassy, and half for myself that I had never seen them, and would probably never pass that barbed-wire barrier.

And then one day, just when the political sky was turning Red, I was invited into the wing of the Embassy which was still "White." Of course, technically it was neither White nor Red nor anything: Russia did not exist for us, diplomatically speaking. There was even a legend around the State Department that when they *had* to refer to Russia they would merely call it "the territory bounded by Latvia, Lithuania, Rumania, Turkey, Persia, China, etc., etc."! I had an invitation into a diplomatic vacuum.

It came about because I wanted to have a Russian court dress made to wear for a group of Russian and Polish songs at a costume recital I was giving for charity. I wanted the costume authentic, and as magnificent as a wealth of Woolworth jewels could make it, so I enlisted Russian help—White Russian, as I had never met a "Red"—in planning it. Some morning, my friend suggested, we would go to see the lady who lived in the old Russian Embassy, as she had some beautiful costumes and rare books on the history of Russian dress.

So I was to get into the Russian Embassy at last! At very last: for although we did not know it then, that very night the lady and her husband, with all their belongings and all the Russian monarchist archives, were to be spirited out in the small hours of the morning by government agents (to avoid unpleasant publicity for the outgoing regime) before the keys to the Embassy were turned over to Mr. Skvirsky of the Soviet government. And after that moment, suddenly it was the White Russians and not the Reds who became "mysterious characters."

Not long after came the Diplomatic Reception at the White House, and naturally the Soviet Chargé and Mme. Skvirsky stole the show. They took it all very phlegmatically, on the outside, although inside it must have been a very exciting moment, after so many years of figuratively keeping to the diplomatic back streets. But after all, the Skvirskys were only the prologue, as it were, to the Troyanovskys. What would a Soviet ambassador and ambassadress be like? Someone had told me that the Soviet ambassadress in Paris had dyed her hair the brightest possible red, and only wore gowns to match, and that at every party she smothered the embassy in bright red flowers. Would the Troyanovskys put on a show like that, everyone wondered, and—even more important— who would be invited to it?

The question of "taking up" the Soviets was solved immediately by the President, through the Secretary of State, who instructed all American diplomats to call at once upon the Soviet diplomats in every capital; and we, meaning official Washington, were obviously expected to follow suit as soon as possible. After all, it was just common sense. Either you have diplomatic relations with a country, or you haven't.

In the lull before the Troyanovskys arrived, interest centered in the redecoration of the Embassy. Could a Soviet ambassador, we speculated, sleep peacefully in the gilded rococo magnificence of the old Pullman mansion? Or would all the cupids and bowknots be torn down and the Hammer and Sickle put up in their place?

Eventually the answer came. No, they would not. Soviet Russia had more important things to do with its money than to waste it tearing down unimportant emblems of a dead-and-gone day. The Troyanovskys would simply ignore the cupids.

As the day of their arrival came nearer, we began to lose interest in the embassy cupids and whether the house had ninety or only eighty rooms, and turned to wondering how soon we would actually meet the Troyanovskys. For in Washington, calling and having your call returned may mean nothing more than leaving the necessary number of cards on both sides, for months. Our interest —or curiosity—was to be satisfied surprisingly soon, for the Japanese Chargé d'Affaires and Mme. Taketomi invited all three of us to a dinner in the Troyanovskys' honor just a day or two after their arrival.

When the Ambassador arrived, preceding his wife and their fifteen-year-old son by a few days, a slight sensation was caused at the station when, as the Washington *Post* wrote the next morning: "Three hands were outstretched to greet him—one belonged to Robert F. Kelley, Chief of the Eastern European Division of the State Department, one to Jefferson Patterson, Acting Chief of the Protocol Division, and one to T. Taketomi, Chargé d'Affaires of Japan." It was Mr. Taketomi who provided the sensation. Why, the papers wanted to know, did Japan have to poke into a Russian-American historic occasion? Mr. Taketomi explained that he was merely there as an old friend of Mr. Troyanovsky, who had served for five years at Soviet Ambassador to Japan, and that his now-famous dinner was merely a friendly affair and in no way official.

At last the night of the dinner came, and we were all at the Embassy, standing around the smaller drawing room where the Taketomis were receiving, and trying to look as nonchalantly as possible toward the door where a butler would soon announce, for the first time in Washington, "Their Excellencies, the Soviet Ambassador and Mme. Troyanovsky!"

When he did, a very unassuming couple came in who were, somehow surprisingly, in perfectly conventional evening clothes. No red hair; not even a red dress. Even though the papers had been telling us for weeks that Troyanovsky had once been a cadet at the Imperial Russian Naval Academy, and was one of the few higher-ups of the Soviet regime who had belonged to the old, aristocratic Russia, he really looked much more like a bourgeois than either a nobleman or a Bolshevist. And so did Mme. Troya-novsky—placid, pleasant, with eyeglasses, but quite pretty, and like her husband, rather small and dark. She spoke hardly any English then, but that isn't a handicap for very long to any Russian, and she spoke a little of everything else.

The Troyanovskys stayed with the Skvirskys for quite a few weeks while the work of restoring the Embassy was going on, and the Ambassadress settled down at once to the business of paying calls in person. No one could have been more *"protocolaire,"* and it should have given us a hint of how formal and magnificent the entertaining at the Soviet Embassy was going to be. But it took their historic first big party to make everyone realize it.

The invitations looked entirely conventional: stiff white engraved cards, with your name carefully written in in the proper place, and the usual embassy gold coat-of-arms at the top; only, if you looked closely, you saw instead of the usual crown or legendary symbol a golden hammer and sickle.

It was to be an evening reception, and Mother and Father were dining that night at the Bulgarian Legation, where, it quickly became clear, a good part of diplomatic Washington was doomed to play Cinderella; for naturally only the diplomats whose governments had already recognized Soviet Russia could go to the prime event of that evening. No party, of course, is half as good as the one you can't get to. So the next day I wasn't surprised when one of the uninvited diplomats asked me to go to Pierre's for luncheon with him and tell all, or when other Cinderella men came to listen in. I told them from the beginning:

How you drove up to the front entrance of the Embassy in an endless stream of cars, to find, instead of the barbed-wire barrier, the festive formal awning-canopy of the best caterer in town, and the broad smile and gleaming silk hat of William, the colored carriage man who used to welcome you to practically every party in Washington. And how you walked over the carpeted sidewalk and entered the great front door, where two inexorable butlers demanded to see your invitation. How the entrance halls are lined with mirrored walls and dressing rooms, and how you walked up the grand staircase covered with a thick red carpet (which reminded you much more of the traditional red carpet of royalty than of Red Russia) into the first of a series of gigantic drawing rooms, where the Ambassador and Mme. Troyanovsky were receiving, as the gold cupids smiled down at them, while "everybody" in town whirled around the ballroom or wandered from room to room and from floor to floor of the enormous house.

For the floor above the state apartments had been made into the Troyanovskys' private apartment, and the floor above that had been made into a separate apartment for the Counselor and Mme. Skvirsky—and the whole house was open to everyone to wander about as they pleased.

And not only open, but on each and every floor there was a complete buffet, groaning with Russian caviar and vodka, in addition to all the usual tidbits and champagne. In the great dining room there was a superbuffet, with a seven-hundred-pound sturgeon which had been brought from the Volga in sections to be put together again here as the centerpiece. Besides, every room of the Chancery, which opens right out from the dining room, had a buffet or a bar of its own. And the last room in the Chancery, the Ambassador's office, which has some really excellent paintings by Soviet artists, also boasts a marble bust of Lenin: which before the evening was over had acquired a frieze of empty champagne glasses all around the base.

The party looked exactly like an embassy scene in a particularly lavish movie, especially from the arch in the dining-room wall, where you could lean over the balustrade and look up and down the stairs as the party went on, on three floors at once. A few philosophic souls took time to wonder why the Soviets chose to give the most capitalistic fete Washington had seen in years. The rest were satisfied merely to be there.

Evidently, the Soviet motto in capitalistic countries was to be: When in Rome not only do as the Romans do, but do it a little bit better.

The Embassy's reputation for magnificent entertaining continued uninterruptedly for several years, and it was really an experience to go to a formal dinner there, with nearly a hundred guests at one long table going through several rooms—so long, I always suspected that two of the butlers had to flag each other with napkins before they could give the host and hostess a simultaneous signal that it was time to leave the table.

Then, in startling succession came the Nazi-Soviet Pact, their double invasion of Poland, and the imminent Soviet attack on Finland—which, because of its unfailing and honorable payment of World War debts, and the heroic resistance it had determined to show, was naturally the most popular foreign country in the United States. And the fact that Finnish Minister Procopé happened to be not only the best-looking but about the best-liked diplomat in Washington at the moment only intensified the feeling.

The new Soviet Ambassador and Mme. Oumansky, who had succeeded the Troyanovskys after their return to Russia under typically mysterious circumstances, had already sent out the invitations for the annual Soviet reception "to celebrate the Great October Revolution," when the Russo-Finnish situation became more acute. Suddenly it became as important who would *not* go to the party, as it once was who *had* gone to that first party at the Embassy years before. A waiting world learned on the front pages of all the next editions that not a single high executive official or ranking member of Congress showed up that afternoon.

Yet a year or so later, when Hitler had invaded Russia and the Russians had resisted so magnificently, the whole situation was reversed again. Even such elusive figures as Speaker Rayburn or Secretary Hull, whose appearance at an afternoon function is practically front page news, would hardly think of missing a Soviet celebration; and the Finnish Minister, when his country turned to the Axis, found himself as shunned as he had been courted before.

One of the charms of Washington is the chance of getting to know people whose names run like a golden thread through the tapestry of European history. Pick up almost any biography or book of memoirs, from the seventeenth century down, and you are almost sure to find some reference to a Prince de Ligne, a Countess Potocka, a Duchesse de Gramont, or a Count Szechenyi. I remember one rainy day in the country coming across the memoirs of the Countess Potocka of Napoleon's time, and sitting enthralled all day with her candid view of Warsaw society's impressions of Napoleon's famous romance with Countess Marie Walewska, which, you remember, Greta Garbo and Charles Boyer brought to the screen in *Conquest*.

To have an old, world-famous name that you have to carry through life like an invisible neon sign must feel—how? A tremendous burden, a tremendous obligation, or a tremendous challenge? It would probably depend on one's temperament: just as they say foreigners arriving in New York for the first time react differently to the first overwhelming view of the skyline. Some feel, "What can *I* ever amount to in such a city!" And others feel, "If human beings have been able to do *that*—then I can accomplish anything, too!"

Among Washington's bearers of proud ancestral names, the Szechenyis have a special interest for Americans not only as one of the legendary great names of Hungary but because, as the newspaper public well knows, the present Countess Szechenyi is the former Gladys Vanderbilt of New York.

Which makes me think of a day not long after we had come to Washington, when our hotel telephone rang and the operator announced, "Countess Szechenyi calling on Mrs. and Miss Bloom. Shall I send her up?" Count Szechenyi was then, and for many years after, the Hungarian Minister to Washington; naturally we had left cards at the Legation, but we hadn't yet met him or the Countess, and were surprised that she should take her Congressional calls seriously enough to return them in person when cards would have done quite well.

Never was there less of an "arrogant American heiress" than the Countess Szechenyi who walked into our sitting room a few minutes later. Almost painfully shy and self-effacing, and (as we were to find out as time went on) always most simply dressed, she was really a very appealing person. In the years they stayed in Washington we went to a long succession of parties at their house on Massachusetts Avenue which they used as the Legation, and where they built a ballroom for the debuts of their five daughters, a new one of whom would be ready for her coming-out party, it seemed, nearly every year.

The Count was as tall and dramatic-looking as the Countess was small and demure, especially since he had to wear a black patch over one eye, which he lost in an accident while he was home on leave one summer.

The portrait that de Laszlo did of him in the Hungarian uniform, all in black, with sable-trimmed cap and swinging shoulder-cape—and the black patch (which always stole the show when he appeared at the Diplomatic Reception at the White House)—hung in one of the drawing rooms at the Legation, with a companion portrait of the Countess in another. Next to the artist's marvelous portrait of a cardinal that we saw in the museum in his native Budapest, I think his portraits of the Szechenyis much finer than any of his that I have seen since he became Sir Philip de Laszlo, court painter to the Court of St. James's. And thinking of de Laszlo tempts me to leave the Szechenyis for a moment to tell a little story on him.

While we were living at the Mayflower, we had a nice Irish chambermaid on our floor, who had the face of a Madonna.

One day she came into our apartment fairly trembling with rage. Naturally we asked what was the matter. But she only kept muttering, "The nerve of him! The nerve of him!"

"The nerve of whom?" we prompted.

"A feller down the hall. The nerve of him—thinks I'm that dumb, as if I'd never been to the movies! I'm on to the likes of them!"

"On to whom?" we asked, now fully intrigued.

"Good-for-nothings who say they're artists, and ask you to pose for them—and as the Blessed Virgin, too! Why, I've seen a dozen movies like that. Artists, indeed!"

"But maybe he is an artist," Mother suggested. "What's his name?"

She dug a card out of the pocket of her uniform and handed it over disgustedly.

Of course, you've guessed the name we saw engraved on it: Sir Philip de Laszlo. But there was no use trying to convince her. She had been to the movies, and she was "on to them"—and that was that.

Naturally, at the Szechenyis', with so many daughters, who were not only charming girls but combined a great title and a great fortune, there was plenty of romance in the air. The eldest, Cornelia, fell in love with Eugene Roberts, an awfully nice Washington man but not a great enough *parti* to satisfy her father, until the Szechenyis had been transferred to London and he found that instead of being "nothing serious," it was so serious that life had no interest for her there. One day the Count picked up the telephone in London and informed a lovelorn young man in Washington that the wedding could take place with the family's blessing, as soon as he could catch a boat to England. At which the lovelorn young man, a husky six-footer, is said to have fainted dead away at his desk! Since their marriage the Roberts' live quite simply in Washington in the wintertime, and in the utmost magnificence in the summer at the Breakers, in Newport, which Countess Szechenyi inherited from her mother, the dowager Mrs. Vanderbilt, and which she seldom has been able to occupy herself.

The second daughter, Alice, had a brilliant church wedding at St. Matthew's in Washington, marrying a young Hungarian, Count Hadek. All the Hungarians in the wedding party were dressed, like the Minister, in that marvelous uniform, which, it was decreed after the First World War, must be all black, as a sign of mourning for Hungary's lost provinces. Some people think it more dramatic than in the days when Hungarian noblemen could choose any vivid shade they wished. All I know is that the black was stunning enough.

Potocki is another name that, like Szechenyi, crops up continually in Continental memoirs. And to me, that was all it was—a name in black and white rather than a person of flesh and blood —until the Washington papers announced one morning that Count Jerzy Potocki (to be pronounced "Pototski") had been named Polish Ambassador to Washington.

Washington needs no other provocation to start the most absorbing speculation. As soon as anyone is appointed, the same questions begin to buzz all over town. Is he young? Is he old? Is he serious? Is he gay? And—quite the most important, of course —is he married, and to whom? And (this is, naturally, to yourself) will I be on as happy a footing at the Embassy as I was before? "Before" in this particular case meant during the regimes of the other two Polish ambassadors since Poland had been raised to the status of an embassy, Titus Filipowicz and Stanislaus Patek, who both had shown us friendship that went far beyond mere official courtesy.

It was Patek—so distinguished, but so infirm that a footman walked unobtrusively behind him wherever he turned at his own parties at the Embassy, in case he should lose his balance, and one of his Secretaries was always by his side at other parties—who brought to so many occasions a truly Spartan courage and old-school charm. With his white mustachios, his elegance, and his jewel-studded walking stick, he was one of the last diplomats who could add a touch of the authentic grand manner to the Washington scene. An outstanding figure in the re-establishment of Poland as one of the great European powers after the war, he could command practically anything from a grateful government; and I understand it was only when President Moscicki urged him to give the benefit of his great experience to the Polish senate that he was induced to give up his post in Washington and return to his treasure-filled bachelor apartment in Warsaw. And who could then imagine that a few years later he would have to make the characteristic decision to refuse to escape from his beloved Warsaw under the threat of almost certain death in the savage German bombardment of the city!

We knew in advance what the new ambassador looked like, for we found that his likeness was already hanging in the Embassy ballroom, in the large portrait of Marshal Pilsudski and his aides, where Count Potocki, as one of his favorite young officers, stands right beside the Marshal. And hardly had he arrived in Washington before everyone realized that the Polish Embassy was due for a totally different regime. Young, modern, dark and dashing, he almost immediately made the front pages by joining one of the smartest Virginia hunts and getting into an argument with M.F.H. because the Master objected to the Ambassador's reckless riding, by American standards, which according to the Ambassador's explanation was quite the usual thing in hunting circles abroad.

The other burning questions were also quickly answered. Yes, he was married, to a petite Peruvian lady whose mother was said to have the most brilliant salon in Paris. (Incidentally, this seems as good a place as any to mention that special Polish custom of almost always ending the masculine version of a family name with an *i*, and the feminine with an *a*. Which often leads to bewildered indignation when a manly Pole hears himself addressed by some American as, say "Count Potocka"—an innocent error that to him can only sound like an intolerable slur.)

The Ambassador came on ahead of the Countess, with only a valet, and a chef who had been at Buckingham Palace. She arrived later with fourteen extra servants to add to the permanent Embassy staff, including three nurses for their one four-year-old son, Stanislaus. None of this ever reached the papers—or was mentioned, as far as I know, by the Potockis themselves. But at the Embassy, where I had many dear friends then, it was a natural part of the talk.

And after all, why not? For large as the Embassy is, it must have seemed about as cramped as a Swiss chalet in comparison to the Potocki estate in Poland, Lancut (they pronounce it "Winesoot"), so famed for its magnificence that during the First World War, it was spared in turn by the Russians, the Germans, and the Austrians, who each hoped to claim it eventually for their own, and who, besides, each had sentimental associations with it, as Potockis have married into most of the reigning families of Europe throughout the centuries. (And to think that Lancut is now in Nazi hands!)

It is a house that might seem more than regal even to a royal bride. So many friends of mine visited there, and never had two meals in the same dining room, never approached a door without finding a servant waiting to open it, were serenaded by the Potockis' private band, and were mounted, if they wished to ride, on Irish hunters from a stable with white marble, red-carpeted corridors. And when the Potockis would give a garden party at Lancut, they would send out the invitations weeks in advance, asking all the ladies to come dressed in one particular color—blue, pink, mauve or whatever the choice might be—and then, when they arrived, have a garden blooming in that one particular shade especially for the party.

Yet no one could be more appreciative of the simplest courtesy, the simplest hospitality, than the Ambassador. I remember that one of the young couples on the Embassy staff, who lived most simply and economically, received a hint soon after he arrived that he would like to dine with them one evening at their small house in the suburbs. He did—and was so gay, so charming, and, apparently, so charmed with everything, no one could possibly have guessed that he had ever dined magnificently in his life.

The matchmaking possibilities that were lacking because the Ambassador was married were more than made up for when, a few months after they came, the Potockis announced that the Ambassador's mother—she had been a Princess Radziwill and a fabulous beauty—and his bachelor brother, Count Alfred, who was the head of the family and considered one of the greatest catches in Europe, would spend most of the winter with them in Washington. But, the newspapers added warningly, there was a hard, solid obstacle to any free-for-all matrimonial sweepstakes in this case, for it was rumored that Count Alfred would expect a dowry of several million dollars, cash, to carry on the family's magnificent traditions.

We met Count Alfred and his mother for the first time at the small dance the Ambassador and Ambassadress gave for them at the Embassay soon after they arrived. He turned out to be just the opposite of his brother—blond instead of dark, quiet instead of dashing. He was kind and thoughtful to everyone, and his manner always seemed the same whether he was host or guest, as we found when he came in with the Ambassadress to one of our Tuesday at-homes.

But although Count Alfred "did" not only Washington but New York, Palm Beach, and Havana as well, he returned to Poland fancy free and without a chatelaine for Lancut.

Then suddenly, with the invasion of Poland, everything was tragically changed. The Nazis occupied Lancut; but the dowager Countess had refused to leave even when escape was still possible —she felt her place was there, where she could still do something to help the people on the estate. Count Alfred stayed, too, and no one seems to know what has happened to them. Fortunately, the young Countess, who had spent much of her time abroad, escaped with her son Stanislaus from France and joined the Ambassador here, and when they were succeeded by our old friends the Jan Ciechanowskis, they went off to Peru, where, I understand, he is busily engaged in modernizing the Countess' estates.

Another with a famous Polish name who came to the Embassy in Washington was Prince Andrew Sapieha, serving as financial counselor. Victor Podoski, who was first secretary at the Embassy, and one of the most popular bachelors who ever came to Washington, and Witold Wankowicz, who, living in Warsaw between two periods of serving at the Embassy here, had casually come back "for the week end" to keep Sapieha company on the way over, brought him out to dinner at our summer house one night.

Sapieha was tall, with a dark, witty face, and he and "Wanky" are about the most hilariously good company I've ever known.

Since he was a bachelor, it was very easy for Sapieha to spend half his time in New York, where, obviously, a financial counselor can do his country the most good. He was dining with us in town a few months later, when he mentioned how astonished he had been that a New York hostess had seated him at her right at dinner, and Richard Whitney, then the president of the New York Stock Exchange, at her left.

"But for heaven's sake, why not?" someone asked him. "After all, just on your own, and without your official position, you would certainly outrank Mr. Whitney."

"Ah," Sapieha chuckled, "but he's so *rich!*"

Neither guest could take his place again now; and for what different reasons! Richard Whitney became the most "distinguished" prisoner at Sing Sing; and Sapieha was one of the great Polish nobles missing—probably "liquidated"—after the invasion of Poland.

No proud ancestral name in Washington has been taken more seriously by its bearers than that of the Prince and Princess de Ligne, who were Belgium's ambassador and ambassadress for some time. Of course, the de Lignes, like the Potockis, are intermarried with all the greatest names in Europe, but, unlike the Potockis, they could never seem to forget it. Refreshingly, however, when a younger Prince de Ligne came to the Embassy as counselor, he turned out to be one of the simplest and most charming men who had come to the Capital in a long time.

De Gramont, one of the oldest names in France, is one of the newest among these memories of mine. With it goes a charming bit of unwritten history about the romantic heroine of both Dumas' *Lady of the Camellias* and Verdi's *La Traviata,* whom we call Camille. And here is the story.

Shortly before the war, Washington was undemocratically delighted to hear than a son of the Duc de Gramont, Count Gabriel de Gramont, was coming to the French Embassy as attaché. And as it happened, before he had been in town a week, we met him at a dinner at the Embassy—a nice young man with that combination of a fresh, pink-cheeked face and a sophisticated manner that so many young Frenchmen have.

After dinner the talk turned to Greta Garbo's *Camille,* and he mentioned how Paris had flocked to see it and how pleased everyone had been that Hollywood hadn't compromised an iota with the original story of the frail lady who was the toast of the Second Empire's demimonde, and of Armand, whom she really loved.

"You know," he added, "I have a special interest in Armand —after all, he was my grandfather!"

"Your grandfather!" we all echoed in amazement.

"Yes, really," he assured us. "You see, there really was a Lady of the Camellias, and so, of course, there really was an Armand. And when the younger Dumas—who much preferred the romantic to the swashbuckling stories that attracted his father— heard that the son of the Duc de Gramont was so madly in love with the notorious and beautiful Marie Duplessis that he actually wanted to throw away the diplomatic career he was about to enter —which, by the way, is the family's traditional career—well, he had to write *La Dame aux Camellias*. It almost wrote itself.

"Of course, it was the most sensational success. But only those 'in the know' realized that the whole story was true—that Marie (the Marguerite Gauthier of the play) *did* sacrifice her love to Armand's future, and she *did* die not only of consumption but of a broken heart.

"Perhaps," he added, after a minute, with a rueful smile, "it would have been better, not only for the two most concerned but for France itself, if Great-grandpapa and the call of duty had not been obeyed! . . . You see, Armand settled down to a most conventional married life and a brilliant diplomatic career, and actually became minister of foreign affairs under Napoleon III; and his policies, quite as much as the Empress Eugénie's famous interference, led to the Franco-Prussian War in 1870 and the worst defeat France had ever known.

"So that's what I mean when I say it might have been better all around if he had been left in disgrace and bliss with his Marie."

"And was he really named Armand?" I asked, wondering why Dumas had made the young man belong to a middle-class provincial family rather than to one of the greatest noble houses of France.

"Oh, yes. You see, the Duc de Gramont, as far back as anyone can remember, has always been called either Armand or Antoine."

"But what if the eldest son should die?"

"Ah, but you forget, in France we always give so many names when we christen a baby that it is easy to tuck an Armand or an Antoine in somewhere—just in case!"

As the party began to break up, the pretty young Countess de Gramont joined our group to say good night.

"You see," her husband laughed, "I took no chances of repeating Grandpapa's story while *I* was waiting to hear if I had passed

143

my diplomatic examination—for I had a wife and three children before I even took it."

For them, too, unguessed tragedy lay in the future. Soon Hitler was to overwhelm France, and Gabriel de Gramont was to leave his little family the very first week of the war, a volunteer soldier for France. He escaped to England after the armistice, and died fighting for de Gaulle when his plane crashed to earth.

These tales I have been telling belong to the days when one could travel; and I have traveled somewhat waywardly in my memories to tell them. Then came the time when frontiers were barricaded; and then overrun.

Hitler marched into Austria. There was a diplomatic party in Washington that afternoon; and although the guests tried to keep up their imperturbable manner, you could see worried groups of diplomats with their heads close together—especially those whose countries stood in the path of the Nazi steam roller.

The next shock came when Edgar Prochnik, who had been the Austrian Minister to Washington since the World War, turned over his legation to the German Embassy and actually appeared in the next month's Diplomatic List, issued by the State Department, as a member of the German Embassy staff with the unheard of title of "Minister-Attaché"—a combination of the highest and lowest ranks he could possibly have.

Things were anxious but quiet on the local diplomatic front until Hitler marched into Czechoslovakia. Then the burning question became whether or not the Czech Minister, Colonel Hurban, who, like Prochnik, has an American wife, would follow his Austrian colleague's lead and turn over his legation at the inevitable demand of the German Embassy.

But Colonel Hurban, with a heartwarming heroism which made him the most admired man in Washington, flatly refused to turn over the Legation when the German chargé d'affaires, Dr. Hans Thomsen, added insult to injury by sending a mere third secretary of the Embassy to demand it.

Colonel Hurban's action not only saved the Czech Legation and established Czechoslovakia as a "government in exile" in this country, but set the example for all the other diplomats who were to be involved in the tragic story to follow. Thus, although the dictators were able to crush one country after another, yet Poland,

Belgium, the Netherlands, Norway, and all the other occupied countries continued to have full diplomatic status here—and continued implacably defiant to Hitler.

All, that is, but France. For the French Embassy, divided against itself into followers of Marshal Pétain and the Free Frenchmen of General de Gaulle, became for a time the great diplomatic mystery. Count de Saint-Quentin, who represented such a different France, had gone, and in his place came Gaston Henri-Haye, who represented who-knows-what? To be sure, he spoke for the French government in Vichy; but no one could doubt that the men of Vichy spoke for Berlin. And so after war was declared, the French Embassy—through all our history the most popular diplomatic mission in America—was closed, and the French Ambassador, with the few members of his staff who did not resign to follow de Gaulle, was interned along with the Germans, the Italians, the Japanese, and the diplomats of the smaller satellite states.

Now upon the soil of France as well as in the south and east of Europe, the liberating armies have rolled tyranny back upon itself. In a kind of predawn twilight, where colors are not always clear, and shapes not always distinct, the restoration of free diplomacy is beginning. Full daylight is to come, when each nation again will know and name its own ambassadors to the world.

7. When Uncle Sam Gives a Birthday Party

Perhaps nine million words on any one subject are enough! In so many words the official volumes tell the tale: how in 1932 Uncle Sam celebrated George Washington's two hundredth birthday, and in 1937 lit a hundred and fifty candles for the Constitution. But all those pages notwithstanding, there are stories—of the kind not thought suitable for an official history—that ought still, I think, to be told.

It is possible that you have almost forgotten the Washington Bicentennial, and the Constitution Sesquicentennial as well. But I can *never* forget! Nor do I quite believe that you can either.

It was in 1923 that my father began to dream of those birthday celebrations; it was in 1924 that Congress took definite action, and later he became Director of the Bicentennial Commission (with a co-director who soon was called to other work); and it was in 1943 that he wrote finis to the record as the Sesquicentennial Commission's director. Anyone who saw much of him was bound to have moments of uncertainty whether this century's date began with nineteen or seventeen. As for his family, we marched with the Continentals and founded the nation a thousand times over.

One man does not make a celebration. These two were made by men, women, and children of all the United States, plus others in at least fourscore foreign countries that joined in the proceedings; and if you consider only the leadership job, the nineteen members of the Bicentennial Commission required a staff which, at the celebration's peak, numbered over two hundred. What they were busy about, the official record is full of. There you can read how new facts of the nation's beginning were brought to light;

how the commission kept in touch with thousands of communities, stimulating and aiding them in their honoring of firm foundations; how a memorial highway to Mt. Vernon was built, special stamps were issued, songs of the Revolution discovered and new music written, plays staged, dances footed, essays put in contest, portraits exhibited, ancient bells rung; how Major James Doolittle went on a bombing flight dropping commemorative mail by parachute into towns the First President visited in twenty-six hundred miles of his travels; how seedlings from George Washington's acres now grow in various earth from Iowa to Uruguay, from Baguio to Istanbul, and from Albania to Japan (except where bombing of another kind may have blasted them).

Many people planned many doings; but one man had to sign most of the commissions' letters and releases. Which gave the newsmen much copy, and the humorists a few gags. Several times a day for weeks on end I dutifully laughed when someone was said to have said: "I know who Sol Bloom is; but who is this George Washington?" Perhaps the best was the story originating at a Gridiron Club dinner, carried on by a Washington columnist as follows:

"One of the visiting statesmen recently in town was asked by an official of the State Department whether he was seeing all the sights of the Capital.

" 'Oh, yes, quite,' the gentleman responded.

" 'Have you seen the cherry blossoms?' the State Department official asked him.

" 'No, but I've seen the Sol Blooms,' the visitor rejoined."

But the true ironic story of the Bicentennial cherry blossoms failed to appear in print.

The sure sign of spring in Washington used to be a flock of newspaper photographers snapping the current Japanese Ambassador under the famous blossoms which the Japanese government had given to ours at Mrs. Taft's suggestion. (If, that is, we happened to be on good terms with Japan when the trees happened to be in bloom.)

In the Bicentennial year the sign of spring, like every calendar event that could possibly be made significant, was to be special. Wishing to pay graceful tribute to George Washington, the plump, genial little Japanese Ambassador, Mr. Debuchi, was to broadcast a nation-wide speech from under the cherry blossoms, to which

Father would respond in the name of the President and the Bicentennial Commission.

Naturally, both speeches were written and released to the press in advance. They mentioned balmy breezes, gentle spring sunshine, and fluttering petals. All very fitting and proper, if the weather had played its expected part. But instead, a more raw, wretched, marrow-chilling spring day never struck Washington.

Mme. Debuchi and her pretty young daughter Taka came bravely in Japanese dress, their only compromise with the weather being fur scarves, which, of course, they couldn't wear for the photographs.

The microphone was moved to the partial shelter of a covered boathouse near the blossoms, and there the Ambassador and the Congressman-Director, valiantly trying to keep their teeth from chattering, went on with their "gentle spring sunshine" and "balmy breezes," praying, no doubt, that no one in Washington was listening in, and that the rest of the country would remain ignorant of the Capital weather situation that day. When they had finished, and Japanese-American relations had been warmed up quite a bit for a while, we were all frozen.

Unexpected rescue came in the person of the proprietor of the boathouse, who with diffidence inquired if Their Excellencies and ourselves would accept some hot tea.

Would we!

It appeared that there was a little soda fountain in the boathouse, where two tables were set together for our party. To be sure, the service was anything but ambassadorial; yet our host supplied spiritual good will and glow enough for twenty embassies, and as for his tangible diplomacy, I am sure no priceless tea in eggshell-china cups had ever tasted so good to any of us. The Debuchis entered wonderfully into the spirit of the thing, so there was a certain balminess about the day after all.

Incidentally, among the best Bicentennial stories is one that came from Japan, where an American consul heard it. Evidently the vast stream of releases that poured from the commission's mailing room provided some usable copy for newspapers in Nippon, as elsewhere all over the world. One Japanese paper even printed the immortal George-and-the-cherry-tree story in picture form, and one small Japanese boy, fired to action, went out and hacked down one of his father's glorious old cherry trees.

Inevitably, papa arrived on the scene. The little hero staunchly declaimed historic words: "Father, I cannot tell a lie. I did it with my little hatchet!"

But father failed history. Instead of clasping his noble child to his breast with tears of joy in his eyes, the Japanese parent said disgustedly: "My son, I had rather you had told ten thousand lies, than cut down my cherry tree!"

Since this chapter is mostly concerned with the plain funny or laughably painful moments of the Bicentennial, I ought to stop just once to acknowledge that it was, seriously, no joking matter. As for my father's part in it: if there was one thing that animated him as strongly as his appreciation of George Washington's character and great life, it was his passion for facts. Current misinformation about the early days of our republic appalled him, and gaps in the information, and the fact that so much of what was known was nevertheless unknown to so many of us. He believed that people everywhere would be glad of a chance to make more real to themselves the sterling humanity of the man whose generalship and statesmanship led a nation into being, through difficulties that, when one looks back at the totality, seem hardly surmountable. And he was right. Perhaps one reason was that the anniversary fell in the worst year of the Depression, when material props had fallen and people had been thrown back onto fundamental qualities of character. As the records amply show, the celebrations were no mere outward ceremonies. They were honor to Washington in the hearts of his countrymen, in which many felt themselves encouraged.

The machinery for bringing it about was as much my father's pride as a clipper ship her captain's. Could he have awarded gold braid to the personnel, I suppose the most gilding would have graced the expert historians of the commission, who were charged with providing the truth, the whole truth, and nothing but. Not one release or pamphlet could be made public until its every statement had been declared pure. I remember stopping in very late one afternoon to pick Father up on the way home, when he was evidently caught on the horns of some documentary dilemma, for I could hear his voice way down the hall demanding loudly and plaintively, "Isn't *one* of my six historians here?"

The very apple of his eye was the line of filing cabinets containing the commission's correspondence with more than forty-five thousand communities: nearly every one in the country that had a United States postmaster, from New York City to a "town" of two people out in the desert. (The only ones missing were the few that failed to answer the initial questionnaire inquiring what local organizations there existed to take the lead in the celebrations, and so forth.) It was Father's boast that anyone from anywhere could walk into the commission's office and within half a minute have in hand the record of his home town: what suggestions the commission had sent, and what the community had done in observing the Bicentennial. Which was often tested, and always proved. (His other favorite boast, equally true, is that Uncle Sam was not one cent out of pocket for the birthday party. The money Congress appropriated for it was more than repaid by what the Post Office Department made on its Bicentennial stamp issues.)

One of the amusing preliminaries was the experience of, literally, putting a town on the map.

The town was Charles Town, West Virginia, and the map was a special one on the history of Washington's travels, being prepared by the National Geographic Society as its contribution to the Bicentennial. The Geographic was insisting that Charles Town didn't belong on the map, and Charles Town was insisting that it did, when Walter Washington arrived from the United States Embassy in Brazil bringing, to me, a gift from the former Brazilian Ambassador to Washington, Amaral (it was a most beautiful Brazilian guitar), and to Father, a letter of introduction—which signified, without saying so, that his present (of course, unofficial) mission was the job of getting the town on the map.

As it happened, Walter (the only member of the Washington family in our foreign service, by the way) came from Charles Town. His mother lives there, and they own Harewood, which was built by Samuel Washington (the First President's brother), and where James and Dolly Madison were married. Not only that, but Maudington, Charles Washington's home, and another family mansion, both of which have passed out of the family's hands, are hardly more than a stone's throw away. We visited the present Washingtons several times, learning the family ramifications by heart, and familiarizing ourselves with the town's historic associations. Charles Town is a charming place that was the retreat of the Washington family when mosquitoes and malaria made Mount Vernon uninhabitable. It is named after Washington's brother Charles; the streets bear the names of a sister and the several brothers. Why, there are more Washington "connections" among the town's not quite twenty-five hundred souls than in any one place in the country; and there is even a legend that Washington held Masonic meetings in a near-by cavern, which in his time was used as the local lodge.

Yet in spite of all this the Geographic had decided that Charles Town did not belong on the map!

The cause of the snub was that no town of that name appeared in Washington's (diary. And for a very good reason, as Father eventually could point out: the town had been called Happy Retreat in those days. It was the old name for one of the family estates, and the name Charles Town was a later gesture.

So the issue of the Geographic came out not only showing Charles Town on the map but with three large photographs of it besides, and we could mail the result of his mission to Walter in Tokyo, where he had been sent in the meantime as a member of the American Embassy.

The evening before the official opening of the Bicentennial on February 22, 1932, *Wakefield*, the masque specially written by Percy Mackaye, was presented in Constitution Hall, with Margaret Anglin in the leading role, hundreds of civic-spirited amateurs and semi-amateurs in the cast, and an audience including nearly all Washington officialdom.

While the producers of the masque were having their own troubles putting up the scenery—for Constitution Hall belongs to the Daughters of the American Revolution, and they would not allow a single tack to be driven into the floor of the stage, which meant that miracles of bracing and bolstering had to be done—the commission's staff were having an equally hard time trying to map out a tactful seating plan so that the performance could be received with happy dignity. In fact, this probably gave the Protocol Division its worst headache in history, for seldom indeed does the whole official galaxy appear at one function. The experts had either to face, or to suggest an arrangement that would allow them not to face, the perennially undecided issues usually avoided by never asking the Vice-President and the Speaker, or an ambassador and Chief Justice, to the same affair. There were some fine points we hadn't met with before. For instance the Presidential box (to which the Hoovers were unable to come that night) is always to the left of the audience, because that puts it to the right of the stage, which is the place of honor. The others follow from left to right. I remember that Mrs. Woodrow Wilson, as the widow of a President (and Mrs. Taft, too, if she had been able to come) had the box immediately next the ambassadors' boxes, before the Supreme Court, the Cabinet, and everyone else.

The time came at last; and it turned out to be one of those raw, wet, windy nights when there's no place like home. But if you knew your Washington, you expected everyone to appear in spite of everything. And they did. For there is a social training, or conscience, in official life that is as rigorous as the actors' immemorial determination: "The show must go on!"

In case you sometimes doubt it, on evidence of that evening I should say that Washington officials are realistic. For the point where one noticed the audience really come to life was when, after the deep mystical atmosphere of the masque, the lights flooded on and national groups, singing folk songs in costume, trouped down the center aisle and onto the stage. All over the house you could hear people recognizing their chauffeur in the Italian group, or their butler with the Norwegians, or their vegetable man with the Portuguese. And the singing itself was rousing good fun.

When the Chief Justice and Mrs. Hughes had arrived and Father was escorting them to their box, the Chief Justice had said to him, rather wistfully, "You know, my boy, I'd love to see that costume ball you're giving tomorrow at the Mayflower, but no one has invited us!"

Father promptly started an investigation, and it turned out that nobody had. Mrs. Walter Tuckerman and her committee for the ball had made excellent and diplomatic disposition of all the boxes; but probably because the dignity of the office of Chief Justice is so overwhelming that one wouldn't naturally connect it with the thought of a ball, it simply had not occurred to anyone on the committee that the Hugheses might like to come. Quick maneuvers were effected, of course; and next night the genial Chief Justice beamed down on the ball.

To our box we had invited the ambassadors of France, Germany, and Poland, in compliment to the three countries which gave most aid to the American Revolution, and in special tribute to Lafayette, von Steuben, and Kosciuszko. It would have been beyond belief, that night, had we been told what the future would

152

hold for our charming and congenial guests. To be sure, Paul Claudel would continue his dual career as poet-diplomat with undimmed distinction—until the fall of France. But German Ambassador von Prittwitz within a year was to sacrifice his brilliant career when Hitler came into power, because he could not, in conscience, represent such a regime. The last we heard of him, indirectly, after his return to private life in Berlin, was that it had been made impossible for him to earn a livelihood as an attorney, and Frau von Prittwitz was trying to help out by telling fortunes. And Titus Filipowicz was to be one of the very last Polish officials to escape the Nazi bombardment of Warsaw in September of 1939.

Father's heart had been set upon having the President and Mrs. Hoover attend the ball, as the President was also the chairman of the Bicentennial Commission. But Mr. Hoover frankly explained that as a Quaker he had never attended a dance in his life, and felt it would be against his principles to be present even at this one; and of course one could do nothing but respect such a reason.

Mrs. Tuckerman's heart had been set on having everyone, without exception, come in costume, as had been done at the beautiful Beaux Arts Bicentennial ball in New York a few weeks before, where even the photographers and the waiters had been obliged to deck themselves in eighteenth-century style.

But it isn't so easy to command things in Washington. In the first place, it is nearly impossible for an ambassador or a minister to appear publicly in costume. And for a Senator or a Congressman to take a chance of being photographed in a powdered wig and satin knee breeches would be to give his opponent in the next campaign a ridicule weapon made to order. Retreating in the face of these troubles, Mrs. Tuckerman asked only that anyone who had the right to should wear a uniform—diplomatic or military. But aside from the question of comfort, there were all sorts of regulations against that. Almost at the last minute she had to fall back another step and simply ask that any man come in costume who could and would.

The diplomatic ladies also retreated from the original idea that they would all come in the eighteenth-century court dress of their own countries, and instead left it a matter of personal choice —not whether, but what kind: which was the question for the rest of us too. I had made my choice weeks ahead, but was so disappointed when I saw the reality that the sketch turned into, a few days before the ball, I didn't know what to do. But Mother's costume, all lilac taffeta and silver, was a complete success.

And then, out of a clear sky, a tremendous box arrived at Father's office, with the request from a New York costumer that we should ask some of our friends if they would like to wear these dresses to the ball. So down to the office I went with Mme. Prochnik, the Austrian Minister's wife, Bee Sokolowska of the Polish Embassy, Blanche Skalicky of the Czech Legation (all Americans, as it happened, and all to become political refugees when their husbands' countries fell victims to Hitler's Germany), and Laura Tuckerman, Mrs. Tuckerman's daughter. Taking over one of the offices for an impromptu dressing room, we opened the huge box, and in a moment the furniture had disappeared under a froth of silks and laces and satins—absolutely perfect copies of historic dresses which had been worn by our First Ladies. There were enough to save two, as I had meanwhile promised: one for Helen Coolidge, Senator Coolidge's daughter, who soon as Harry Woodring's wife became the youngest and prettiest Cabinet lady in the Roosevelt Cabinet, and the other for Reine Claudel, daughter of the French Ambassador and Mme. Claudel.

Lacking a full-length mirror, we had to take each others' word about how becoming the dresses were as we tried them on. In the end Mme. Prochnik chose Dolly Madison's costume of yellow and silver, complete even to the plumed turban which Dolly always wore. Bee and Laura decided on two different Martha Washington gowns. Blanche took a charming Abigail Adams flowered dress with an organdie fichu and high mobcap. It happened that they were four of the prettiest women in Washington, and the costumes seemed made for each of them. Mine was a replica of the gown Mrs. James Monroe wore when she was presented at the Court of Louis XVI, as the wife of the American Minister to France. It was a flowered ivory-taffeta, trimmed with cherry-colored bows, and intricately stitched and spangled in gold. But I paid for my grandeur—it was so heavy, with the countless yards of material, to say nothing of a three-quarter-inch iron hoop sewed into the underskirt, that I could hardly move a step all evening without taking an escort's arm in the good old-fashioned way.

After the ball the whole set of costumes was exhibited all over the country, for they were really works of art. Then, having accomplished its purpose, the Monroe costume was sent to me as a souvenir of the silk manufacturers' fine co-operation in the Commission's suggestion to reproduce Colonial silks and create modern ones with patriotic motifs—stars and stripes, liberty bells, and so on—which had an enormous success.

For weeks before the ball Washington had been a Babel of animated talk about who or what everyone was going as. The fed-up friend of mine who declared savagely, "I'm going to go as *Benedict Arnold!*" may be quoted as unknown spokesman for all the host of silent sufferers. Probably the climax of sufferance, however, was when even museums were prevailed upon to lend their eighteenth-century American treasures to descendants of the original wearers, who came to the Capital from all the original thirteen states and appeared in the pageant as their own ancestors. Moreover, besides the official ball at the Mayflower, there was a smaller one at Gadsby's Tavern in Alexandria that same night, attended only by people whose ancestors had danced there in Washington's time. All in all, the Bicentennial opening night was one of the greatest opportunities the "professional descendants," to whom the past is so much more important than the future, had ever had.

Both Father and Mother, of course, had to be at the Mayflower early; but by the time Stanley Hornbeck and I arrived, just at the moment when the men's floor committee, all in buff and blue uniforms, came careening around the corner of Connecticut Avenue on top of an old-fashioned stagecoach, we found the huge front lobby, and the mezzanine which looks down on it, so jammed with people watching the arrivals that it was almost impossible for the police to keep an entrance lane open. The papers next morning said that surely several thousand people were crammed into the lobby.

And they gave me one of the thrills of my life—for as we were passing through, they burst into applause. I turned to see what the excitement was about, but could discover nothing. And I thought Stanley was just indulging in a little State Department diplomacy when he said, "It's for you—and your costume!" I suppose a movie star at a gala opening can take such a thrill as her due; but to me, it took some believing!

The strange part about that ball was that the costumes and the occasion really commanded people's moods. Everyone felt a sort of simultaneous urge to live up to the elegance and the dignity of the period. There were no hip flasks in the pockets of satin or brocade coats; no white wig got the least bit askew all evening. The usual effects of a public party during Prohibition were entirely lacking, and all quite voluntarily, too.

The ball, of course, only climaxed a day of continuous celebrations, which began with President Hoover's speech before a joint session of the Senate and the House in the morning, with the diplomatic corps, the Supreme Court, the Cabinet, and other high officials all attending. And this was prelude to a series of observances lasting many months, from Washington's Birthday until Thanksgiving.

Music, that great indispensable of all patriotic occasions, can cause some of the worst moments to those responsible for the program. The best such story I know belongs to another year than the Bicentennial, but I cannot resist telling it here as a consolatory offering to all who have ever been "stuck" for the words of our national anthems.

The cornerstone of the National Press Club in the Capital was about to be laid, with grand ceremony. John Philip Sousa was to conduct the band, and Frances Peralta, the Metropolitan Opera singer, was the American prima donna of the day.

We were sitting on the outdoor platform with the guests of honor and the artists, when the leader of the Marine Band came up to Miss Peralta and whispered to her, "You know, you're singing 'My Country, 'Tis of Thee.' "

"No, no!" she whispered back, "I'm singing 'The Star-Spangled Banner'! I don't *know* 'My Country, 'Tis of Thee'!"

"But the band does 'The Star-Spangled Banner' at the end, and the program says you do 'My Country, 'Tis of Thee.' "

"All right," said Miss Peralta, resignedly, "I'll do it, if you'll give me the words."

"My country 'tis of thee, Sweet land of liberty, Of thee I sing," the leader of the Marine Band began confidently; but there he petered out. "Good heavens! What *does* come next? 'Land where our fathers died' or 'I love thy rocks and rills'?"

"I don't know!" said Miss Peralta helplessly. All this time, of course, the program had been going on, drawing nearer and nearer the crucial moment when she would have to sing.

"Do *you* know?" they asked me. I admitted that I just never could get beyond that third line on my own steam, and suggested that they ask Mr. Sousa, who was sitting near by.

The March King made a businesslike start; but he, too, stuck at the third line! Just then, when everything looked quite black, a newspaperman who was standing close by and had heard all the whispering, quietly passed a slip of paper to Miss Peralta, on which he had scribbled all the verses of "America," and moved away, hardly waiting to be thanked for having saved the day.

With superb dignity Miss Peralta rose, and merely glancing casually at the paper in her hand, sang "America" as I'm sure she never did before.

The next day she phoned me and said that Mr. Sousa had sent her his photograph, with all the verses of "America" written out in his own hand.

Mr. Sousa, near the end of his career, nevertheless did his part for Washington's two hundredth birthday. The specially composed "George Washington Bicentennial March" turned out to be the last of his immortal marches; and his conducting of it with the Marine Band at the Capitol on the first morning of the celebration was his last public appearance.

One sidelight of the Bicentennial which has never been mentioned, since it was a dark secret, was the unprecedented Sunday when the Mount Vernon Ladies Association made a special dispensation allowing the commission to invade the Sabbath stillness of Mount Vernon in order to take the official photograph of the Houdon bust of Washington. (Later the rule was swept away entirely, and Mount Vernon was at last open to the public on Sundays—a great boon to visitors, and to the many Washingtonians who could not go at any other time. But on that Sunday in 1932, as I say, we were sworn to secrecy.)

Arthur Jaffé, of Vienna, who was acknowledged to be the greatest photographer of art masterpieces in the world, and who traveled to America occasionally to photograph the new treasures of the Metropolitan Museum in New York or the Athenaeum in Boston, had come this time to Washington, especially to photograph the Houdon bust.

He was a slim, well-dressed young man, with the face of a poet, and with his mind plainly bent on the work at hand, for he was not very talkative on the way down to Mount Vernon

157

early that Sunday morning with us and several others from the commission.

It was a strange and beautiful feeling to ride into the estate (at a side entrance, so that no one might see a car enter on the forbidden day) and find only courtly old Colonel Horace Dodge, the custodian, who was at Mount Vernon since 1885, awaiting us. It felt almost as if we were about to visit "The General" and "Lady Washington" themselves.

The Houdon bust—which is, of course, only the plaster cast that the great French sculptor made at Mount Vernon for the full-length bronze statue at Richmond, Virginia, completed in Paris from the measurements and notes he had made during his visit to General Washington—is kept in one of the little museum-like outhouses at Mount Vernon. Mr. Jaffé tried to take his photograph without moving the priceless bust; but it was obviously impossible to do it right in that small room, and the leaders of the conspiracy decided to take the serious chance of moving the bust over to the mansion. Fortunately it was a beautiful day, for even the most carefully treated plaster is still plaster, and might be hurt by even a drop of rain.

And when they began to move the precious statue, I'm sure that everyone wished it were marble or bronze instead, for one mis-step, and— It was too awful to think of, especially when Colonel Dodge, in spite of the fact that his steps were not so firm as they once were, although, at eighty, he was unbelievably strong and erect, insisted that it was his obligation and his duty, as custodian of Mount Vernon, to carry the bust himself. Certainly it was his *right,* but the grassy ground we had to cross to reach the mansion was uneven and dangerous for such a delicate undertaking, and I shall never forget the sight of the Colonel, the bust clutched tightly in his arms, carrying his treasure, while the other men formed such a close and anxious cordon around him that they were almost carrying him. I don't think any of us really breathed until the bust was deposited safely in the great dining room, where Mr. Jaffé decided he could get the best light.

You would imagine that to take a photograph of an immobile subject like a statue would be only the work of a second. But I realized why Jaffé is the great artist he is, when literally hours passed during which every possible height of camera and object had been tried, and every possible change of lighting, with all the men assisting by holding cloths up to the window in endless different arrangements—and still Jaffé was dissatisfied.

Finally he placed the bust right on the floor, stretched himself full length on that same floor with his camera, and at last breathed a sigh of complete satisfaction.

Just at that moment some workmen in the next room began hammering away on the floor to attach one of the brass railings, that had been loosened, no doubt, by daily thousands of leaning tourist elbows.

Jaffé let out an agonized shriek of "Stop!" that brought two amazed workmen's faces to the door. But not too soon, for, as he said, one tremor passing along the floor might have struck the statue in such a way as to shatter it to bits.

It took hours more until the final perfect plates were made, so Mother and I left the others to their patient work, and stepped out on the portico overlooking the river. After a while Father joined us, and we walked slowly down to the river landing, enjoying lawns, groves, and rolling fields, fragrant and warm with sun, surely not greatly different from the outlook that so delighted the General when he would walk down to greet friends coming by boat from their estates across the Potomac. And for me, I know, the best of the Bicentennial will always be that quiet Sunday, when everything at Mount Vernon, from the lovely design of the buildings themselves to the music score open on the clavier, spoke of a way of life built equally of grace and strength: the home of the man who did more than any one other to establish the home of the free.

The Constitution provided an inconvenience right at the beginning of the Sesquicentennial by having its birthday on September 17, when Congress was not in session, and when indeed most of official Washington, after the stifling summer, was away on vacation at last.

In England, when the king's birthday falls in a month inauspicious for the traditional royal garden party and the trooping of the colors, His Majesty simply chooses an "official" birthday on which even the British climate is apt to be kind. In such a matter our once-rebellious country is more conservative. No cavalier shifting of anything to do with the Constitution!

President Roosevelt, who, just as President Hoover had headed the former commission, was chairman of the Sesquicentennial Commission, thought of the solution himself. He would open the celebration by speaking at the Washington Monument the night of September 17, with boxes for high government officials and the diplomatic corps, several thousand reserved seats for invited guests, and all the monument grounds for the general public.

This left only two large problems: rain and protocol. For even when ambassadors are away, their countries must be accorded due honor in the persons of lesser representatives. By and by a design for seating had been developed, and the invitations—eight by ten inches of creamy cardboard, steel engraving, and the gold Seal of the United States—were sent out in the name of the commission. Whereupon Mother and I could expect no moment's peace until the birthday was over. The telephone at home rang from morning until night, with strangers who had "a special reason" for expecting an invitation, or with friends of ours who, quite naturally, didn't know whether or not to "dress" for a speech by the President in the open air on what might turn out to be—and did—a cold, damp night. To Washington, which dresses in the evening for almost anything except a twosome at the movies, it was quite a question.

No one seemed to want to answer it, so Mother and I, by the time the newspapers were calling us up regularly to find out, concluded it was up to us to decide on "a black dinner dress with a black velvet evening wrap, and a little black theater hat." The papers recorded this momentous decision in time, and believe it or not, practically every woman in the boxes appeared answering exactly to that description. The men, of course, were "black tie."

By this time, public interest ran so high that the police were expecting a quarter of a million people to be at the Monument that night. Which was just about exactly how many came.

When the invitations were sent out, Father gave us just a few to send to people away from Washington who might cherish them as souvenirs. One we thought of at once was Della, a sweet Irish cook we had had years ago in New York, whom misfortune had lately shadowed through an accident to her husband. Perhaps that piece of engraving would be of some cheer to her and her family.

When it came to making up our box, it was natural—and strange—to think back to the box party of five years before, at the Bicentennial Ball. Of them all, only Stanley Hornbeck, at

© Acme

President Roosevelt and His Mother Leaving the Capitol

Wives of Four Speakers of the House—Mrs. Garner, Mrs. Longworth, Mrs. Gillett, and
Mrs. Bankhead

the State Department, remained in Washington. This time the diplomatic chiefs of mission were to have their own boxes; and our guests were to fare far better than those earlier ones. The Stanley Reeds are now a Supreme Court family. Mr. Frank Hogan, who came with Mrs. Hogan, found a term as president of the American Bar Association not difficult to survive. And nothing frightful has happened to Stanley Hornbeck or to Noel Trentham of the British Embassy, who rounded out the party—on the contrary, they are now both happily married.

The seventeenth dawned gray and drizzly. Father went off to test the loudspeakers which had been installed all along Constitution Avenue so that the overflow crowds could hear the President's speech. We were told later how people for blocks around heard a voice that seemed to come from the sky, commanding the rain to "turn off up there!" What's more, it did.

At home, Mother and I were swamped under a crescendo of telephone calls. "Will the celebration go on anyhow?" "Will we *still* 'dress'?" "May I bring a friend who just came to town?" "My tickets haven't come!" "This is the Associated Press. May we have the list of your box party now?"

One call turned out to be Evelyn Gordon, the society editor of the *Washington News,* in search of some kind of a story.

Just as I was answering, the butler appeared: "Excuse me, Miss Vera, but someone named Della is at the door with her son. She said she was invited to meet the President tonight! What shall I tell her?"

Della! The invitation had been taken seriously, at who knows what financial sacrifice!

"Oh, Evie," I said, "will you forgive me if I ring off? I can't explain it all now, but our dear old Irish cook from New York has come down for tonight, and I must take care of her."

Without realizing it, I had given Evie the perfect lead for "human interest." That night she found Della, careworn but radiant, where Father had ensconced her with her Jimmy in an unoccupied box right behind the Cabinet, with someone to point out all the celebrities to them, for the newsreel floodlights made night as bright as day. And Evie wrote her entire column the next night to portray such an occasion as it must have looked through Della's eyes. Usually the most brittle and sophisticated of all the

Capital society editors, she made it a little masterpiece of tenderness.

The best of it was that a warmhearted constituent of ours, who had come down for the event, read the story, sent for Jimmy in New York, and offered him a desperately needed job in his plant, where, draft board willing, he is still working today. Not long afterward a letter came from Della's sister, who is a nun, to tell us that Della had passed away quietly, still happy in the memory of that glorious trip, and in the knowledge that her Jimmy was taken care of. There seems to be a moral in it somewhere. Perhaps it's that sometimes it's wise to be foolish.

The Sesquicentennial was to continue for almost two years, celebrating the great events of the years 1787-1789 through which the government of the United States was established. Mother and I had wondered (to ourselves) whether real public interest could be aroused over something as impersonal and inanimate as the Constitution. As it turned out, conditions in Europe, where constitutions and all they stand for were going by the board as one country after another succumbed to the dictators, created an appreciation of the Constitution here that was both sober and enthusiastic. Free speech and a free press were not mere phrases any more, and orders for the compact little book *The Story of the Constitution,* which Father had spent years in doing, poured into the commission's office by hundreds of thousands.

The next national birthday party (eleven of the thirteen original states having celebrated, meanwhile, their respective anniversaries of ratifying the Constitution, with North Carolina's and Rhode Island's still to come) was March 4, 1939, the one hundred and fiftieth birthday of the First Congress.

It was an ideal date for a joint session of the Senate and the House, at which the President, of course, would be the principal speaker; and a wonderful opportunity, besides, for something new under the sun: an address at the same session by the Chief Justice. The tremendous personal ovation Chief Justice Hughes received made headlines throughout the country; but as he told Father afterwards, he had been so ill that morning that he had hardly known what was going on. No one could have guessed it from his magnificent voice and bearing. And the event was a news photographer's dream: the President's lost fight over the Supreme Court reorganization still a fresh memory, and the Chief Executive and the Chief Justice posing together on the rostrum of the House.

The fighting on this great occasion, however, took place in the music department. We thought the arrangements made in advance would meet the requirements beautifully: which were that the soloists of the day should be American singers, who would perform with great dignity. We had found two who not only filled the bill but were available on the historic date, Gladys Swarthout and John Charles Thomas. They were to sing "The Star-Spangled Banner" as a duet at the finale, and each to sing a solo earlier in the program. Father relied on my suggestions in this, which quite sensibly but unfortunately were as follows: Mr. Thomas ought to have the chance to sing something dramatic, like "Columbia, the Gem of the Ocean." Miss Swarthout, in that case, would sing the opening number, which as usual would be "America"; an arrangement all the wiser, I thought, because Mr. Thomas would probably not be satisfied to open the program, whereas Miss Swarthout, known to be as sweet as she is beautiful, probably would. No hitch developed upon broaching these plans to the artists. All seemed well, right through the afternoon of March third, when Frank Chapman, Miss Swarthout's husband, telephoned to let us know that they were in Washington, and to tell Father "how grateful Gladys is for this wonderful experience, and that she is saving her voice for tomorrow."

But there was no word from Mr. Thomas—that is, until the next morning, at practically the last moment, when he flatly refused, to Father's amazement, to let Miss Swarthout sing before him! The fact that the arrangements and the program were all ready, and that the President of the United States was satisfied to be the last speaker, made no impression. Only, apparently, the realization that the entire civilized world would be listening in by radio finally moved him. Of this crisis, and its apparent last-minute resolution I was unaware, being already in my gallery seat ready for the fruition of well-laid plans.

Miss Swarthhout sang "America" thrillingly, and sat down again beside Mr. Thomas. At last, the time came for his solo, just before the President was to speak. I listened for the introduction to "Columbia, the Gem of the Ocean." It never came. Instead, his accompanist began "America"—again. There was no sign of absent-mindedness; piano and voice were firm and unfaltering. I could only conclude my ears were playing tricks. Even after hearing of the last-minute show of temperament, I wondered: Why? So did the papers next morning. He must have been getting even, in a curious, literal way, with Gladys Swarthout, no matter if it marred a great historic observance. His explanation, afterwards, was that he had some extra verses of "America" that he wanted to sing, and that was that.

Even fairy tales, where "the feasting and the merriment lasted forty days and forty nights," were exceeded by the long span of Constitution celebrations, although, to be sure, feasting and merriment were not exactly the words to describe it, until after the fourth of March.

But the next historic red-letter day, April 30, when the New York World's Fair opened, was quite a picnic. (It even rained.) The fair—although everyone, apparently, had forgotten it—was originally intended to celebrate the inauguration of President Washington in New York, a hundred and fifty years ago that day. In the meantime someone had thought up the theme "'The World of Tomorrow," and by opening time even the fair's president, the glamorized Grover Whalen, had probably only the vaguest remembrance of the original idea. There was a rumor about that the symbols of the fair—the newly named Trylon and Perisphere—had been inspired by the Washington Monument and the dome of the Capitol. But no one seemed to know just who had had such a quaint and far-fetched idea.

Quite possibly no one would ever have connected Washington's inauguration with the fair again, if the Director of the Sesquicentennial had not been faced with a problem. The March fourth celebration had been such a success that there could hardly be another historic joint session of Congress only six weeks later without its being a terrible anticlimax. Moreover the President, it appeared, had agreed to be in New York to open the fair on the thirtieth, and obviously a joint session without him would have been like Hamlet without Hamlet.

Even Father was stumped for a minute when he realized that. Then, he decided, why not have Congress "convene" in New York? as, indeed, it had on the day of Washington's inauguration. The fact that ninety-six Senators, and four hundred and thirty-five Representatives—and, of course, their wives—would have to be transported, fed, and amused, to New York and back, and not at

164

government expense, didn't faze him for a moment. After all, he figured, if gratitude is really a lively expectation of favors to come —and the fair still had a very lively expectation of a Congressional appropriation of several million dollars—it should have been very grateful indeed for the opportunity to invite all its potential Santa Clauses to be guests on the opening day.

And sure enough, a few evenings later he announced with glee unbounded that the Fair had agreed to charter a special Congressional train (although, to be sure, it would only be made up of day coaches) which would leave Washington at seven o'clock on the morning of the thirtieth, take us right into the station at the fair late in the morning, and bring us back to Washington about two o'clock the next morning—at least what would be left of us after such a day, and doing a World's Fair in between.

It sounded perfectly terrible to me; but of course I didn't say so. Besides, I knew only too well that once the excitement of it got in the air, I'd be up at dawn with the best of them. Mother and I did persuade Father, though, that something definitely social should be done for such a delegation. After all, you wouldn't put Santa Claus on an ordinary Sunday excursion train the day before Christmas, unless you had arranged a really good time for him at his destination, now, would you?

So it was arranged for the Congressional group to join the buffet luncheon at the Federal Building, to which the diplomatic chiefs of mission had already been invited, and which turned out to be beautifully served by Sherry's at small tables overflowing into the large and lovely patio of the building.

A tremendous percentage of both Houses had accepted the invitation, and as the Vice-President and Mrs. Garner decided not to come, the Speaker and Mrs. Bankhead headed the delegation. Father had insisted that one drawing-room car should be put on the Congressional Special, so that the Bankheads could have a compartment to themselves; and in the other compartments he installed popular Dr. Calver, the Physician of the Capitol, and his assistant, just to be ready for any emergency. Fortunately, nothing more serious happened than some bad cases of "Fair feet" and the bad effect of the weather on a thousand drenched dignities.

Mr. Whalen, for some reason or other, although he invited the four society editors of the Washington papers, had absolutely refused to include just three other press invitations which would have enabled the three great news services (Associated Press, United Press, and International News Service) to cover the picnic. As a result, what should have been almost the biggest news story of the opening, and priceless nation-wide publicity for the fair, was barely mentioned except in the Capital society columns.

Most amusingly, the Washington morning papers carried stories which were all sweetness and light. But the evening papers fairly sizzled with reports of hurt feelings and minor misfortunes.

The explanation was simple. The trip down had been pleasant, the skies were blue, and we were met not only by special buses but by Julius Holmes, formerly the protocol expert at the State Department, who had left to fill the same niche for Grover Whalen, and who greeted us in all the top-hatted splendor which Mr. Whalen had requested of the Washington group, but in vain. . . . Yes, this was the same Julius Holmes who was to become Colonel (later Brigadier-General) Julius C. Holmes, and General Mark Clark's right hand man and official interpreter in the invasion of French North Africa in 1942; thus proving that even the most dandified sector in American government can produce an authentic war hero.

The luncheon was lovely; there was a special section of the grandstand reserved for us in front of the Federal Building to hear the President's speech—and then, at two-thirty we were thrown on our own until a nine o'clock traintime. Which *might* have been fine, except that neither the transportation, the restaurants, nor the amusements which Mr. Whalen had so blithely promised Father, materialized.

The sun went in, the deluge came down, and kept coming down for hours. Senators were soaked, Congressmen were congealed, and not a cup of coffee or a conveyance were to be had for love or money. We were even politely but firmly put out of the huge Federal Building (where the Federal legislators might at least have expected to find shelter) because another party had been planned there!

The President and Mrs. Roosevelt arrived by special train from Hyde Park just in time for the President's speech. When this was well under way, Tallulah Bankhead, beautiful in black, dramatically swept down the center aisle of the grandstand to where her father and stepmother were listening to the President in the first row, thereby putting herself in perfect focus for all the cameramen.

As the crowds swarmed around the grandstand later, it became obvious that we were in New York and not in Washington. Hundreds of autograph fans besieged Tallulah, who was then starring in *The Little Foxes*, while her father, who was merely the Speaker of the House of Representatives, stood proudly beaming but neglected near by.

That was the last we saw of the Bankheads or of Father for hours. The crowds separated us like flotsam on a flood. Mother and I, with one faithful escort, managed to find at least some shelter at a covered bus stop, where we stayed for four solid hours while one rare overcrowded bus after another rushed by. At last, in sheer desperation, we tramped, drenched and dismal, all the way back to the station, where, since there was no waiting room, we stood for an hour or so longer. Soon we were joined by more and more of our delegation, who, wet, weary, and wild, had managed to get back to the station in spite of the directions of the most courteous but most completely blank information guides the world has probably ever seen, who had been especially trained (for what?) for at least six months.

At last, the stationmaster announced through a megaphone that the Congressional Special was now on the tracks. We found out later that Father by superhuman effort had reached a telephone and registered insistence that the stationmaster bring the train in ahead of schedule and see that some sort of supper was served in the dining car. It was after nine before we had any word of Father, but at last we got a message asking us to join him in the Speaker's compartment.

We reached it after passing through at least six cars fairly sizzling with wrathful tales of the day's adventures and misadventures, and there found Tallulah putting on one of the best acts of her career. All the way in from Flushing to the Pennsylvania Station, where she and her handsome actor husband, John Emery, left the train in a final barrage of news photographers' flashlights, she told us the story of their afternoon's adventures with emotion in that husky voice of hers that would have utterly shaken the most heart-hardened first-night audience. Rage, hurt, pity, revenge, followed each other so fast, and with such intensity, that the train seemed to tremble with it.

She wound up with a final vow to "let the world *know* how disrespectfully my Daddy was treated, sending him off to the *swamps* outside the farthest gate, and taking *hours* to get back in the rain, in spite of all that poor *darling* 'Uncle Sol' could do!"

And then, with a tragic good-by kiss for each of us, she was gone. The last glimpse we had of her, she was making a sweeping curtsey to us all on the cold station platform, as the train pulled out. In the compartment it was calm again, as it must be when a tornado has just passed.

P.S. Somehow or other Congress continued to neglect making appropriations for the Fair.

8. All Roads Lead From Washington

That all roads lead to Washington is a commonplace; a picture familiar and exciting. Turn the notion around, and it's rather a dim surprise. Oh, obviously, those same roads also lead *from* Washington; but does one really picture the outbound traffic? It moves, nevertheless, as fateful, as ordinary, as incessant as the in-going parade. For official life has always been a constant to-and-fro, what with state visits, international conferences, and good old prewar garden-variety, dollar-a-day Congressional "junkets"—which it's always been more polite to call "official inspection tours."

We have taken the roads that lead from Washington to a dozen different capitals: which hardly seem to be the same cities when visited officially as when taken in on tour. I know, because we've "done" most of them both ways.

Even a round of official Washington is no preparatory school for official entertainment abroad, where for centuries it has been traditional for governments, parliaments, and the city fathers themselves to put on a magnificent show for foreign "visiting firemen," who usually arrive for an international conference and are likely to be old hands at that game, trained by experience to expect wining and dining, morning, noon, and night, in one magnificent government building after another.

Not that we haven't magnificent government buildings in Washington. No place in the world, I think, could supply a more stately background than the Capitol or the Library of Congress; but so far as I know, Congress, as such, has never been expected to offer even a glass of fruit punch or a cookie to a group of visiting dignitaries. Washington leaves its official entertaining to the White

House and the State Department, and usually only our Latin American visitors are entertained at the Pan-American Union, which, with its romantic Aztec garden, is surely one of the loveliest buildings in the world.

A state visit, here as anywhere, usually lasts only two or three days, and the visiting royalty, or president, knows pretty well what to expect on his social schedule: a White House dinner the night of his arrival; a luncheon or dinner given by the Secretary of State and Mrs. Hull the next day; a dinner at which he will be host at his own embassy or legation the following night; and, if the visit should last longer, usually a dinner given by the Undersecretary of State and his wife. During the war Senator Connally and my father started something new when they instituted giving a luncheon for distinguished guests like Mr. Churchill and Mme. Chiang following their addresses to Congress—the first time, so far as my knowledge goes, that any official visitors have had a mouthful to eat in the Capitol. But this is still not Congressional entertaining, as, of course, Congress makes no appropriation for it.

For an international conference—which may run into hundreds of delegates and last for several weeks—the White House usually gives a tea, or a garden party; but no one dreams of expecting a party at the State Department itself, such as was always on the program in London at the Foreign Office, or in Paris at the Quai d'Orsay. The reason, of course, is simple: in most Continental capitals the highest cabinet members live in gorgeous apartments in the government buildings. The Secretary of State and his family would live on one floor of the State Department, and so on down the line.

And just compare, for instance, what is expected of the mayor of New York and of the lord mayor of London, in the way of official entertaining. New York's mayor, from time immemorial, has received official guests of the city on the steps of the beautiful City Hall; and that is all anyone has ever looked for from him.

But the lord mayor of London—who, of course, is mayor only of the old City, the great financial district, while lesser mayorlings preside over the various London boroughs—normally entertains on a scale so nearly regal that his term of office only lasts a year, and usually even a rich man's bank account is by then badly depleted. In fact, it's the expected thing, in peacetime, for a lord mayor of London to spend in this way about a hundred thousand dollars of his own money during the one year of office.

The lord mayor, quite unlike the mayor of New York, is a figure of almost ritualistic solemnity, king over his domain, which His Britannic Majesty himself may enter only after formally having been granted the freedom of the City. The palatial Mansion House is the lord mayor's official residence, and the Guild Hall, where he used to entertain on behalf of the City of London, was surely the most magnificent municipal setting for a reception that one could think of, until it fell in ruins—one of the great casualties of the London blitz.

The rare chance of seeing a reception there came to us when the Interparliamentary Union, of which my father was one of the American officers, met in London one summer.

Five or six separate entertainments in honor of the delegates took place at the Guild Hall that night—everything from a solemn reception by the Lord Mayor and Lady Mayoress, Sir Wilkins and Lady Waterlow, and the Chief Sheriff and his lady, in full regalia, standing on a dais to receive the guests, to a ball in a hall as vast and as beautiful as a cathedral, and, like the whole building, nearly nine centuries old. A chamber music concert was going on in another hall, a popular concert in another; endless art galleries were open for us to stroll through; and half a dozen supper rooms, from the lowest crypt to the highest hall, offered the most lavish suppers I have ever seen, served on the Guild Hall's priceless collections of gold and silver plate, to which each lord mayor is expected to present an important addition.

The Interparliamentary sessions were held in a gorgeous room at the House of Lords, where King George V and Queen Mary looked down from their portraits. There were a lot of grand parties, including one at Lady Astor's; but the most amusing time for me was the afternoon we were all invited by the King to be his guests at tea at Windsor Castle.

Meeting in the little triangle opposite the House of Lords, we found it crowded to the limit with what we call sight-seeing buses and the English call char-a-bancs, waiting to be filled by senators and deputies from every nation in the world, and their families.

There were no special places, and you piled in where you pleased. I beckoned to one of our delegation to sit with me, but a slightly cockney voice behind me said, "Oh, I say, would you mind saving that place? I am trying to keep it for Lord Strickland." So I canceled my signal, and the Englishman went on to tell me that he was a newspaperman and that this was his one chance to get hold of Lord Strickland, who, as the prime minister of Malta, Britain's great Mediterranean naval base, was at that time on the front page of every paper, every day, for some very sensational thing he had done in direct opposition to both the Maltese parliament and England, and, I think, the Vatican as well. I was rather vague about it, but I did know that he was pretty much the man of the hour.

In a moment the newspaperman whispered, "Here he is—but don't let on I told you!"

Lord Strickland, like so many latter-day lords, looked anything but lordly. He was round and tubby, with twinkling eyes behind gold-rimmed spectacles, and looked more like a good-natured innkeeper than a peer of the realm.

The conductor started doing something to the top of the bus, and the Prime Minister made an exclamation in Italian, *"Ma perchè!"*—as we would say "What's the idea!" The spirit of the occasion being altogether informal, I chimed in laughingly, *"Ma perchè no!"*—"Well, why not!"

He turned around and loosed a flood of fluent Italian, and was delighted that I could come right back at him, so we kept it up for the whole hour and a half to Windsor. For a long time he gave no hint of who he was.

But he was so funny that I couldn't stop laughing, and naturally Mother, in the seat ahead, wanted to know what it was all about. I got tired of saying, "He says—" so I finally said, "Oh, Lord Strickland says—" and of course he demanded to know how I knew who he was.

I couldn't go back on the newspaperman, especially as he was sitting right behind us, so I had to say innocently, "You shouldn't have so many pictures in the papers!"

He went on to tell me that his mother had been a Maltese lady, hence the perfect Italian, and for that reason he felt that he was particularly suited for his post in Malta. Then came a tragicomic lament about the woes, financial, of having a peerage conferred upon you. You must have a town house and a country house, you must go to the best hotels, you must expect to be overcharged in every shop as soon as they discover who you are, and so forth.

We arrived at Windsor all too soon; the newspaperman claimed his prime minister, and I saw him no more.

After tea in the Orangery and a tour of the castle, I boarded another bus for the ride back to town. And there, as it happened, was Count Visconti (an Italian senator) and his son. The Senator was over six feet tall, with a black spade beard and handsome features, so Italian-Renaissance-looking it seemed a pity that he should be in a morning coat and derby hat instead of velvet and plumes.

"We didn't see you coming down," he said politely.

"No," I said, having no idea what a political bombshell this would be, "I was in the bus with Lord Strickland."

"Lord Strickland!" Count Visconti cried, as incredulously as if I had said Oliver Cromwell. "Is *he* here?" And he jumped over the side of the open bus without another word to go to look for him. The Prime Minister, however, had disappeared without trace, thus forestalling whatever international unpleasantry might have developed.

So my ride back was in Italian, too, with young Visconti, who was, surprisingly, studying agriculture instead of the politics or diplomacy which had occupied so many of his family since centuries ago when they ruled Milan.

He was anxious to compare English impressions with me. "Have you met a lord?" he asked, and I said grandly, "Oh, yes, lots." Then he wanted an itemized list, which fortunately I could honestly produce.

He said, "I met one yesterday!" And I rejoined clairvoyantly, "Oh, you mean Lord Luke," because he had given a tea for all of us the day before, at his house.

"And that," said Visconti, "is what I consider a really nice house."

I blinked, with the mind's eye at least, wondering if he was serious. For the Villa Visconti on Lake Como is marvelously beautiful even for Italy, and Lady Luke's house was just a comfortable, unimaginative London town house, with no artistic claims at all. And then I realized that he was quite sincere, and that too much of anything, even beauty and art, can pall.

In spite of all the teas we'd been to in beautiful houses and famous clubs like Ranelagh and Roehampton, I felt that a London season couldn't be complete without tea on the Terrace of the

House of Commons. We were invited there on what turned out to be a hopelessly dismal day. We went anyhow, hoping the sun would come out, but it got wetter and wetter, and we had to have tea indoors. Finally, I got up the courage to suggest to our host that perhaps we might at least peek out at the terrace, wet or not.

He solemnly counted us, "One, two, three, four, five, six, seven, eight, nine," before we left the restaurant. At the head of the stairs he did it all most carefully again, and at the foot of the stairs we met a bobby who, unwilling to rely on a mere M.P., counted us himself. At the door of the terrace our host counted us once more to be sure he was right, and then let us out on a deserted, dripping place, right on the Thames, which went the whole length of both Houses of Parliament, with seemingly hundreds of little iron tables and chairs covering the entire terrace except where a wide empty space signified a sort of no man's land between the Commons and the Lords. Once inside, we were solemnly counted again, and I wondered what would have happened if it had been a sunny day and we had really had tea on the Terrace. I suppose we would have been put in the Tower of London a while, for observation, first.

It was such a contrast to the utter informality, not to say confusion, which reigns in the Senate and House restaurants, and to the complete freedom with which anyone could come and go in the Capitol; until the war, of course, when it became necessary to check all packages and cameras at the door and show the guards the contents of your purse.

We left the London conference a few days later, and headed on our own for Paris, where quite Americanized André Tardieu was then the premier of France, temporarily, as usual. He had invited us to spend the week end as the guests of the French government in Nancy, where he was ceremoniously to be given the freedom of the city; and at the same time had come an invitation from Marshal Lyautey to visit Mme. Lyautey and himself at their chateau near there. The double invitation was doubly tempting, but we didn't see how we could make train connections from London to Nancy in time, so we sent a telegram regretting.

Then in Paris, Marcel Knecht, one of the editors of *Le Matin,* who was making all the arrangements for the celebration—no doubt because he was a Parisian of Parisians from Nancy—convinced us that we could make it, and promised to have someone meet us at the train.

We arrived in Nancy just before luncheon, to find not a soul in sight who could possibly be looking for us. I even asked the stationmaster if there was any message for "Monsieur le Deputé Bloom." He shrugged expressively. I asked if he knew what the plans were for the Premier's entertainment, and he did know that there was a grand luncheon going on at the Hôtel de Ville—the city hall.

Feeling very neglected, we decided to storm the Hôtel de Ville —a peacetime version of Joffre's glorious taxicab advance, on a very small scale. But when we dismounted at the entrance of a very magnificent building, some gendarmes (the only people in sight) politely but firmly insisted that no ladies were allowed.

All I could do, as the family's official interpreter, was to make one of them promise that he would not leave Monsieur le Deputé until he had delivered him safely to either the Premier, Marshal Lyautey, or Marcel Knecht. Then Mother and I disconsolately retreated across the square to the Café Stanislas, luggage and all, for luncheon.

We almost forgot our forlornness, eating the famous *guiche lorraine,* a sort of glorified omelet, and the historic macaroons of Nancy, and looking out at the lovely Place Stanislas, named for the last Duke of Lorraine, and as exquisite as a Louis XV ballroom designed with the sky for a roof: like a smaller Place Vendôme with France's finest wrought-iron and gilt gates and arches at every opening.

After lunch all Nancy began to stream into the square to hear the Premier over the loudspeakers which had been put up everywhere, and a double cordon of soldiers materialized standing a few feet apart all around the square as soon as there were signs of activity inside the Hôtel de Ville. Just then a spatted and silk-hatted delegation dashed across the square and up to us, breathlessly explaining why we had been so cruelly deserted. At the very last moments some bright young secretary had produced our regretful telegram from London; in the confusion, no one had thought of looking for the date; they accordingly took no for our answer and canceled all their plans for us.

After almost overwhelming us with apologies, they said that as soon as all the excitement for the Premier was over, we were to motor with Marshal Lyautey to the Château de Thorey, stopping on the way at the Princesse de Beauvau's for tea.

By the time we started there were five cars full of distinguished people, and all I saw of the Marshal was a flash of a tall figure, white hair, bristling eyebrows, a sky-blue uniform, and surely every decoration in the world. That is, until we reached the Princess' château—an eighteenth-century one with huge windows flooding every salon with sunshine and showing off the marvelous tapestries and works of art at their best. The Princess was young and charming: half American and half Italian, and, she agreed with me, "all French."

Just when we were having a lovely time at tea around the dining room table with the Princess and her mother-in-law, an exquisite old French lady, a booming voice behind us said, "*Madame Bloom et Mademoiselle Bloom! Je vous prie de partir toute suite avec moi dans ma voiture!*"

It was Marshal Lyautey, commanding, rather than inviting, Mother and me to leave with him in his car at once. And when the Lion of Morocco roared, everyone obeyed, I can tell you!

Perforce, we bade a hasty farewell, the Marshal growling all the time how long we were taking, and soon we were off, Mother sitting at his right on the back seat, a civilian aide and I on the folding seats, and an orderly and the chauffeur in front. And the Lion roared, all the way through the peaceful countryside of Lorraine to his lair.

Marshal Lyautey was seventy-five, but one could still easily visualize him as the great gallant he had been, and he still had more energy than all his young aides put together. It was said he wore them out completely within a few months. I can well imagine it, if he directed everything as he did that ride to the château, for he could have defended the Western Front with half as much energy.

He was very worried lest the other cars lose the road, and every other second he would thunder at the aide—in French, of course— "You can see them all, all four?" The aide could look out of the little window in the back, and the Marshal could not.

But I could, and though half of the cars might be out of sight on the curves, the aide looked at him with the angelic expression of a naughty choirboy answering an archbishop, and kept repeating meekly, *"Oui, Monsieur le Maréchal! Oui, Monsieur le Maréchal!"* in answer to a hundred questions on the subject.

Evidently his staff was trained to obey three contrary orders at the same time. He would say *"Arrêtez!"*—"Go slow!" to the chauffeur, *"Avant!"*—"Go ahead!" to the orderly, and *"Attendez!"*—"Wait!" to the aide, all at once, and they somehow kept their heads.

Hoping to distract him, I called his attention to the fact that Mother was dressed in the same shade of horizon blue as his uniform, in compliment to him. He assured her gallantly that, on the contrary, he had worn it in her honor.

Between commands, he showed us the historic places we were passing, and even found time to tell us that he was a Royalist while Madame Lyautey was a Bonapartist, her father having been one of Napoleon III's closest counselors.

So I told him that I had been almost the last person whom the Empress Eugénie received before she left Paris for the last time.

He inquired who had presented me to the Empress (it was her nephew, Count Primoli) and let me know how much it would interest Mme. Lyautey to hear of it.

Intermittently, all along, the bombardment of commands and countercommands had gone on, and I could believe in the colossal energy which had enabled him to hold and modernize Morocco for France through the worst days of the First World War, and had made Lyautey a doer of the impossible. I could hardly wait to see Madame la Maréchalle; it was impossible to imagine what woman had been able to tame the Lion.

Arriving at last at the château, we were greeted by a kind, calm and dignified lady, whom the Marshal had married late in life, who proceeded to scold him for bringing us so late that the tea was cold!

But we soon had fresh tea in the library, under a huge portrait of another Lyautey who was also a marshal of France, under Louis XVI; and later the Marshal showed us, in his treasure chest, the bit of blue ribbon which poor King Louis had cut from the decoration he was wearing at his last meeting with his faithful counselors, as a sad souvenir for each of them. Now it was framed, like a miniature, and rested against the Marshal's baton which linked the Lyauteys through the centuries.

The Château de Thorey was quite modern but enormous, and

dominated the little village of Vazilize, which only existed to serve the château. On the top floor the Marshal had made a perfect setting for his Moroccan trophies and souvenirs, even bringing huge timbers of Moroccan wood to make the rafters. The electric lights were shaded by enormous ostrich-eggshells, in typical Moroccan style, to harmonize with the rugs and furniture, and even the kit and camp cot which went with him through all his campaigns was in a reminiscently bare little room near by.

He seemed to prize most highly a dress sword which the Moroccans had given him to celebrate his recovery from a very serious illness—and the story that went with it.

Every day in all the mosques they had prayed for his recovery, and when he was finally out of danger and sent them his thanks, they begged that, instead, he should go, the first time he was able to go out, to the Great Mosque and there give thanks to Allah for having heard their prayers.

The Marshal said that it was a very difficult thing to refuse; but he told them frankly that, though he would go most reverently the second time he was able to go out, first of all he must offer thanks in his own church, just as he would expect them to do in theirs. They were so touched by his devoutness and his sincerity that they gave him the jeweled sword as a memento of the occasion.

Everything in that vast room had a history; but while the Marshal was still making the grand tour, Mme. Lyautey motioned silently to me to follow her, and, without the others' realizing we had gone, we left "Morocco" and went down flight after flight of stairs and through corridor after corridor until we came at last, as I had suspected, to her secret Bonaparte shrine—a small room done in simple Empire style with a portrait of Napoleon III and personal souvenirs of the days of both the Napoleonic empires everywhere.

Next to it was an Empire bedroom. "And here," said Mme. Lyautey kindly, "is *your* room, *chère Mademoiselle,* when you come to pay us a real visit, the next time." I hardly knew how to thank her for bringing me into the very heart of her memories, but she said that she was more than repaid by hearing of my visit to the Empress Eugénie.

"You see," she said smilingly, opening a connecting door into a little study of the Marshal's which was filled with souvenirs of the Bourbons, "this is how we can have a Royalist and a Bonapartist in the same house and still keep harmony! We keep our treasures separated!"

After a while we joined the others, who were so busy with Morocco that they hadn't missed us at all, and then we went back to the library, where the Marshal kept us busy for hours with anecdotes—interspersed with constant commands to do something or other to the four or five military aides and secretaries who had been in the other cars with Father and the rest of the guests. One of the commands was to remind him to send me two of his latest books to Paris, which duly arrived, with handsome dedications.

But he had an even grander souvenir in mind, for a few days later we came into our hotel rooms in Paris to find a beautiful bust of Lafayette, after the Houdon one in the Louvre, white wig, uniform and all, standing on the middle of the floor, a gift that appeared anonymous until, searching in a mass of mail on the desk, we found a card, "With Marshal Lyautey's compliments." Searching further, by going around the statue on our hands and knees to look for some mark, we found that it was made of the rare, pure white Biscuit de Sévres, and we learned later that there are only two others in America, one in the White House, and the other in the French Embassy. Truly a magnificent souvenir of a magnificent man.

When we left the Château and returned to Nancy, we found that there was a private dinner on for about twenty local lights and prominent Parisians who had come down with the Premier. That turned out to be a complete education in French cooking. And far into the night we had a marvelous time finding out how important Frenchmen relax. Everyone did some perfectly ridiculous stunt. One of the greatest newspaper owners in France did an imitation of the Spanish Consul in Paris trying to speak enough French to propose a toast to the then King of Spain. A famous writer did a marching army with the aid of his knuckles on the edge of the table and a comb in his mouth. A great sculptor did his specialty, An English Maiden Lady Crossing the Channel on a Rough Day—with an orange quickly carved into a caricature, teeth and all, and a napkin manipulated somehow into a glass of water, with all the expected dreadful details. Colonel Weiss, one of France's outstanding aces, recited funny poems; and so it went. I understand that in Paris even Monsieur le Président and ministers of state got together now and then in just such an un-self-conscious, simple way. For if there's one thing the French have always seemed to abhor as much as stupidity, it's stuffiness.

Yet the next day, when we all met again to go back to Paris, it was hard to believe that they could be so dignified again—except, of course, for the telltale twinkle in their eyes.

Another summer, we had a chance to see how Paris entertains officially—quite a different side of the City of Light from the gay night life which spells Paris to almost everyone.

I met France's jovial bachelor President Doumergue, quite by chance, when he received the Interparliamentary Union during its meetings in Paris one summer. He gave a reception for us at the Elysée, the French White House, which was—and here's a fine French touch for you—originally built by Louis XV as a town house for Mme. de Pompadour or Mme. du Barry, I forget which. Imagine our choosing for the President's official home a house originally built for a Mme. Jumel or a Peggy O'Neill!

Before the President arrived, while we were inspecting the over-ornate palace, which I found disappointing except for the superb tapestries, Fred Purnell, a jolly Congressman from Indiana who was one of our delegation, came up in great distress. Wouldn't I help make the footman who was checking the wraps see reason? He flatly refused to take the Congressman's stiff American straw hat, which he had fondly expected to check out of sight so that he could otherwise appear in faultless formal dress before the President.

I never found out the exact reason, but I suspect it was that a Frenchman takes his top hat, gloves, and walking stick with him into a drawing room when making a visit of ceremony. Anyhow, no argument I could think of would make that footman take that inharmonious hat. Finally the Gentleman from Indiana whispered to me, "Let's just drop it and run!" Which we did, barely in time to get back to the Grand Salon before the President's entrance.

A few nights later the shaggy-haired Minister of Foreign Affairs, M. Briand, gave a grand farewell dinner for the Interparliamentarians, serving a different marvelous wine for every course. A certain Senator in our group considered himself a great connoisseur of French wines, and held forth so patronizingly all through dinner that some of us couldn't resist playing a joke on him. When he wasn't looking, we mixed the dregs of all the glasses together in one horrible mixture of Bordeaux and Burgundy, sparkling and still, and had a glass of it solemnly offered him by one of the footmen "with Monsieur Briand's compliments, from his private cellar!"

Such ecstacies over the bouquet, the body, the vintage—until we thought we had let him go far enough! Well, at least it was a most eloquent swan song to a career in amateur wine tasting.

Our first official visit to Switzerland followed the International Copyright Conference in Rome and our last talks with Mussolini, and our appearance in Berne, the picturesque Swiss capital, had an amusing element of shock.

At that time we didn't know Hugh Wilson, our Minister to Switzerland, who later served as Ambassador to Germany, resigning on the day Hitler invaded Poland; but Warren Robbins, who was then counselor at the American Embassy in Rome, had written the Wilsons that we were coming.

Before the tea they arranged in our honor Mr. Wilson wisely and cautiously called the legation staff together and told them that for their own good they had better remember that Sol Bloom was a member of the Foreign Affairs Committee, and a Democrat, and they would be well advised to avoid controversial haberdashery. Under the circumstances, he decreed, No Spats had better be the order of the day.

But we always managed to take enough to wear for any conceivable occasion in a few suitcases and a hatbox. And I have never heard such a howl go up in polite society as when my father stepped out on the lovely terrace at the Legation, where they were all waiting to meet us—*resplendent in spats!*

We were in Switzerland again a few summers later when the Interparliamentary Union met in Geneva. But as Geneva would probably have been bankrupt in no time if it had tried to entertain on the scale of Paris, London, or Rome for all the councils and conventions constantly meeting there, we found ourselves left to our own devices and our own delegation most of the time. In common with many another in the long parade to Geneva, we enjoyed the services of its premier self-appointed guide, M. Guillaume Fatio, the J. P. Morgan of Geneva, whose enthusiasm for his country was such that almost any day you could see this great financier going around Geneva piloting a group of tourists, to whom he would make Swiss history and Swiss institutions unforgettably clear and admirable.

We had expected to go down to Madrid that summer to visit Alexander Moore, our ebullient Ambassador to Spain, and we never regretted anything more than missing this opportunity, and only getting to Madrid too late to witness the outrageous things he did there—but so genially and so naturally that the king he called "Chief" and the queen he called neither Madame nor Your Majesty but just plain "Queen" came to see him off at the train themselves, when he left for America, with a trainload of flowers and a jeweled cigarette case with the royal monogram for souvenirs.

At first I used to think that the tales of Mr. Moore's doings in Madrid were pure fiction, but having heard them from more than one eyewitness, I know they must be true, and I can imagine he was as welcome to that formal court as a fresh mountain breeze.

His own tradition, according to the stories, began early, with his presentation to Spain's British-born Queen.

He was told that on being presented, he was to bend over and kiss the Queen's hand while he counted eight, and then rise. He remembered the bending over, and the hand-kissing, but forgot how many he was supposed to count—so he just kept his head down, and murmured, "Say when, Queen, say when!"

Someone who was present told me about the time, soon after his arrival, when King Alfonso was holding a cabinet meeting and had given strict instructions that it was not to be interrupted for any reason whatsoever. Shortly after the session began, the American Ambassador telephoned the palace to speak to the King, only to be told by his secretary that His Majesty could not possibly be disturbed.

"Oh, but I must speak to him," Mr. Moore insisted. "It's of tremendous importance, and I don't think you ought to take the responsibility of not putting me through."

The poor secretary, probably having visions of another Spanish-American War on his hands, slipped in and whispered to the King, who picked up the telephone at his elbow.

"Is that you, Chief?" came the Ambassador's cheerful voice. "Sorry to trouble you, but I thought you might know a good real-estate agent in San Sebastian. I'm looking for a place for a summer embassy, and thought you might be able to help out!"

The King replied that an agent wouldn't be necessary; a friend of his had a beautiful place there that he was anxious to rent for the summer; he, His Majesty, would make the necessary arrangements himself, and see that the Ambassador got it at the right price!

Afterwards the King remarked that he was delighted with Ambassador Moore's way of doing things: if we live in the twentieth century, we ought to do things in the twentieth century way, and using the telephone was certainly the most obvious way of all.

It sounds like Alice in Wonderland but it's all quite true, and Poland lost a great experience when lovable "Alec" Moore passed on before he could take up his new post in Warsaw.

It seems just a step in my memory, from Old Spain to New Spain and a visit we made at La Fortelesa, the great castle that is the residence of the governor of Puerto Rico.

We had known Governor and Mrs. Horace Mann Towner in the familiar atmosphere of Washington, when he was a member of the House: which did not at all prepare us for the pomp and circumstance surrounding them in Puerto Rico—all very necessary, to be sure, to accord with both the prestige of the United States and the importance of Puerto Rico.

La Fortelesa, the most palatial building in the island's capital, San Juan, is a real palace, old and magnificent, built, so the story goes, by Ponce de Leon himself. It had everything a well-regulated Spanish castle—or even a castle-in-Spain—should have, from turreted battlements to dungeon-keeps and ghost stories.

There were people continually coming and going as guests at the palace, all of whom were entertained to a perfection of stateliness. I used to think it was rather an imposition to look up our diplomats and governors in out-of-the-way places, but the more of such places I get to, the more I'm convinced that anyone from home to break the monotony and bring some news is really more a godsend than a nuisance.

It was rather hard to be so formal and so hot at the same time. I remember one morning we went shopping with Mrs. Towner —"shopping," for the Governor's lady, consisting of sitting out in the car in the blazing street while the shopkeepers respectfully brought out their wares for her inspection, as it was simply unheard of for the Governor's lady or her guests, while they were with her, to enter a shop.

I was so hot that I unthinkingly pulled off my hat, and then immediately felt that certain something in the air that makes you realize you've done something your hostess doesn't want you to do. I turned around questioningly to Mrs. Towner. "Yes," she said with a smile, "you'd better put it on. You see, the people wouldn't like our being informal."

Another day I went for a ride alone with the Governor, and getting into the car first, quite by habit I sat down in the right-hand seat. Immediately the Governor, who was really the simplest and kindliest person imaginable, said, "I'm sorry, Vera, but I shall have to sit there. To the Puerto Ricans, you see, I am the person of the President of the United States, and they would consider it a great affront if I were not in the place of honor, although, of course, under any other circumstances, it belongs to the lady." So along we went, according to protocol, to frequent cheers of "*Viva el Gubernador!*"

It was Governor Towner, by the way, who made me promise to write my experiences; it was really a duty, he insisted, to leave some record of the people I had known as I had known them. So here it all is, Governor, with a bow to your memory!

We made our pilgrimage to the Fountain of Youth in the course of a motor tour through the island, a trip that to me was indescribably sad, in spite of the beauty all around us, because of the almost unbelievable squalor in which so many of the poorer people lived, although I understand that since then the government has accomplished miracles on their behalf.

Our official guide was the Commissioner of Agriculture for the island, who was a Cornell graduate; and the Commissioner of Health, also American-trained, accompanied another carful from the palace.

Late one evening, about seven o'clock, hot, tired, and hungry, we drew up at a building and found the smiling Health Commissioner waiting for us.

"This," he announced grandiloquently, "is the Fountain of Youth!"

"Not the real one?" we asked.

"On Ponce de Leon's word of honor," he assured us. "Hurry!

you must bathe in it before dinner. We are keeping it open especially for you."

Eternal Youth appealed to me much less just at that moment than a nap in a cool room, but there was no use arguing with the Health Commissioner. Taking Mother and me each firmly by an arm, he led us down what seemed literally endless dark flights of stone steps, until we finally came to some baths, evidently hollowed out of the living rock, which were presided over by a sleepy Indian woman in charge of two bath towels; and there he left us.

Obviously, there was nothing to do now but sample the magic waters, which turned out to be some thick dark mud in which we had to stretch out full length. And so went glimmering my mental picture of a Fountain of Youth throwing diamond sprays into the sunshine, somewhere.

But there was so much beauty in Puerto Rico, that one lost illusion hardly mattered.

And one lovely island makes me think of another, and of Christmas holidays in Cuba. Friends at the Cuban Embassy easily convinced us that the joys of the season in Havana were something not to be foregone.

We hadn't been in that siren city twenty-four hours before we realized that the chic Cubans—and they certainly are chic— would consider us hopelessly dowdy if we appeared at their parties or at their magnificent clubs in the resort clothes we had fondly hoped were "the right thing for Havana." The dark town clothes we had tucked in for a possible rainy day became our mainstay. For Cubans think of Havana as what it actually is, a sophisticated city, not merely a resort for northern sun-worshipers. During the winter they simply ignore the soft sun and the warm surf, and go their way dressed for promenading on the palm-lined Prado as if it were Fifth Avenue on a cool spring day.

We have had official engagements made for us at almost any hour of the day; but when we were told that the President and Mme. Machado would receive us at eight o'clock in the morning, we were for once surprised. We had been hearing of those late Havana evenings, which, by all accounts, the President enjoyed more tirelessly than anyone in Havana. He had even created an energetic new dance called the Són, which was being danced in every Cuban night club just then.

What worried me was that I might have to be interpreter for

the meeting, at that hour when my English flows none too quick and a rather sketchy Spanish might flow not at all. But I needn't have worried. For with a grand presidential gesture, our host had commanded not one but two ambassadors to be on hand as official interpreters—the retiring Ambassador to Washington, Sanchez-Aballi, and the newly appointed Orestes Ferrara, who, with Mme. Ferrara, was to treat Washington to the most magnificent entertainment it had seen in many a moon. Later they returned to Cuba when he was appointed Secretary of Foreign Affairs, and barely escaped with their lives during the revolt which overthrew Machado, while bullets whizzed through the wings of their plane.

How President Machado, who was known never to get home until the not-so-wee hours of the morning, could be ready to receive anyone three or four hours later was a puzzle. It took but little discreet questioning to find that he prided himself on needing less sleep than anyone in Cuba, although he did bow to the custom of the country and disappear at siesta time, which for most of Cuba, as for all Spanish countries, appeared to be from just after lunch to just before cocktails.

Machado, of course, fled from Cuba after having proved himself the most ruthless and unscrupulous dictator the island had ever known. But what we saw when we arrived at the huge and magnificent Presidential Palace with our two ambassadors at exactly eight that morning, was merely a stout, mild-looking, middle-aged man, whose eyes beamed benignly from behind horn-rimmed glasses as he waited for us with his whole family grouped around him. You would much more likely have taken him for a nice Rotarian than for a ruthless dictator.

He led Father and the other men in the party off to his private study, while passive, motherly Señora de Machado and her daughters took Mother and me up to the private presidential apartments. There was a whole series of splendid salons, and the largest was enhanced by a most exquisite Crib—the scene of the Nativity in miniature—which is the Latin American equivalent of our Christmas tree and has the holiday place of honor in every South American home, whether the figures are of rough clay in a poor peon's cabin, or of jewel-encrusted gold in the President's palace.

Mme. Machado and her daughters were kindness itself, but the conversation was quite constrained, for though one of the daughters could add a little English to my Spanish, the President's wife didn't speak a word of English, nor Mother a word of Spanish.

Mme. Machado proposed "some refreshments," but I hastily declined for both of us. I had a suspicion that the servants might appear with a *tierce*—literally a traditional Cuban snack of thirteen separate dishes. Politeness demands that a guest sample every one, and as light breakfasts are our habit, I was sure we would be unequal to that situation.

Just as the others joined us and the moment of leavetaking was upon us, Mother remembered that she *did* know a word of Spanish—*muchos*—and that it means "many." So, taking Mme. Machado's hand, she repeated cordially, *"Muchos, muchos, muchos!"* Mme. Machado laughed delightedly and exclaimed, *"Si, si! Yo comprendo!"* She understood that it was many, many thanks, and her warm response needed no translation.

Remembering Cuba reminds me of my father's most dramatic constituent's case in all the more than a quarter of a million he has taken care of.

One night, in Washington, about ten o'clock he was called long-distance from New York. It was a plea to save the life of a naturalized-American doctor who had gone back to his native Cuba, become involved in politics, and been sentenced to be shot at sunrise!

"Shot at sunrise" is not a phrase you can easily believe in, coming over your everyday telephone. But there it was, a stark reality, and what could be done in those few hours before the early tropic dawn? The State Department, through which the case should have gone, was, of course, dark and deserted. He tried to reach some of the officials, but none of those concerned were at home.

In desperation, he put in a call direct to the President of Cuba. The connection was interminably slow, but at last it was ready, and—well, there was no shooting at sunrise that morning.

We have memories, too, of an island half across the world, of the merry month we spent in Dublin and motoring through the truly emerald beauty of Ireland.

In London one summer Frederick Sterling, who had just been appointed our first Minister to Ireland, asked Father to go along to Dublin and lend his moral support in all the ceremonies, as Mrs. Sterling was back home visiting her mother, the inimitable "Ma" Williams—Mrs. John R. Williams—Washington's pet dowager.

Mother and I wanted to go along, but so many returning Americans had "warned" us that one couldn't get anything decent to eat, a room with a bath, or even a closed motorcar, that Father thought it wise for us to stay behind in London until he could look things over. Of course, not a word of it was true. I don't know whether it was deliberate anti-Irish propaganda, or just that "Gulliver's Travels" complex which seems to come over people the minute they get the slightest bit off the tourist beaten track —or beaten tourist track—making the most safe and civilized places loom wild and dangerous.

But a message came promptly, "Come over tomorrow. It's grand. You'll love it!" So over we came, across a beautifully behaved Irish Channel, in a much larger boat than its English Channel sisters. Father met us at Kingston, the port for Dublin, and we motored—in a closed car!—to the new Grafton Hotel in the heart of the capital, on the very spot where some of the worst of the last fighting took place.

The Grafton was modern and charming, if perhaps without so much atmosphere as the Shelbourne, an older and more famous Dublin hotel. In fact, the table d'hôte meals at the Grafton were so good, and so ridiculously inexpensive compared to London, that we aroused by our praise Mr. Sterling's personal and professional interest. He'd like to see for himself, if only he could be sure of sampling just an ordinary everyday meal, so that he could recommend the hotel to Americans who would be coming over.

As he hadn't been in Dublin long enough to be recognized at sight, it was easily arranged without a word of warning to Miss Mullins, the only lady hotel manager I had ever met. But when afterward we told her who the guest was, and the Minister congratulated her on the excellent luncheon, she didn't half enjoy the triumph, so keen was her distress over not having provided something special.

We went out to tea one day at our Legation, which, as a special compliment to the United States when the legation was established, was located in the historic Secretary's Lodge near the Viceregal Lodge, home of the governor-general of Ireland, in beautiful Phoenix Park.

We arrived to find a great discussion going on. How should the Minister dress at the Dublin Horse Show, high spot of the year?

Governor-General Tim Healy, once the young firebrand of Irish politics and now its grand old man, who was the first *Irish* direct representative of the king of England, was doubly in mourning at the time, for his wife and for his brilliant young nephew, Kevin O'Higgins, who had been tragically murdered just a short time before. He had therefore offered the viceregal box at the horse show to Mr. Sterling, and now the point was how he was to dress. I was all for going as "Ascot" as possible, with surely a gray topper, and, if possible, a gray frockcoat too, on the theory that the greater the style, the greater the compliment implied.

Unfortunately for Mr. Sterling and for my own peace of mind at the show, I won. For when he appeared in all his Ascot glory, he found himself surrounded by all the Irish aristocracy wearing the most disreputable-looking old tweeds, evidently the time-honored correct thing to wear at the Dublin Horse Show, where the *horse* is king. Never again shall I pronounce on "What the Well Dressed Man Should Wear."

I did better with another Dublin Horse Show problem when we got back to Washington. It happened that an American Army cavalry team was being entered there for the first time the next summer. The White House aide in charge of it, who was a great friend of mine, asked me what special stunts they would be expected to do. So I, who have never been on a horse in my life and hardly know the difference between a bridle and a stirrup, showed the American team—by "jumping" with two fingers on a cigarette box—how they do the tremendously difficult jump up on a high, wide, grass-covered mound, and how the horse must change feet before jumping down again. Either because of it or in spite of it, our team won!

Most of the social letters of introduction which we had brought to Dublin found the people out of town for August, but AE, the great Irish poet and economist (George Russell), who was reputed to be "an intimate friend of the fairies," was in town, and in response to a note we sent him along with an introduction from our former consul-general to Dublin, he wrote back simply asking us to come "at half-past seven on Sunday."

Unable to divine whether the prospect included other than spiritual nourishment, we prepared ourselves with an Irish high tea, and at half past seven stood at the top of a broad flight of steps before a front door equipped with a huge bell and a still huger knocker.

"I wonder which we should use?" said Mother, when a deep voice startlingly answered "Neither!" and AE, his massive, gray-bearded head peering through a crack at the door, let us in himself.

We only saw two rooms, and they were hung ceiling high and stacked half a dozen deep with his own paintings of Irish scenes —and Irish fairies. Sofa and chairs were ready for us in the back room, and with no preliminaries and practically no pauses, AE held forth until midnight on art, politics, the rise and fall of civilization—every subject in the world except the fairies, to which nothing could draw him. We were, he felt, merely "curious" about them, and not "sympathetic."

Another time, we went up to see him in the office of his magazine, to find the walls of his sanctum, on the top floor, completely covered, as by a landscape wallpaper, with fairy pictures. But never a word about them would he say, although he is, I suppose, the most brilliant and prodigal word-user I have ever met.

A totally different type of Irishman was President Cosgrave —"president" in deference to the American-mindedness of the Irish, but actually prime minister of the Irish Free State. He received us, red-headed, frockcoated and friendly, for a long, formal talk in the magnificent old town palace of the Dukes of Leinster, Ireland's premier dukes, which is now the seat of the government offices in Dublin. President Cosgrave's dignified self-possession provided a vivid contrast to the associations of the place. We had known the present Duke of Leinster in London, an attractive personality but with the fateful carefreeness of all his line, which, they say, led his father to gamble away the use of their marvelous country seat for the lifetime of the gambler he was playing with: who, I believe, is still in possession, and if the estate had not been entailed it would have been gone forever.

But of all the fine Irishmen we met, the Governor-General, Tim Healy, was the finest—and I can't think of a much nicer afternoon than the long one we spent with him at the Viceregal Lodge, formerly the summer palace of the viceroy, who surely found it a cheerful, sunny retreat from the grandeur and gloom of the winter palace, Dublin Castle. Now the Lodge, in the heart of lovely Phoenix Park, where the largest and tallest and most perfect flowers I have ever seen are cultivated for everyone to enjoy, is the year-round residence of the governor-general.

Tim Healy was a mellow little old man, a veteran of a hundred political battles, simple, humorous, and unassuming, but blessed somehow with a natural dignity that made his plebeian presence in the atmosphere of those traditionally royal rooms not at all out of place. Afterwards we were told that our visit must have done him a lot of good, for it was the first time since his double loss that anyone had heard him laugh, which he did wholeheartedly and often as the afternoon wore on. And it was the first renewal of enthusiasm for the collection of china, Waterford glass, and old silver that filled his private apartments. He even asked for the long-unused key to a little corner closet where he kept his old Spanish silver, now black with the tarnish of a long-forgotten hobby. He showed us, too, a rare old coin, the first to be minted when Ireland, over a century ago, was granted the right to issue her own currency; and he pointed out the blackness in one corner, from acid used by the mint to test the quality of the silver. This he insisted on my accepting as a souvenir.

Then he exhibted a pair of old Waterford water pitchers, and chuckled like a boy successful in villainy when he told us how he had had one of them for twenty years while he searched everywhere for a mate to it, finally found one in a tiny antique shop, and was so afraid something might happen to take it away from him after all those years, that he threw the money on the counter and bolted with the unwrapped pitcher clutched in his hand, leaving the shopkeeper to wonder at sudden idiocy, while he recked not, rested not, until the prize was safely lodged.

Standing at the window of the viceregal throne room, we could look across the soft Irish hills to the Governor-General's own home, which from the wistfulness in his voice, was much dearer to him than splendors. Then we went out into an old walled garden with fruit trees trained against the walls, a tapestry of living verdure. Leading off from it were the hothouses, and there I found out again that no one is so rich or so powerful as not to walk softly before the gardener. I have seen a woman with thousands of roses afraid to pick a single one.

His Brittanic Majesty's representative in Ireland said: "I'd love to pick you a bunch of grapes, if the gardener isn't around!"

He tiptoed off, and was back in a moment with the spoils; just then a head appeared over a hedge, and a grim voice said, "Hey, Yir Ixillincy!" No denying it: His Excellency was caught red-handed taking his own grapes! The gardener looked at the bunch a moment, and then added with a twinkle in his eyes, for after all he was Irish, "Well, if ye had to pick one, why didn't ye pick a good one!"

We sat in the sunlight eating our grapes, while the Governor-General reminisced on the old viceregal days gone by.

"Just think," he said, pointing to the great entrance to the Lodge: "when the great Lord Chesterfield was viceroy here, no one without a title was ever allowed to pass those gates!"

"Then," said Mother cheerfully, taking another grape, "if he were here now, *none* of us would be here!"

"That's right, we wouldn't!" said Tim Healy, roaring with delight.

And we would all have missed a beautiful Irish afternoon.

Our farthest official visit in Europe was to Poland; and we will always be grateful that we took the chance, on a sudden decision, to see something of the old Polish life before it disappeared under a rain of Nazi bombs.

It happened that we arrived in Warsaw the very last night our Minister, John B. Stetson of Philadelphia, was to be in the Lega-tion, as the Polish nobleman who owned it wanted it back. And no wonder, for it was a fascinating old palace, though, like most of the palaces of Warsaw, quite inconspicuous from the outside, for the great Polish families, long under Czarist Russian domina-tion, had found it wise to conceal their wealth as much as possible.

Mr. Stetson took us there almost straight from the train, to dine with him alone and to share his last bottle of Château Yquem. In fact, he was so good to us that we literally could not find a moment in which to break away and leave Father's card for him at the Legation, so we simply stuck it in the vanity case in his car!

Since we had made up our minds at the last second to take the

Warsaw Express from Berlin, there hadn't been time to provide ourselves with exchange. The day we arrived was a bank holiday; the next day was Sunday; then came a patriotic holiday, and then a religious feast. No chance to get a bit of Polish money; but also, pleasantly, no time to worry about a day of reckoning.

The last day of our visit the Charles Deweys gave a luncheon for Mr. Stetson and for us. Mr. Dewey, who later came to Congress representing Illinois, was then financial adviser to the Polish government. Perhaps he gave financial advice to a countryman that day. Anyhow, after lunch Father passed around a hat and collected a few zlotys from everyone so that we could at least tip the porters at the station; Mr. Stetson assured the Europeski Hotel that our credit was good; and so we were enabled to depart unpursued.

I still have the little notebook in which I wrote down the names of the Polish people we met, that were so difficult to learn. It is terrible to think how many of those kind, charming people are now, after Hitler's invasion and long terror, homeless and destitute, or worse.

Yet in spite of the most unbelievable hardships, Poland kept her proud spirit high for a century and a half until she achieved her independence after the First World War; and surely that proud spirit will live on, no matter how cruel her present trial.

Our latest and least expected experience in parts unknown was when the Mexican government included us in the official American group invited to the inauguration of President Avila Camacho on December 1, 1940—of which group the Vice-President-elect and Mrs. Wallace were to be the very bright particular stars.

We had just come back to Washington from New York after the Roosevelt-Willkie campaign, and the tumult and the shouting had hardly died when we received the invitation from the Mexican Ambassador, Dr. Castillo Najera, through the State Department. A moment before, we had thought the only thing in the world we wanted was a few weeks of peace and quiet; but hardly had Father finished reading the letter before we all were agreeing that what we really needed was a little more excitement; and what could be more exciting than a Mexican inauguration? That we had never been to Mexico, except just over the border to Tia Juana, made the invitation twice as tempting.

The Wallaces were to motor the whole way to Mexico City
—as post-campaign relaxation. Father suggested that the rest of
the American delegation should meet at Laredo, Texas, since we
were all expected to get that far "on our own," and cross the
border together to Nuevo Laredo, where retiring President Car-
denas was sending his private car to take us on the two nights and
a day to Mexico City.

We pulled into Laredo the Wednesday night before the Sunday of the inauguration, not knowing just who would be waiting
there or what we were to do, except find the naval attaché of the
Mexican Embassy in Washington, Commander Araica, who had
been sent as an honorary aide to take care of us in Mexico. And
there on the platform were the friendly faces of the former Secretary of War and Mrs. Pat Hurley, Representative Marvin Jones
of Texas, who later was to become the War Food Administrator,
and Mayor Maury Maverick of San Antonio (who formerly
served in the House) and Mrs. Maverick, with Commander
Araica. They bundled us into waiting motors and across the International Bridge to a dinner in Nuevo Laredo which had been going
on for hours, where we learned that Senator and Mrs. Chavez of
New Mexico and Senator Downey of California were to join us
in Mexico City.

The President's train, which had been attached to the regular
Mexico City Express, was due to leave late that night, and we
found it was made up of a sleeper and a combination lounge and
dining car, decorated in Spanish style with heavy oak beams and
wrought-iron brackets. Our luggage was all in place, and there
was nothing anyone could ask for that wasn't provided in a second.
For us, it was the first trip across a border since Father had become
chairman of the Committee on Foreign Affairs, and we found
that at each stop from Monterey early the next morning to the
capital itself, Ambassador Josephus Daniels had ordered each
consul to come and pay his respects, no matter what time the
train was due! It was just what such a kind, courtly soul as Mr.
Daniels would think of doing.

The consul at Monterey brought not only a bright morning
smile but also engraved invitations from the Ambassador and Mrs.
Daniels for us all to lunch at the Embassy the day we arrived, to
which we were requested to "r. s. v. p." That was quite a problem,
as none of us opened the envelopes until after the train pulled

out: we were so engrossed with the brilliant, exotic movement at the station, and with our first sight, among the crowds dressed in ordinary clothes, of Indian men in huge sombreros and sarapes and Indian women dressed in multicolored full skirts and blouses, with blankets wrapped about them in every conceivable way. The "r. s. v. p." problem was solved when someone thought of asking the Commander, as the only one of us who could cope with the Mexican telegraph system, to wire the Embassy when we next stopped, saying on everyone's behalf that we had the honor to accept.

We went on all day through the strange, wild beauty of the Mexican mountains, climbing higher and higher endlessly to the great plateau. Everyone was feeling perfectly fine until someone said ominously that we had reached 7,300 feet above sea level, when we all began to feel strange symptoms of the altitude—our main topic of conversation and concern from then on.

Ever since our decision to go to the inauguration I had been using every spare moment to brush up on my Spanish. And then, just as we were pulling into Mexico City Friday morning, Maury Maverick, our self-appointed mentor, declared that none of us were to speak any Spanish at all! His reasoning was that an innocent mistake might create an international incident; and I obeyed until, with Mr. Wallace's example and Ambassador Najera's encouragement, I concluded that even limited Spanish would add to the Good Neighbor feeling, and that one should do one's bit.

Incidentally, all Mexico was chuckling over a joke on Mr. Wallace; a linguistic windfall, or pun. You see, "Wallace," in Spanish, would be pronounced *Vaya se* (the *se* like our *say*), and *Vaya se* happens to mean "Get out of here!" But it was a very friendly insult, for the Mexicans fell in love with the Wallaces for their sympathetic sincerity and friendliness, and were overjoyed when they decided to stay on a month or so unofficially after the inauguration was over.

No one had prepared us for the magnificence of Mexico City, which is very much like a Spanish version of Washington. It is laid out on very much the same plan of stately circles and avenues, and with the same wealth of splendid buildings, but with the added patina of Spanish viceregal days and of Maximilian's court: an atmosphere that still clings to the great palace, where the new

President and his wife entertained us at luncheon the day after the inauguration, and to beautiful Chapultapec Castle, set in a lovely park on the heights above the city, where we were the guests of the retiring President and his lady at tea the day we arrived, and where, it seemed, at any moment we might see the shade of the unhappy Empress Carlotta flitting from one regal room to another.

Hardly had we unpacked and pressed and dressed for the luncheon at the Embassy before we were overwhelmed with good advice of what to do and not to do about the altitude. Don't rush —even to answer the telephone! Take your dinner at noon: only a snack at suppertime! Be careful going up stairs, especially grand staircases (which seemed to be everywhere)! Take a fur jacket if you're going to be out after sundown—and don't grieve the Mexicans by intruding tropical sports clothes into their beautiful city when you should dress as you would in New York or Washington on a perfect October day! Don't carry an umbrella: no raindrop falls, from October to June! And above all, take it easy, 'cause the altitude will get you if you *don't watch out!*

How to take it easy while on a split-second schedule, and being wined and dined morning, noon, and night, was something only you yourself could work out. Most people find that three short siestas during the day are better than one long one; but no one is surprised if you suddenly make for the nearest chair when your heart begins to thump, your head begins to spin, and you think you're "gone." In five minutes you've forgotten all about it and are having the time of your life again.

The Mexican government gave each official guest his own car with an excellent chauffeur-guide, and two motorcycle policemen who cleared the way wherever one went, with shrieking sirens, even if it was only to the drug store for a coke, and who had orders to stay with us until they saw us safely into the Hotel Reforma every night.

The whole experience there was so kaleidoscopic and crowded with impressions that I can still hardly separate them in my mind. The days were so full of contrasts: from the luxury and elegance of the great Spanish families to the pathetic poverty of the poor peons . . . from the Southern kindliness of Ambassador and Mrs. Daniels, which made our enormous Embassy seem so home-like, to the stupendous pageantry of the outdoor fiesta which the

Mexican government gave one night on the lake in the park below the castle, with singers and dancers in costumes from every part of Mexico drifting by on beautifully decorated floating barges beneath a sky ablaze with fireworks . . . from the cozy friendliness of small, quiet parties with old Washington friends, to the gala grandeur of the "diamond horseshoe" at the national opera, with its curtain of Tiffany glass showing the fantastic beauty of the view of snow-capped Popocatepetl from the castle heights . . . from the exciting danger of Inauguration Day, with the whole city a seething sea of soldiers with bristling bayonets and every inch of space crammed with cheering crowds, to the stillness of the floating gardens of Xochimilco, broken only by the boatmen's poles as we drifted up and down the canals past island after island, one all violets, another all heliotrope, all carnations, or lilies, or roses in scented succession, while the strumming of guitars, or snatches of a song or laughter, floated back across the water as another boat went by . . . from the silent immensity of the Aztec pyramids to the stately formality of a diplomatic reception at the Palace . . . and from the few stolen seconds in the shops and the colorful markets to buy a little Mexican silver and pottery, to sharing the Wallaces' welcome while apparently all Mexico joined in a thrilling and heartwarming cheer for the United States.

9. The Seamy Side of It

We call it "the seamy side." The French, a bit more artistically, call it *"le revers de la medaille"*: the other side of the medal. But however you say it, it means the same thing—the side with rough edges, which never shows from the front. Here it may be just a social pinprick; or it may have all the makings of a slanderous whispering campaign to wreck a great career.

I don't mean to say that Washington has a monopoly on the seamy side. Goodness knows, every town in America has its quota of "visiting firemen," bores, sight-seers, buffalo moths, busy-bodies, leaky faucets, and subversive elements. But Washington, in the very nature of things, has its own oversupply of very specialized blights—the lobbyists, the high-pressure boys, the propagandists, the social "sponsors," the party crashers, the foreign secret agents, the sensational columnists and commentators, and the fortune hunters.

The one character dear to fiction that I have yet to see (or perhaps only to recognize) is the alluringly beautiful lady spy. Probably she would be so incongruous against the conservative Capital background that her very allure would defeat its own purpose.

The nearest Washington has come to an authentic feminine foreign agent, so far as I know, is Constance Drexel, who is one of the six Americans indicted for treason since the war because of her propaganda broadcasts from Berlin, where she has been the Nazis' American version of the renegade British Lord Haw-Haw. Constance Drexel used to be quite a familiar figure among the newspaperwomen in Washington; we knew her, too, in Paris and Geneva, where she used to specialize in covering the League of Nations for a Philadelphia paper and various big news services.

And perhaps the most unpleasant sensation I have had in all these years in Washington came with the knowledge that I knew an outright traitor, who will rightly have to pay the supreme penalty we can impose on war criminals when we can lay our hands on them.

It is a horrible feeling to know that you have actually called a traitor by her first name (although, of course, nearly everyone first-names everyone else in Washington, unless they are much older or of high official rank.) It makes you feel so stupid and so naïve to think that you accepted her as just a rather pretentious and ambitious newspaperwoman, without the least suspicion that there was anything even sinister, let alone treasonable, about her. The only consolation is that apparently no one else did, either.

In her Berlin broadcasts which were beamed to America, I understand, the announcer always introduced her as "the famous American heiress and social leader, Miss Constance Drexel, of Philadelphia," obviously hoping to give the false impression that the cream of American society was pro-Nazi. She was not a Drexel at all, as nearly everyone in Washington and no doubt some people in Berlin knew. Her real name was Dreisel or something like that, and she had cleverly taken Drexel as her pen name when she went to work on a Philadelphia newspaper. Since she had acquired a certain grand manner, and was very ambitious socially, it undoubtedly did a great deal to help her in that way, especially abroad.

But I don't think even the Nazi announcers described her as either beautiful or glamorous, for she was neither, although she must have been quite good-looking when she was younger. She was thin, with sharp features and reddish hair, and went in for very dressy clothes and too much rouge. She hadn't appeared in Washington for several years before the war, that I know of, and I never heard of her having any political connections with Germany, although she said her mother had lived there for years, as she was an invalid and needed to take the waters at Wiesbaden.

Whenever anyone would ask her what her relationship was to this or that Drexel, she would just say airily, "Oh, I don't like to talk about my family!" Perhaps that would have gotten by, if she hadn't been so hard put to it, occasionally, to cover up her failure to be noticed by Drexels when in town. Her deceptions, at least of the social kind, were pretty thin; but of course for work as a Nazi propaganda agent, that would be no great drawback.

For all the secret agents who have been unmasked, it's frightening to think how many more must still be undiscovered. If that sounds overnervous, remember where we live. People who know Washington know how wary anyone in public life must be, and that no matter how careful you are, you can still get into the most unpleasant and false situations through no fault of your own.

For instance, about a year or so before the fall of France, during the time when some people thought it funny to call it "the Bore War," a youngish Frenchman suddenly appeared in Washington, and setting himself up at one of the fashionable hotels, proceeded to cut a wide social swath. His teas, luncheons, and dinners, all with really quite impressive guest lists, appeared regularly in the society columns, and apparently he had plenty of money.

It annoyed me that he regularly sent me invitations to his cocktail parties, although I hadn't met him. I never went, and never even sent a card of regret, as ordinarily I would have. Knowing France and Frenchmen as well as I do, it just struck me that there was something wrong with the picture of a rich young Frenchman, without any official status, coming over here and putting on such a "show," when everyone knows that no Frenchman ever left France except to go into business or on some official duty.

Then one day a lady European refugee with wide social connections came in to one of our Tuesdays at home, and in the middle of all the excitement while I was trying to help Mother take care of fifty people at once, she asked me if I would go with her the following Monday morning to Mrs. Townsend's musicale at the Mayflower. I had no other engagement, and could think of no excuse; and when she asked me to plan to lunch there afterwards, as nearly everyone did, I accepted that, too, and arranged to stop by for her that morning.

Only as we were going into the hotel did she mention, casually, "Oh, by the way, you're not lunching with me. We're lunching with a *charming* Frenchman—" and she named the man I had been avoiding so long.

I was furious. But what could I do, when I was obviously perfectly well and had said I had no other engagement! Belatedly I found out that the lady was acting as his "social secretary"; through her wide connections *she* had been inviting people to all those luncheons and dinners, and they had only found out who their host was when they arrived.

What intrigued me at lunch was trying to guess which of the other guests had been roped in as innocently as I had. What about the American naval officer who was seated to my right?

By and by our host called across the table to me, "And who do *you* think will win the war?"

I could hardly believe my ears.

"The Allies, of course!" I said.

"But why 'of course'?" he laughed. "You speak as if it's a foregone conclusion! Do you mean you cannot picture the world unless the Allies are victorious?" He sounded like an impatient adult trying to convince a child that there is no Santa Claus.

"No, of course I can't picture a world under the Nazis! Life just wouldn't be worth living, for anyone."

He laughed again. "Well, it's a possibility you may as well face! After all, with France under a crooked scoundrel like Daladier—"

By that time, I was too angry to talk. But the naval officer came to the rescue.

"I happen to be your guest," he said bitingly, "but I cannot sit here any longer and allow a Frenchman to insult and malign the Premier of France! Either we will change the subject, or I must ask permission to leave the table!"

A few minutes later, the luncheon broke up, and one of the women guests—an American army officer's wife—asked me in the "charming Frenchman's" presence if she could bring him in to our day-at-home the next afternoon. Of course, since it was an "open" official day, to which anyone could come, I could hardly refuse, but I said coldly, "If he cares to," never dreaming that he would, after such a discouraging assent. But he did, and made himself so conspicuous, getting tea for people and passing things around, that several guests remarked how surprised they were that we were so chummy.

It happened to be our last at-home of the season, and when it was over, Mother decided that it was the last open day we would ever have. And it was.

After the fall of France, the charming Frenchman disappeared from the Washington scene as suddenly as he had appeared. I found out afterwards that the name he had used was not his real one; but whether he was up to anything actually subversive or not, I don't know. That's what you're up against. Trickiness, and not knowing.

But don't think you only need to keep your eyes and ears open to avoid being taken in by possible foreign agents. The lobbyists are up to every trick they ever knew, and probably a few more.

The most high-handed tactics ever put over by lobbyists that I can remember were in a "kidnaping" a few years ago, when a whole private-trainful of Senators and Representatives were spirited off to Florida by the sugar interests without knowing a thing about it! I know it's true, because we were on board.

It started when the governor of Florida and the president of the Florida Chamber of Commerce wrote to high-ranking Congressional groups in both the Senate and the House asking them and their wives and daughters to be "the guests of the State" on a special train which would be their home for the several days the trip would take, except for one night at the Miami-Biltmore, which would take them on a tour specially planned to show them the outstanding industries of Florida.

The invitations came during a particularly long, cold winter in Washington, and I don't think anyone even tried to resist them. Besides, even the most cautious and seasoned politician could hardly see anything suspicious in such an invitation.

We were already speeding through Florida when a young man came through the train, his arms piled high with expensive boxes of candy and copies of "So This Is Florida!" which he smilingly proferred to each lady "from your host!"

"How sweet of the Governor!" I said innocently.

"But they're not from the Governor—" he answered.

"Oh, you mean from the President of the Chamber of Commerce?" I asked.

"Oh, no!" he explained patiently. "They're from your host, Mr. So-and-So. He will be along in a few minutes to welcome you himself!" And he was gone.

We couldn't imagine whom he was talking about, for we had never even heard the name.

A few seconds later we were enlightened, when a group of Congressmen burst into the compartment, purple with rage. When they stopped spluttering, we learned that our mysterious host was the multimillionaire head of one of the great cane-sugar companies and that they, being from beet-sugar states, were on a terrible "spot" politically. Apparently the feud of the Hatfields and the McCoys was a love feast compared to the feeling between the two sugar groups.

A few minutes after they left, a smiling, rotund, urbane gentleman came along, said how delighted he was to have us as his guests, and went on his welcoming way. And I immediately christened the train the Sugar-Daddy Special. Of course, there was nothing anyone could do but finish the trip. The full light of publicity had already been shed upon the guest list, the itinerary, functions planned for us, and everything else; the damage was done, so even the beet-sugar group finally relaxed and decided to get all the good they could out of the Florida sunshine, come what might on the next election day.

Back in Washington, I spent a dinnertime with two cynical newspapermen as neighbors, who teased me unmercifully about our gullibility. But I still don't see how anyone could ask a more bona-fide invitation than from a governor "on behalf of the State."

But one thing I shall never understand is how any Washington-wise person can get himself involved in anything like the famous case of the Red House on R Street! After all, when you get an invitation from someone like the mysterious Mr. John Monroe, it's just plain common sense to find out who he is and what he's after. True, some people in Washington will go anywhere to a party; but why high-ranking officials, who in the nature of things have more invitations than they can accept, will go to someone they know little or nothing about, is one of those Capital conundrums that I can't solve.

The Washington-wise are even a bit leery of people they have known for years, when, never having made a great social splurge, they suddenly erupt with a geyser of invitations, one after another; especially if the parties are very lavish. I remember one retired American diplomat and his wife who had lived quite modestly, then suddenly started entertaining continuously and on a wholesale scale. Not long afterwards it came out that he was representing the oil interests. All perfectly legal and respectable, of course, and no great surprise to those who knew their Washington.

It is only fair to add that there are good lobbyists, as well as bad, and that "the right to petition" is set forth in the Constitution. If Clara Barton had not persisted in her one-woman lobby during the Civil War, the American Red Cross might not be what it is today; and Miss Cunningham, that indomitable little invalid, worked single-handed for years to persuade an apathetic Congress to permit the Mt. Vernon Ladies Association to save Mt. Vernon as a national shrine. It all comes back to Bernard Shaw's remark that when you teach a child to write, you teach it at the same time to compose a sonnet or to forge a check.

At the bad end of the scale is the most despicable lobbying of all—the terroristic kind, with which we have had all too close experience. This is the kind that flourished just before Pearl Harbor, when the fight over neutrality revision and lend-lease brought so many subversive elements into the open. The more subversive the group, the more fine-sounding a patriotic name was flaunted.

I suppose it was inevitable that since my father had to lead the fight in the House on those measures, he would be one of the prime targets. But still that didn't prepare me for the shock I had late one afternoon, at the time the Neutrality Act was due for revision, when I heard a commotion at the front door, and Amanda, our devoted colored maid, rushed upstairs to my room, pale with fright, to tell me that some women wearing mourning veils and carrying placards were demanding to get into the house to see Father.

Senator Pepper, of Florida, had been hung in effigy outside the Capitol just a day or so before, and a woman had suddenly appeared in the House gallery wearing a skull mask, which was dreadful enough; but to have a group actually try to force their way into our house was just too much.

Mandy and I were alone in the house and she had securely bolted the front and back doors, but I began to worry what such people—who, of course, were obviously hired nuisances, no matter what pious names, like the Mothers of America, they used—might do to my father when he got home from the office. I decided the better part of valor was to telephone the police; and within two minutes a radio car had arrived, with three comfortingly brawny policemen. One stayed inside the house, and the other two stayed outside; for the women refused to disperse, and stood on their Constitutional right to picket the house.

They insisted to the police that Mandy had only "imagined"

that they were forcing their way in when she opened the door; and as they were well behaved (from a legal standpoint) while the police were on guard, nothing could be done about them. Of course, once the police were called in, the case inevitably got into the newspapers; but I felt that was far preferable to taking the chance of their doing something violent.

The women finally left late that night, vowing to be back in the morning—which they were. Nevertheless, one of the policemen stayed on guard outside all night long, in case. And just when we thought we could settle down to an exhausted sleep, we discovered that our vicious visitors had other plans for us.

About half past eleven the telephone rang, and a sepulchral female voice said: "The Mothers of America warn you that you are first on Hitler's list—and he will avenge us soon!"

The printed page cannot reproduce that ugly sound; but you can probably imagine how horrible the effect became when the phone continued to ring every five minutes on the dot, with some similar message of what would happen unless Father gave up the fight for neutrality revision. They were evidently phoning from pay stations, for we could hear the coins being dropped in the machine, so the calls could not be traced.

At last, it got just too much for anyone's nerves, and Father rang up the telephone company to ask them to disconnect our phone until morning. They said it was impossible, and that we were not even allowed to leave the phone off the hook. But after another half hour of those terrible calls, he rang up again, and said that something had to be done.

They agreed then that we could leave the phone off the hook, and Father left off the extension by his bed. But somehow, in the middle of the night, one call did get through, for he woke up to hear a muffled, ghostly voice repeating: "Hitler will get you!"

When we arose in the morning, the pickets were there already, with new bloodcurdling placards, and anyone who came to see us had to pass the line. Those telephone calls continued at longer intervals throughout the day. It was impossible to avoid them, for any one of the rings might be a legitimate call.

Of course, by that time, the press photographers were on the scene. Unfortunately their pictures could not bring out the amazing sight of a crepe-draped mourning "Mother" wearing a bright red sweater—the only touch of comedy to relieve a miserable memory.

After a day or two more devoted to us, they transferred themselves to the Senate and House galleries, where they continued to sit in mournful groups (but without the placards, of course) during the rest of the neutrality debate, on which their tactics fortunately had not the slightest effect.

For years my father's office—like that of every member of both the Senate and the House who was not an outright isolationist—had been swamped with scurrilous mail and besieged by high-sounding isolationist delegations, and we were accustomed to receiving insulting, anonymous telephone calls at home, every once in a while. This, however, was the first time we had been besieged at home by an organized group. But people in public life have to get used to the idea that not only the head of the house but the whole family is bound to be the target for such unpleasant things, as well as for untrue and sensational publicity.

Most of the Washington newspaper people are the finest and fairest-minded in the world, but there is a certain group of columnists and commentators who will stop at nothing to get what they consider a good story. It's bad enough when there isn't a word of truth in it, but to me it's even more infuriating when there is just a grain of truth—so that you can't deny it flatly—but so distorted that it has absolutely no relation to the original event.

Take, for instance, the story Drew Pearson wrote when we went to Mexico for President Avila Camacho's inauguration. He said that my father had left the luncheon at the President's Palace in a "huff," for two reasons: because we weren't seated at the President's table, and because we had had to ride to the inauguration in the same car with the Pat Hurleys.

In the first place, there was no President's table—there was only a buffet. In the second place, we were overjoyed to be with the Hurleys, who have always been among our most treasured friends in Washington.

The grain of truth in the story was that we did leave before the luncheon was over; but not for the reason Drew Pearson adduced.

In simple fact the cause of our leaving was that bugaboo of all

206

newcomers to Mexico City, the altitude, which, as I've said, can play the strangest tricks, so that you feel perfectly well one minute and sure you're going to faint the next. Father's one concern the whole time we were there was that, if he should suddenly feel faint and have to sit down at some official function, someone might magnify it into an "incident" embarrassing to the Mexicans; and he made up his mind to get out into the open air immediately if he should feel it coming on, rather than do anything conspicuous.

The state apartments of the palace were crowded and very warm, and there was a long, unavoidable wait while the new President and First Lady received the regular diplomatic corps, as the rest of us had only "courtesy" diplomatic rating for the inauguration. A few minutes after we were received by the President and Señora de Camacho, Father noticed that ominous feeling coming on, and said quietly to Mother and me that he thought we had better slip out, if I could find someone from the Protocol Division and explain. I searched out the assistant chief of protocol, Señor Franco Lopez, and he took us down the seemingly interminable grand staircase and found the car in the courtyard for us himself.

Then sure enough, as soon as Father was in the fresh air, the dizziness disappeared, and he was only concerned lest the Hurleys be stranded without the car. But Franco Lopez assured us he would look out for them himself—and we started for the hotel.

Whereupon we realized that it was nearly three o'clock, and that none of us had had a mouthful since eight that morning, so we decided to stop at Sanborn's, Mexico City's famous American tearoom, for a sandwich and a cup of coffee, since we knew it would be open and we could be served right away.

When we got back to the Reforma, there was a message that "Vice-President Wallace called in person to inquire about Congressman Bloom, having missed him at the reception." (This incident, too, somehow got into Drew Pearson's story. It was made to appear that Father had added insult to injury by being out "gallivanting" at Sanborn's when the Vice-President was calling on him!) We rang up the Vice-President at once and explained just what had happened; and then the Hurleys came back, quite concerned about Father, and relieved to make sure it had been nothing more than the usual touch of altitude.

Who sent Drew Pearson that lurid version we never did find out. It was a distortion that could easily have strained the Good Neighbor Policy we had gone so far to help strengthen, to say nothing of our friendship with the Hurleys, had that not been on such a firm foundation. And the facts could easily have been checked, for the story was not published until several weeks after we returned to Washington.

Fortunately there were no really bad results; but another experience we had with a Washington columnist led to stark tragedy. Sensationalism had it that our Italian chef, Vincenzo, had chased Colonel Pennaroli—the Italian military attaché, who was also an honorary aide-de-camp to the King—out of our kitchen with a meat cleaver in an argument over Fascism!

The true story was quite simple—far too simple to have spread over front pages throughout the country, as its melodramatic version did, with some of the milder headlines screaming, "Anti-Fascist Chef Routs King's Aide in Sol Bloom's Kitchen." The time, by the way, was long before the Rome-Berlin Axis, when Italy's government, as well as its people, enjoyed the friendliest relations with the United States.

The kitchen was the cause of what little foundation there was to the story. We had had a Czechoslovakian artist come down from New York to decorate it in authentic Czech peasant style —walls, windows, woodwork, and china—in vivid freehand painting, the technique of which is passed secretly from father to son; with the result that everyone who came to see us wanted to see the kitchen, too.

Vincenzo had reigned in it for four years, meeting everyone who came in with deference and a broad smile. He was fiery but good-hearted, and we never paid much attention to his long harangues on politics that a long-suffering succession of Italian maids had to listen to. Nor had we any idea that his occasional flares of "temperament," which all good chefs seem to have, could ever lead to insanity. Perhaps they never would have, except for what that sensational story brought about.

All of the Italian Embassy knew Vincenzo, for whenever any of them dined with us, from the Ambassador down, they would always go out to the kitchen to congratulate him on his wonderful cooking.

On the day that was to become a sensation, I had about twenty people in to tea, and someone suggested that I show the kitchen to Pennaroli, who had recently been transferred to Washington directly from Czechoslovakia. So off we went. I introduced Vincenzo to the Colonel as an Italian "artist," and Pennaroli, in his charming way, gripped Vincenzo's hand and said how glad he was to meet an Italian who was so much appreciated away from home.

Then I explained to Vincenzo that the Colonel was the new military attaché at the Embassy. Whereupon, Vincenzo, emboldened, no doubt, by the American citizenship he had lately attained, proceeded to say how wrong the Fascists were, and what he thought of the treatment he had received when he was in Italy that summer as a war veteran with six wounds, and his opinion of Italy in general.

I was stupefied to hear him talk to a guest in that way, and I begged him to remember that the Colonel was our guest, and also that he belonged to the Embassy. Pennaroli put his hand kindly on Vincenzo's shoulder and told him to "be a good boy," and we went back to the drawing room where we had left the others.

When we came in, Mother looked over from the tea table and said to me, "What's the matter? You look pale!" I must have —not from fright, but from embarrassment. I thought that they might have heard the loud talking and perhaps imagined it to be something much worse than it was, so I said, "Oh, we just had a little argument about Fascism"; and that was all—or so I would have thought.

Pennaroli had his tea, and the incident was of so little concern that he stayed on after everyone else had left, admiring and discussing paintings and prints and bibelots, for he was quite as much a connoisseur as a colonel. When he left, about seven o'clock, Mother and I told him that Father was in New York for several days, but that we would have him bring Vincenzo to task for his discourtesy when he got back. Pennaroli, however, begged us not to give the matter another thought, and we didn't even think it important enough to mention to Father when he spoke to us long-distance that night..

Next morning, just I was going out to luncheon, the phone rang. It was Marco Pennaroli, who chatted a few moments, and then asked me if I had seen the *News,* the Washington evening tabloid which was piling up circulation with a society column by George Abell called "Capital Capers," which was packed with dynamite nearly every night—most of it, probably, sheer invention on George's part. So when Pennaroli said "the *News*," my heart sank, and when he told me the gist of the story—the headline was enough—I was dumbfounded. Most of all, because George Abell had been a friend of ours for years, and had telephoned me the night before without asking me anything about the story which someone must have told him had happened that afternoon. It seemed unbelievable that George, who comes of one of the best families of Baltimore, and who was amusing and witty enough to write a better column than almost anyone in Washington on nothing but the truth, could not have resisted writing such a story, even for the doubtful satisfaction of seeing a lurid front page headline over his signature.

Our first thought was how dreadful it was for Pennaroli—to say that a military attaché had run away from a cook! It might even have ruined his career, except that it could be definitely and unequivocally denied. Our next thought was for poor misguided Vincenzo, for his flare of temper might cost him any other position as a responsible servant, and he had a nice wife and a little boy dependent on him, too.

So I began what turned into two solid days of telephoning to and from every important newspaper and news agency in the country, in an attempt to vindicate them both. First I phoned Father in New York, so that he should know before any newspapers and interviewers might shock him with the story, the exact truth of what really had happened. Then I tried to get in touch with George directly, but without success. So I had to go over his head to his editor, who, I had heard, enjoyed having a society column that tore down "pink teas" and the people who went to them, so I expected little help from him. He refused point-blank to take the story out of the later editions, but finally conceded to put in a correction—very lukewarm—that absolved Pennaroli of running away, but not Vincenzo of attacking him. That was absolutely all he would do. As I say, for two solid days I denied that story over the telephone, for every newspaper wanted to have its own story of "what really happened."

I began to feel like a witness in a murder trial establishing an alibi. For only by showing that, instead of running away, Pennaroli had actually stayed on after all the others had gone, could I prove without a doubt that the whole story was false. Obviously, someone there had told George something about it. It's quite possible, of course, that whoever it was merely told him the facts, and that George did all the elaborating himself.

It would probably have ended then, if a horde of Washington's seamy-side fly-by-night lawyers hadn't gotten hold of Vincenzo and given him visions of untold wealth to be had by suing the *News*. Poor Vincenzo, who could hardly read and write English, and whose head was full of ideas for making the world over, began to picture himself with all those millions as the Savior of the Oppressed. Mother and I tried to reason Vincenzo out of his fantastic ideas; at least, to make him promise to do nothing about the lawsuit until Father's return. We weren't nervous about him then; we just thought he was naturally a little more excited than usual. Shortly before Father came back, however, Vincenzo came in to speak to me, and suddenly the way he was standing, all disjointed and limp, like a scarecrow or a rag doll, sent a chill of apprehension through me. I remembered reading, in a book about pantomime, that such a posture meant there was no mental control.

When Father came back, he tried to reason with Vincenzo. He explained how unscrupulous those lawyers were, and that even if he did win such a lawsuit, he would probably only be given the traditional six-cent damages, since he had not been hurt, or even lost his position (for to discharge him, of course, would have been tantamount to admitting that the story had been true).

Vincenzo went back to the kitchen unconvinced, and while he prepared a marvelous dinner—the last one, poor fellow!—he gaily told what he was going to do with all his millions.

First of all, he was going to give Pennaroli a gold and diamond sword as a pledge of his regret—for he was really heartbroken over having brought such unpleasant publicity on us all, and he had already sent the Colonel a letter of apology that his wife had written for him and he had signed. Then he was going to make Father the American Ambassador to Italy, and he was going to give me half a million dollars. He was going to kiss Mussolini on both cheeks in the Piazza del Popolo in Rome, to show his good feelings toward him, and give him enough money to carry out all his reforms, besides. And he was going to give the Pope enough money so that all the priests and nuns would have nothing to do but help the sick and the poor. Then he was going to cancel the entire Italian national debt left over from the war. It was heartbreaking. There wasn't a mean thought in his poor head.

When he went home that night, we still did not realize that he could be seriously unbalanced. But shortly after midnight his wife telephoned, weeping, to say that he had gone raving mad and had been taken away to the hospital.

I rang up Pennaroli the first thing in the morning so that he would know the tragic end of it before the newspaper men phoned him, as they surely would when they saw that Vincenzo had been entered at St. Elizabeth's. He wanted to go to see him at once; but poor Vincenzo was past knowing that anyone was there. He stayed in St. Elizabeth's until the doctors permitted him to be taken home to die. Photographers somehow got his picture in the hospital, in spite of all we could do to shield him, and of course, the aftermath was written up as much as the fictitious incident itself.

The fine newspaper people of Washington were very unhappy that any Washington newspaper story should have been even an unwitting cause in such a tragedy; for, as I've said, there is no higher code of newspaper honor than in Washington. George, of course, could not have known what the aftermath would be. But what I could never forgive him for was his failing to ask me about the story when he telephoned me that night.

Besides the columnist, you also have the Capital commentators to worry about: under which heading comes an experience I had once when the Congressional Club asked me to give a talk on Mussolini. It was just before the Italian war debt settlement was to be voted on by Congress, and feeling for and against Italy was running high. Despite which I felt fairly equal to the occasion, until I looked down in the first row and saw Miss Janet Richards. She had been lecturing on world current events throughout the country for thirty years; I not merely saw but, so to speak, *heard* her listening around and between the words of my talk.

At the conclusion Miss Richards—who was "specializing" in Fascism at the time, and had met Mussolini—rose to ask a question: one of those searching questions that came from her searching mind.

"What," she inquired, in her best Spanish Inquisition manner, which succeeded in giving anything she said the worst possible implication, "does Mussolini call you?"

There was nothing to do but answer, so I said, "He calls me Vera." Sensing immediately an avidness of gossip-scenting all around, I thought it best to add good-humoredly (I hoped), "But he treats me like a daughter."

"I *see!*" said Miss Richards, as though she didn't at all. "And one question more." She paused a moment impressively and then went on, "Did your mother *always* go with you when you went to see him?"

If a better world is ever made, one will be able to ignore such a question; if a perfect world, no such question will be asked. But there I stood before hundreds of friends from the official families of Washington, and if such an innuendo were let pass, no telling what it might grow to. I have seldom done anything more difficult than to answer her pleasantly and matter-of-factly: "Yes, Miss Richards, Mother *always* went with me. In fact, Mussolini would tease her every time we came about not learning Italian, and she teased him in turn about not speaking English —until he learned it, and they could chat without needing me as an interpreter."

To descend from topics of spies, meat cleavers, insanity, and the sublimities of commentators: there are other seaminesses in Washington, which all seem to come back to the one theme that someone is on your trail, with as determined a desire to "get" you as the Royal Mounties every showed in getting their man. How much or how little they bother you depends partly on your own slant. To women who are unhappy over what the mirror says, the ubiquitous photographers probably rate as chief pest, while to others they are more than welcome.

Some varieties of bloodhound are after nothing more important than an invitation; and here that great Capital institution, the party crasher, comes into the picture. The dyed-in-the-wool crasher prefers to arrive at a party invitation in hand; but if he can't wangle one by hook or crook, he just comes anyhow.

He, or she, belongs to a certain group of people with no official position and no social distinction except a queer kind of ambition, who especially love to descend on each new and unsuspecting diplomatic arrival and, if they can, make good before the diplomat realizes what's what and who's who. There is certainly no snobbery implied in describing them as they are. The great percentage of the greatest people in Washington, are, and always have been, simple people of simple background, good and fine people who have risen to eminence on just these qualities. The pursuers are vulgar and conscienceless people who are determined to go, by fair means or foul, where they are not invited. They have been known to live on, or even in a legation for as long as the three or four years of the usual diplomatic regime; and naturally they not only spoil the atmosphere there but give the country a bad tone generally. Of course, this could only happen in one of what a baseball fan once described as "the bush-league legations."

Most of the important embassies and legations pass their guest lists on from one regime to the next. True, official Washington, due to the ups and downs of political elections and the routine comings and goings in the State Department and the diplomatic corps itself, changes so rapidly that no list is usable for very long. But usually there is at least one diplomat left on the staff from the former regime who can tell the newcomers what to do. Which is, of course, pretty hard on the professional crashers, who will resort even to mild blackmail. That sounds fantastic, but it's the truth. I know two different ministers' wives who received letters of the "Invite us, or else——" type when they announced they would give a tea dance and a ball.

From the moment a diplomatic hostess announces a party, her life is just one long subjection to pressure for invitations, some of it subtle, but most quite ruthless.

The commonest method, they tell me, is to telephone the hostess or her social secretary, saying sweetly, "This is Mrs. So-and-So, and I feel sure that you would want to know that our invitation for your party *must* have gone astray, for we were always at dear Mme. What's-Her-Name's parties!" (Mme. What's-Her-Name was of course, the hostess' predecessor, and if the truth were known, dear Mme. What's-Her-Name was probably told the same fiction about dear Mme. Somebody-Else.) Some people have been known to r.s.v.p. their acceptance to a party to which they know perfectly well they were never invited! And many, after having been politely but firmly refused an invitation over the telephone—"We are *so* sorry, but the lists have been closed. You know, the Legation is so small for a dance!"—callously walk in anyhow, sometimes bringing friends. It finally got to the point where most of the diplomats had to ask the society editors to refrain from any mention of their parties whatsoever until the day after.

That's why I was quite surprised when "The Three Bachelor Secretaries of the Italian Embassy"—the invitations were engraved that way—didn't send out little cards of admission to be presented on arrival at the famous masquerade ball they gave at the Embassy one Spring.

Tommasi, one of the hosts, was dining with us a week or so before the party, and I asked him if they hadn't thought of the marvelous opportunity they were giving all the crashers.

"But who would walk in?" he protested, incredulously.

"Don't you know," I said, "that Mme. So-and-So had forty crashers out of one hundred and fifty invited guests at her little dance last week; and there were no masks being worn at that party!"

The result was that the Italian bachelors sent out little cards of admission printed on a weird salmon-pink paper that couldn't be casually counterfeited; and that although I arrived at the ball with two of the men from the Embassy, and we entered through the Chancery so they could park the car in the courtyard, and went in through the private Chancery door to the Embassy dining room, still unmasked, and although the butlers knew us all as well as they knew the Ambassador himself, they still demanded our cards before we could pass into the ballroom, and right they were, too.

It is only what you might call the supercrashers who have the courage and the nerve to try to break into invitational evening parties. The average uninvited guest in Washington used to find all-too-easy opportunities in the old Washington custom of official days at home, which were almost universally abandoned even before the war because they were so much abused. It became very unusual to find a diplomatic hostess at home on Fridays, as you used to do. She usually sent out cards to her friends to come on a day of which the general public was unaware until they read about it in the papers the next day. The British Embassy gave up days at home long before, when it found that pieces had actually been cut out of the portieres by avid souvenir hunters.

My first first-hand experience with a crasher happened right after we came to Washington, when we were conscientiously making our first calls on the Senators' wives who had announced in the papers that they would be at home that Thursday.

We began at Mrs. Swanson's; it was when Mr. Swanson was still Senator from Virginia, before he became Secretary of the Navy.

As we came to the head of the stairs which led to the drawing room where Mrs. Swanson was receiving with Mrs. Woodrow Wilson, we were greeted by a portly, unctuous, and rather clerical-looking gentleman, who had a handclasp and a word of greeting for each newcomer.

"Ah," we said, "that must be the Senator. What a nice custom."

By the time we arrived at Mrs. Kendrick's, however, who was the next Senate lady on our list, we found our ministerial friend doing the same act there!

"But good heavens," we said, "he can't be Senator Kendrick, too!"

Of course he was neither, as we soon found out after having him welcome us at a few more places. He was just a particularly virulent type of crasher. If he had only come quietly "for to admire and for to see," we neophytes at least would have been none the wiser; but one of the earmarks of your dyed-in-the-wool crasher is to make himself the most conspicuous person in the place.

A more tenacious crasher than the unctuous gentleman was a strange-looking old lady, who, in addition to other eccentricities, wore her hair in two long iron-gray braids hanging over her shoulders. The poor soul carried a black marketbag in which she was suspected of storing away enough teatime tidbits to feed her for quite a while.

The first time I saw her, I was pouring chocolate at Mrs. Peter Goelet Gerry's one Thursday, when bus loads of boarding-school girls—who had probably been promised "an insight into Washington's official and social life" as part of the school curriculum—backed up to the door at intervals all during the afternoon.

The queer old lady pushed her way through the crowd, came up to me and demanded, without a single "please": "Send me two cups of chocolate, a plate of sandwiches, and a plate of assorted cakes, over there to that chair by the sideboard, so that I can sit down!"

The next time I saw her, she quite outdid herself, at the Czech Legation where Mme. Veverka was receiving, and where the Czech cakes and pastries were almost too good to be true. She came up to the table just as Nella Veverka, the pretty debutante daughter of the house, was beginning to cut one of those incomparable Czech layer cakes. To her amazement, Nella heard a voice behind her say peremptorily, "Don't do that!"

Nella stopped in sheer surprise, and turned around to find the gray-braided old lady at her elbow. "But why not?" she asked, nonplussed.

"Because," said the old lady, firmly, "I'm taking that cake home!"

"Oh, no, you're not," said Nella kindly, but with admirable firmness of her own. "I'll cut you a great big piece and you can eat it here—but that's the best I can do for you."

The old lady accepted the piece of cake, marched across the room, and sat down on the floor against the wall to eat it.

Perhaps the Colossus—or rather, Colossa—among all the crashers I ever heard of, was the one who pulled off her masterpiece a few years ago at Mrs. Henry F. Dimock's, who then ruled Washington society with an iron hand from her big old-fashioned house on Scott Circle.

Passing by one day, the crasher in question, who was a nice-looking middle-aged woman, saw that a tea was going on; and although she didn't know Mrs. Dimock, and must have known that there is not even a shred of an excuse for crashing an unofficial party, she walked under the porte-cochère, up those brownstone steps, and into the Presence, which was intimidating enough when you *were* invited.

All went well, evidently, for she reached the dining room where two of Mrs. Dimock's close friends were presiding at either end of the tea table. And that must have been when the idea of her masterpiece came to her. It was no less than an urge to take the place of one of the ladies who was pouring—which is always, of course, the proof of special friendship with the hostess. Perhaps she waited a while, hovering near by, until she mastered that inevitable phrase of the next lady who is to pour to the one who is still pouring, "I think I'm to relieve you now!"

It must have sounded too temptingly simple; anyhow, she said it, and suddenly there she was behind the silver tea service, pouring at a tea to which she hadn't even been invited! I never heard what Mrs. Dimock said when she found it out, but it must have been well worth hearing.

(By the way, if you want the most infallible test of whether someone actually belongs to the charmed, if not always charming, diplomatic circle, just listen to how they say "Mr. Ambassador." The overawed can't seem to resist saying it something like a butler announcing names at a party: "Mis-ter Am-*bass*-a-*dor*!" But if ambassadors are part of the daily routine, to be treated with due respect, but not with painful reverence, you will probably hear all the syllables blurred together, something like this: "Mist'r Ambass'dr.")

Then there is the phenomenon one may call phantom crashing, in which people go to extreme lengths to try to induce society editors to include their names "among those present." One woman would send her long-suffering husband around to the newspapers day after day, pleading. A fantastic couple used to send out invitations to important personages in town—with whom, of course, they hadn't the slightest acquaintance—and then nearly drive the society editors mad trying to make them print a story that "Mr. and Mrs. So-and-So have invited the following guests to dinner," a list including the Chief Justice, the Secretary of State, and as the smaller fry, five or six ambassadors! The little matter of whether they had accepted or not was looked upon by the couple as entirely immaterial.

The only cure for crashers which has been discovered so far is to engage an exceptionally adamantine social secretary; but sometimes, in that case, the cure is hardly better than the disease.

Washington social secretaries are really a story in themselves, and of course, they, like everyone else, come assorted—good, bad, and indifferent. Incidentally, we have never had a social secretary, for Mother and I found that between us we could manage.

There are the conscientious, conservative ones—usually members of distinguished old Washington families—like Miss Anne Squire, whose little book *Social Washington* is every newcomer's bible, if there is still a copy to be had. In this same group would be Miss Mary Randolph, who was Mrs. Coolidge's secretary, and her sister, Miss Anne, who held the same post for Mr. Mellon when he was Secretary of the Treasury.

Then there are others like Rebecca Wellington, who capably and tactfully steered several embassies through the social shoals before the war. And there was Marian Trumbull—the only social secretary to "marry the boss"—who became the bride of Loring Christie, the Canadian Minister.

All of these were always realistic: by which I mean, they realized that "official" guests' lists must include officials, and not be made up entirely of a social secretary's personal friends, no matter how smart or amusing the latter may be. In fact, many foreign governments would not pay the bills for their diplomats' official entertaining until they received the guest lists and saw that the proper percentage of the proper officials had been included.

It was among the social secretaries specializing in debutante parties and what Washington calls "residential society" that one found those who really had themselves a wonderful time. The queen of this group is Mrs. Rose Wallach Merriam: the F Street Club's beloved "Rosie," and the lady dictator of the smartest debutantes; and there is Mrs. William Laird Dunlop, who for years shepherded the more run-of-the-mill debutantes, who depended on her apparently endless stag-line list for the huge debut dances that were a feature of Washington winters until the war.

Many "social secretaries" are a great deal more than that. Some are really social sponsors, who agree, for a set and secret fee, very much as certain impoverished London peeresses used to do, to launch newcomers socially. Sometimes they do not come into the picture as the social secretary at all but are merely introducing some "old family friends." One very distinguished Capital woman had the most amazing succession of "god-daughters" to present each season.

Of course, it's an old, old, trick for rich and ambitious newcomers to pay for parties given by some secretly hard up but socially solvent hostess, at which they are apparently just one of the guests; but that is an entirely different situation from the sort of thing that was done by the "charming Frenchman." After all, no one but royalty can ask for a guest list in advance, and fellow guests, whoever they may be, are in rightful place if the hostess is the one who actually sent out the invitation.

One of the outstanding social secretaries is known to be absolutely ruthless when it comes to her clients' guest lists, and will not allow them to include a single person of whom she doesn't approve! I know as a matter of fact the story of one debutante she was sponsoring, who promised to assist at the debut of a school chum, and added the girl's name on her own debut list, without thinking to consult the redoubtable lady beforehand. The upshot was an ultimatum that if she didn't send her regrets to her chum's debut, and strike her name off her own list, the secretary would not only resign but would see to it—as she unquestionably could —that her erstwhile protegée was not asked to a single smart debutante party all season.

After much anguished family conclave about "loyalty" and "being realistic about it," the poor girl resorted to one of those diplomatic indispositions that are the only way out of so many social dilemmas; sent her regrets and a beautiful basket of flowers to her friend's party, and, I suppose, just couldn't understand how the invitation to her own debut could have "gone astray." Not a very edifying story; but a girl of eighteen with her whole social future at stake could hardly be expected to stand up to a social dictator with real power of oblivion.

A few years ago another social secretary sued the young husband of a multimillionaire Senator's daughter on the ground that he had failed to pay her the amount agreed upon in advance for introducing him to the heiress and engineering the match. Even to people who feel no surprise at such dealings, this one has a surprising angle. The young man was not a foreigner, but a member of what the papers referred to as "a distinguished Southern family."

That brings us face to face with another category of seaminess, the fortune hunter. Probably no girl who has been in Washington very long, and who is not known to be actually on her way Over the Hill to the Poorhouse, hasn't run up against one of some kind or other.

We usually associate the species with Europe; but to be fair, one should remember that since time immemorial *le mariage de convenence*—the marriage of *convention,* not "the marriage of convenience," as someone mistakenly translated it long ago—has been one of the great Continental institutions. Most Europeans have felt—and quite rightly, from their point of view—that either a titled name or a life in diplomacy was very fair exchange for a substantial dowry, whether the bride happened to be American or European. In most countries on the Continent, especially among the upper classes, marriage has been much more a matter of the head than of the heart, and "marrying for love" has always seemed a quite dangerous kind of madness, especially to the older generations, who have had time conveniently to forget any romantic delusions they may once have suffered themselves.

What I am trying to say is that it seems only fair to judge anyone by what they consider honorable and above-board according to their own code. It should be added, too, that one can think of many European diplomats who have married American girls for love and not for money. And I can never forget the heartbreaking and beautiful devotion of those same couples when Hitler's war made them homeless and penniless refugees.

But the men that belong to this chapter are the outright fakes, whose titles were usually nonexistent, and whose promises of a brilliant diplomatic life were nothing but will-o'-the-wisps.

Some of them even resorted to bigamy, believe it or not. For instance, during the Philadelphia Sesquicentennial Exposition, a very handsome and dashing young man came over to take care of the pavilion of one of the great European countries. Naturally, he came to Washington too, and proceeded to pay court to the charming daughter of the minister of one of the smaller European states. The poor girl never dreamed that anyone representing his country —and so fascinating and romantic, too!—could possibly be anything else than he represented himself to be. So—she ran off and eloped with him, only to discover too late that he not only had a wife at home, but had acquired another in Virginia! It was a real tragedy. The girl's family were transferred from Washington, and we lost track of them, but I hope she has found genuine happiness since.

Then there was another man, who suddenly appeared on the Washington scene some years ago as plain "Mr." The next winter he came back with the aristocratic "de" tacked on before his name, and the third year he blandly called himself "Baron," from what country it was never made clear. He seemed to have plenty of spending money, but no visible source of supply, and he started out on a candid matrimonial campaign.

One day I was lunching at the Mayflower with five or six other girls, and when his name came into the conversation, we suddenly discovered, by a sort of spontaneous combustion, that he had proposed to every one of us! We visualized a very piquant paragraph in the *Washington Post,* something like this: "Baron de ———— has offered to bestow all his worldly goods (if any) on the following fortunate girls . . ."

Finally, no doubt after approaching the last one of the Capital's matrimonial possibilities in vain, he married a very sweet and naïve young girl from some small town. She must have had money, for they put on quite a social show in Washington for a season or so, and then disappeared completely. I've often wondered what happened to her, and whether there wasn't something much more sinister about him than fortune hunting; otherwise why did they disappear so suddenly and so completely?

Another "titled" character—who ended up in jail for blackmail—gave us a very unpleasant jolt, when he announced to Mother that he was divorcing his wife to marry me, when I had never spoken more than ten words to him in my life! He went around telling other people, too, but fortunately they were wise to him, and he soon went after more gullible game.

Perhaps the most astonishing of my experiences in that line came when I was sitting for a portrait by a well-known European artist, at his own request, and he suddenly begged me to let his wife come to see me, as she had "something very important to say to me."

"But what does your wife want to see me about?" I asked.

He answered in all seriousness, "She wants to ask you to marry me!" I had had only the most impersonal conversations with the man, and now thought he must be crazy. I stopped the sitting then and there, and naturally refused to see or talk to either of them. Madame, nevertheless, telephoned me day after day. Finally she sent me the most amazing letter. She had fostered his genius as far as she could, was the passionate purport; now I "owed it to Art"—with a capital A, of course—to carry on from there!

It did not help my vanity very much to read in the papers a few weeks later that they had been evicted from their studio apartment. Just another one of those things.

Another time, a Central European baron (bona-fide, this time) thought that I was out of my mind because I couldn't see the "marvelous opportunity" he was offering me to become his baroness on the extraordinarily reasonable terms of Father's agreeing to pay all the household expenses with "only" fifty dollars a week spending money for himself.

Of course, when you have been around Washington very long you learn to take these things pretty much in your stride—but there is a certain subtle danger in them, too. A girl waiting for "the real thing" to come along may become too well acclimated to the substitute notion that there is always one of these "brilliant opportunities" to fall back on, and so fail to see the real thing when it offers.

Which sad thought would be merely laughable to many Europeans. I remember the time when the twice-divorced Courtney Letts Stillwell Borden married the Argentine Ambassador, Felipe Espil, and one of the young Balkan diplomats said to me impatiently, "How stupid you are, my dear girl! How on earth do you expect to get an ambassador for your *third* husband, if you don't start with an attaché like me for your *first?*"

But enough of these "sentimental" souvenirs!

A far more everyday angle of the Capital's seamy side was the endless stream of sight-seers who arrived daily, before the war. As I've said, everyone in Washington seems to be on someone else's trail; the only difference with the sight-seers is that they want you to hit the trail with them. They are essentially kind and harmless, except in their ignoring that human feet can only stand so much, and that what is a new and exciting experience to them is an old and exhausting one to you.

To dwell in marble halls may be lovely when dreamed in a song; but it's a very hard reality when it comes to the endless miles of them that one must tramp in Washington. The girls in my father's office found that the only way of reducing the ruin from unexpected sight-seeing assignments was to keep a pair of stout walking shoes in their desks. As someone said to me once, "You only begin to enjoy a trip three months after you're back home—when you've forgotten how your feet hurt!"

The only stratagem I know is to stop the damage before it starts, by being too busy, or indisposed. Once I attempted a more subtle tactic. One of my best friends, who ordinarily is just about as lazy as I am, visited Washington for the first time and felt that she had to see the usual things, and I felt that I had to go along. At some distance in our pilgrimage we came to the Lincoln Memorial, which has always been, to me, the most beautiful and impressive spot in all of Washington. But after the strenuous day we had put in, to look up at all those marble steps produced only the following shameful inspiration.

"Listen, Berthilde," I said, "I'll wait here in the car, for it's really so much more impressive when you go up *alone!*"

She started off docilely enough, but at the bottom step she turned and said, "You didn't think you really put that one over on me, *did* you, dear?"

It's quite impossible to tell of any side of Washington life without coming back to protocol, which is as much a part of the Washington air as the fog is of London's. And protocol is part of the seamy side, too, as a setup peculiarly favorable for the innocent making of mortal enemies. Take, for instance, the feud-making possibilities of that fundamental Washington chore, paying calls.

A few years ago, a new New England Congressman's wife, who happened to be a close friend of a friend of ours, came in on one of our days at home, and we immediately seemed to "click." A week or so later, I was in her hotel one afternoon with Bee Sokolowska, and we stopped at the desk while I dutifully turned down the corners of our cards, to show that we had returned her call in person.

The next time we saw the lady she gave us a very cool greeting. We supposed she was just preoccupied; but each time Mother or I saw her, she was chillier and chillier. When even the heat of a summer session of Congress didn't thaw her out, Mother asked her point-blank, when we saw her the next winter, if anything could be the matter.

She answered that there certainly *could*—we had never returned her call! Even after Bee had corroborated my story, she wasn't convinced; but she said that she had taken all the cards of the people who had called on her back to New England, where she would send for them, and then we would see—

Well, of course, our cards were there, and she apologized, and that was that. So much ado about nothing. But that's Washington for you.

Most fertile ground for deathless protocol feuds is the seating arrangement at dinners. The silliest part of it is that blame never falls on the hostess, who made the mistake, but on the hapless, helpless guest who has to sit where he is told.

One day a Senator's wife who was a close friend of ours telephoned me to help her seat a large dinner party. I asked her who the ranking guest was, and she said the Bulgarian Minister. "And," she added, "I'm seating you next to him, to keep him amused in French, because, you know, his English is pretty hazy."

"Oh, *no,* for heaven's sake!" I begged. "Let him flounder along as well as he can, but you know what will happen to me if all those official wives see me up at the top of the table!"

I thought I had convinced her by the time we rang off, but no: she sat me by the most honored guest, and I suffered a martyrdom of dotted-line looks from the higher but temporarily lower ladies. It turned out that misery had company, for a few days later I met the Bulgarian Minister wearing a worried look. He took me off to one side and said, "About that dinner the other night, Vera. Will you tell me something frankly—is my English really *that* bad?"

One of the oldest feuds in Washington, to this day not really settled, concerns whether foreign Ministers are outranked by Senators, or vice versa. Long ago—I think almost as far back as the Civil War—it was decided that a minister and his wife would call first on a Senator and his lady, while a diplomatic couple would be seated ahead of a Senator at dinner. It was one of those compromises that satisfies no one; but it is still religiously adhered to, as far as it goes, which is not so far as to prevent some funny situations.

For instance, if the law says a minister has precedence at the dinner table, shall this be taken to mean that he outranks the Senator throughout the occasion? Or shall we, taking a perhaps larger view, conclude that any rights not specifically delegated are reserved to the people, and remain fair ground for battle?

One night we had the Greek Minister and British-born Mme. Simonpoulos and Senator and Mrs. Copeland as the ranking guests at the same dinner. Both men were very easygoing, but neither of the wives could possibly be described as a shrinking violet or clinging vine. They both had an often embarrassingly salty sense of humor—in both cases completely soluble when it came to a question of protocol.

All evening there was a noticeable failure of sweetness and light

225

between them, and when it came near time for the party to break up, I saw that they were keeping a wary eye on each other across the living room—much as two boxers watch each other from opposite corners of the prize ring.

At last Mme. Simopoulos made the first move to leave. In a flash Mrs. Copeland was on her feet. It happened that we had a stepdown living room in the house we were in at the time, and the hall at the top of the steps made a perfect stage set for the little tableau that followed, as the two belligerent ladies matched each other stride for stride, so that they both reached the top of the steps, where Mother was waiting, at the same instant.

It was, at least figuratively a case of Greek meets Greek, for they marched grimly out of sight to the coatroom, still in step.

Mrs. Copeland gave us a much more vocal version of her protocol complex another night when she and the Senator were dining with us. Recently one of the South American ambassadors, an elderly widower, had been giving a terrific rush to one of the Capital's smart divorcees. So much so that he insisted on her sitting with him in the ambassadorial front row at the musicales which used to be such a popular way for diplomats to pay off social obligations wholesale. Now, no one but the highest-ranking American officials would dream of sitting in that sacred front row; and the young divorcee should have been much too worldly wise to have been foolish enough to sit there, unless her engagement to the ambassador (which never did come off) had actually been announced.

But still, I was dumbfounded at dinner that night to hear Mrs. Copeland loudly demanding across the table, "Since when does an Ambassador's lady friend outrank a Senator's wife?"

People just don't say that sort of thing at an official dinner, and the men on either side of me gasped when they heard it.

But imagine how I felt the next day when the young divorcee's aunt—whom we knew quite well—telephoned me to "demand an apology" for *my* making that remark about her niece at our dinner the night before! Blame, as so often, came down on the wrong head: this time quite by intention, for the lady's information came "straight" from Mrs. Copeland! Of course the others remembered well enough who had made that remark, so it was easy to prove my innocence.

Another innocent-bystander storm blew up one night about a

year or so before the outbreak of the war, at a musicale given by Senator and Mrs. Vandenberg.

At that time, Frau Thomsen, the wife of the German Minister —their ambassador had already been recalled to Berlin—was the enigma of the diplomatic corps. She was hysterically, publicly "anti-Nazi"; in fact, she went around wishing the most blood-curdling things to happen to Hitler. How anyone could have fallen for the performance, I can't imagine. It stood to reason that the Nazis must have wanted her to do it, for surely she was under constant Gestapo surveillance. Nevertheless she managed to arouse lots of sympathy around town, where you would hear people saying, "Poor Bébé Thomsen—she's so sensitive, and she *suffers* so about all that's going on in Germany!" She even gave out an interview declaring why she would never return to Germany. (But of course she did.) There was simply no avoiding her. She would dash up to you anywhere and buttonhole you with a long hysterical tirade.

That night at the Vandenbergs' she rushed up to me practically in tears, saying that Lady So-and-So had deliberately refused to take her outstretched hand. I only wanted to get away from her, but I said, "Why, Frau Thomsen, I really can't believe that she cut you deliberately. She probably didn't even see your hand."

I moved away, and thought no more about it, until a day or so later, when I was shocked to get a very brusque letter from the lady I had tried to defend, asking for an "explanation" of how I could have dared to say that she had publicly snubbed Frau Thomsen at the Vandenbergs'! These mix-ups can generally be straightened out almost as good as new; but in the meantime, they can be made most unpleasant.

The Thomsens figured (though as far as I know, not directly) in another annoying episode I remember.

Rather late one night during the lend-lease hearings early in 1941, our telephone rang and the wife of one of the most rabidly isolationist Congressmen asked to speak to Mother.

"I just wanted to ask you," she purred, "whether your reception in honor of the German Minister and Frau Thomsen is this Sunday or a week from Sunday—I was stupid enough to mislay your invitation!"

The very thought of our giving a reception in honor of the Thomsens was so fantastic that Mother was literally speechless

227

for a minute. Then she denied any such plan and hung up. When she told Father about it, he insisted that she ring back, make it extra emphatic that we wouldn't allow the Thomsens in the house, and also find out more about the invitation itself.

"Why, my dear"—the voice at the other end sounded astonished—"the invitation was written on your double visiting card. I had it here just a minute ago. . . . Dear me, what *could* have have happened to it!" Mother asked her please surely to bring it to the hearings in the morning, as they were both there every day. Although she promised to several times, somehow she always "forgot."

We never could make out what the plot was. The most logical explanation seemed to be that the isolationists were trying to "bait" my father and get him annoyed just when he needed all his wits about him to conduct the hearings. Or perhaps they merely thought it would be "amusing" to see what our reaction would be. Whatever the case, it was just another one of those unpleasant shocks you're likely to get any time you pick up a Washington telephone.

In telling about protocol, I'm afraid I may have given the impression that only women take it seriously, and that the men—especially American men—don't let it bother them at all. It can't be left at that!

For instance, one summer when we were on our way home from Europe, we found that three other members of Congress were on board. We thought it would be nice if the fellow members all dined together one evening, and the chief steward arranged a special menu and a special table for us.

And then, as we were ready to be seated, Protocol reared its head. You might think that you could leave it behind on the high seas; but not at all. Two of our three Congressional guests flatly refused to sit down until their relative rank was settled. The third —Piatt Andrew, of Massachusetts—had been in the House so much longer than they had, that he was undisputedly the ranking guest.

The other two had entered Congress on the same day; and when that happens, the year that a Congressman's state entered the Union is the deciding factor. As it happened (what Fate arranges these meetings?), both their states had been admitted to statehood in the same year. Neither was sure of the exact month, and there was no Congressional Directory on board.

It actually looked as if they were going to stand there squabbling about it until that delicious dinner was ruined; but finally they agreed to toss a coin to decide, and then to "table" the question until they got back to Washington! Both, I'm sure, were convinced there was nothing personal about it; just "the principle of the thing." In a way they would have been right: protocol *is* entirely impersonal, in that it's the position and not the person that counts; but people can get more "personal" about it than about any other question in official life.

While we are unraveling Washington's seamy side, there is one one more seam to finish off, and that is the peculiar phenomenon that nobody ever really listens to anyone else.

Someone said long ago that no one has ever actually finished a sentence at a Washington cocktail party, and it's hardly an exaggeration.

It all comes back again to the old Washington theme song, "On the Trail." He who talks to a Congressman has his eye out for a Senator; she who is exchanging a word with a minister is already looking for an ambassador; and one of the hardest things a newcomer has to learn is not to be disconcerted when he finds himself stranded with his mouth open in the middle of a sentence.

And I for one believe literally in the old legend: That if a woman walked up to someone at a Capital cocktail party and announced, "I've just murdered my husband!" nine chances of ten the answer would be, "Oh, my dear—how *lovely!*"

10. Royal Close-Ups

I made my first curtsey before royalty to an old, old lady receiving her last visitor in the capital which was no longer hers: Eugénie, Empress of the French.

Paris, giddy, forgetful, carefree, was on a crescendo of cheerfulness working up to the first really gay, good old "Reveillon," the first carnival Christmas Eve, since World War I. Today was queen, and yesterday, even the war, was deliberately forgotten. And in the midst of that debonair democracy was the one woman who had been not only Empress of France but queen of Paris—that Paris of modes, manners, and menus that was now vibrating to someone's new whims as it once had to hers. For Eugénie was beginning the last chapter of her story, that was to end where it began so long ago, in Spain. She had reclaimed her privilege from the French government to pass through Paris to her beautiful villa near Monte Carlo; but she had been lingering quite a while in vain consultations with Parisian oculists. . . . In the title-spattered pages of the Hotel Continental's register, the "Comtesse de Pierrefonds" meant nothing in particular. Perhaps no guest in the entire hotel had an inkling of being under the same roof with a former Empress of France.

But in Eugénie's private hall were the symbols of royalty: the guest book on a table, and a secretary or valet continually on guard. A private elevator connected with a private entrance on the side street; but the Empress, suffering, yet still superior to her ninety-four years, seldom left her rooms. The guests who came and went were few. The Queen of Spain, the god-daughter whom Eugénie loved so dearly, would come for a simple tea; her nephew, Count Primoli, had left Rome to join her, as he so often did for months at a time, and Mme. d'Attainville, her cousin and companion, came every day.

Eugénie's retinue was small, but with imperial traditions. Mme. Pelletier dressed her Empress with as much care and ceremony as in those glorious days when Eugénie went forth gowned to dazzle and lead the women of the world. Madame, a silent, black, bird-like little figure, bustled through the halls now and then taking sober bonnets from hatbox to wardrobe, but still quickening to the touch of new clothes. Eugénie was suffering badly with bronchial trouble and could barely speak above a whisper. The weather was raw and rainy, most of the time; but with the passionate piety that ruled her whole life, and that often in the days of the Empire used to impel her to leave the most splendid functions and shut herself in her oratory to kiss her sacred relics and to pray, there was never a Sunday, no matter what the weather, that Eugénie was not at Mass. Every ounce of her failing strength was concentrated into that Sunday morning pilgrimage. With true Parisian contrariness, crowds on one Sunday would wait at the Madeleine or Nôtre Dame on the chance of seeing her, while on the next, Paris would apparently be quite oblivious that Eugénie was still alive.

Count Primoli, whom we had met through mutual friends, had promised I should know in time, if it were possible, where the Empress was to go. On a certain Saturday evening an unsigned card saying simply, "Comtesse de Pierrefonds, at 10:40 o'clock, Rue de Rouget de l'Isle," told me that Eugénie would leave her private entrance at that hour.

Very different was her last Mass in Paris from that one of sixty-six years before, at Nôtre Dame: her first as Empress—unsurpassed day!—when all Paris paused for her to pass, and when the cathedral, as if not magnificent enough in itself, had been glorified by an enormous glittering vestibule, while inside thousands of tapers showed a breathless congregation and an orchestra of half a thousand men; and every bell in Paris was set in motion, for her. Now in place of priceless jewels and lace, and the dazzling white coronation gown, she wore a sad, somber mourning dress, and a thick crepe veil; and in place of the ineffably lovely, triumphant young empress was a careworn, shaken old lady, pitifully fragile-looking as Mme. d'Attainville and the secretary helped her into the car, but still, somehow, the Empress. The bow, the smile, were still electric, imperial.

She had waited past the time for her nephew to arrive, then decided to call for him on the way to church. The street was entirely deserted when her ugly automobile and our own taxi started off. We drew up to the rear entrance of St. Paul–St. Pierre's, and, it being late already and the church crowded to the walls, Eugénie's party, unrecognized, was painfully jostled.

There was not a seat to be had, and Eugénie stood, until finally, after some maneuvering, my father found two little cane-bottomed chairs and slipped them into the aisle for the Empress and her companion. She was restless, continually fanning herself with an infinitesimal black fan, smoothing her black gloves, changing her cane from one hand to the other, and often leaning over to whisper to her cousin. The Empress could no longer kneel, but bent her head humbly.

At last the service was over, and there was a great surge toward the doors; it was all that her nephew and Father could do to keep Eugénie from being swept along with the rush. Even then, no one recognized her. Count Primoli stood on the sidewalk with his hat raised. She bowed to him and to us; but for all people knew, she was merely any lady nodding good-by to some friends.

Count Primoli turned to me and with half a smile, half a sigh, said, "Now you have your wish. You have been to church with the Empress."

Eugénie's last public appearance in Paris was over. Bonapartes and Bourbons alike could only stay in France on special permission, and already she was yearning for the visit to Spain. On Tuesday the valet and the secretary took their posts and, in the immemorial custom of "Eugénie's Court," she received those few who had the entrée through the private entrance. She was holding her last salon not two hundred feet away from the site of the Tuileries, the court where she, brilliant, witty, beautiful, surrounding herself with the prettiest women in Europe, supreme in the consciousness that only against their beauty would hers be truly appreciated, used to set the fashions and stir the imaginations of the world.

On her last day in Paris, I was permitted to bring her the last bouquet of violets: the Napoleonic emblem that in the days of the Empire had filled every florist's, when violet became the prevailing perfume and the popular color, and all France wafted back the fragrance of Eugénie's flower.

In the undiminished etiquette that surrounded her, she expected a court curtsey, and the title of "Majesty." I made my bow and offered her the bouquet. She took it falteringly, and felt it. "They are flowers," her companion told her.

"Yes, Your Majesty," I ventured; "they are violets—your flowers!" Her smile showed instantly that she had understood, and she took my hand, whispered her thanks, and said that she would take them with her to the train. Kissing her hand, I curtsied again and backed away.

An hour later, unheralded and unobserved, Eugénie, Empress of the French, left Paris for the last time: to return with her memories where she had started with her illusions, to the Spain she had left so long ago as the regally lovely though far from royal young Countess Eugénie de Montijo, who was sure that she would someday wear a crown, because an old gypsy woman had told her so.

That poignant encounter was part of the after-school trip abroad by means of which I had promised to do such wonders for American journalism. We had just come from the Italian adventures related in an earlier chapter, and soon were on the way to London. The next intended victim for interviewing was Queen Mary.

What her private secretary, Sir Harry Verney, thought when out of a blue sky came my letter suggesting as much, I cannot imagine. But he telephoned almost immediately bidding me come to see him about it. Yes, Mother might be admitted, too; he would tell the officer of the guard to look out for us.

As we stepped out of the Carlton in plenty of time for our three o'clock appointment, not a single conveyance was in sight but surely the most disreputable-looking old taxi in London. Even the old paint, however, seemed to brighten for a moment under the expression on the faces of doorman and driver when we called for "Buckingham Palace, the right hand gate!" As we careened through the great iron gates to the palace in our ramshackle cab, the guards, in their red tunics and high black bearskin shakos, stood stiffly at attention. There was even someone waiting at one of the ground-floor entrances to escort us in to Sir Harry.

The royal family was away at Sandringham; but we could hardly have enjoyed our talk with him more than we did, even if a royal climax had been in sight. Sir Harry is one of the most distinguished and one of the kindest men I have ever met. There was certainly no official imperative for his cordiality that day; and in all the years since, he has proved himself, again and again, the most thoughtful and delightful friend.

He told us then, and on several visits later, a great many interesting things about Queen Mary. The beautiful Chinese room in which he first received us led naturally to the subject of her great love for interior decorating. She had made a hobby of redecorating the royal palaces, and her taste was so sure that she turned many an ugly room into a place of beauty, like that around us, with treasures she found tucked away in royal attics.

Once, for charity, she sponsored an exhibition of Bad Taste in Decorating as a horrible example of how not to furnish an English home. The prize winning "work of art" was, I think, a statuette of the Venus de Milo with a clock set in where the goddess' vital organs should have been.

Antique dealers in London had special hiding places where they laid aside unusual pieces for Queen Mary to see, and two or three times a year, until the war, she visited her favorite shops to make her choice of hidden treasures.

Queen Mary put her hobby to great use for others when she assembled the Queen's Doll's House, that absolutely perfect replica of a twentieth-century palace, from infinitesimal Rolls-Royces in the garage to the almost invisible crimson crowns on the tiny replicas of the Queen's own writing paper. On view at Windsor Castle year after year, it earned great sums for the Queen Mother's favorite charities through the admission charged to see it. As it happened, we knew Sir Lawrence Weaver, the great art connoisseur, who helped the Queen to assemble the Doll's House; and he not only gave us two enormous volumes he had written about it, but showed it to us himself one day.

The doll's palace, with its many rooms, stood almost as large as an average real life room. He pointed out to us especially the portraits (not so large as a postage stamp!) that had been done by great English painters, and the tiny books, which were even smaller—perhaps a sixteenth of an inch thick—complete copies of the best modern English literature, signed on the fly leaves by the authors themselves, and dedicated to the Queen. Probably only the Queen of England could have accomplished anything so perfect. There was even a minute carpet sweeper, which actually worked.

Americans always think of Queen Mary as a rather austere person; but in reality, she has a tremendous sense of humor, and her entourage lived in constant fear that she might murmur something funny at a most ceremonious moment and make their so necessary dignity impossible to maintain.

Sir Harry told me that Queen Mary was blessed with the most amazing memory he had ever known. Without, apparently, the slightest effort, she could recall anyone who had even been presented to her, even people she might have met only once, twenty-five years ago, perhaps at the Durbar, in India, or at some great Court function in London. Not only that, but she remembered their families, their hobbies, or whatever else she may have heard about them.

It was a year or so later that he presented me to Queen Mary for the first time, at a garden party at the palace.

At the Royal Garden Parties it is all sheer chance whether or not you will see the King or Queen pass very near by. They separate in different directions through the palace gardens, and the Gentlemen of the Court, who precede them, make wide lanes through the guests, in whatever direction the sovereigns happen to go.

All day the skies were threatening. But although most of us looked unpicturesque and practical, wearing warm coats over our frocks, the garden party was bravely in full swing by four o'clock, when the King and Queen came out of the palace as the band played "God Save the King!" Sir Harry had told me in advance to find him in the garden, and to be sure to tell anyone who might try to stop me that he was expecting me. By good luck I reached him before Her Majesty came that way, walking a few yards behind the gentlemen in attendance, stopping to speak a few words with a curtseying lady now and then. The Queen had just been talking to someone directly opposite us when she turned and Sir Harry was able to signal her. She came toward us, as he had almost assured me she would, and in a moment I had been presented.

Her Majesty spoke for a few moments, and then, suddenly looking up at the sky, which was definitely clearer, she said, quite colloquially,

"Not so bad!"

"No, Ma'am," I answered. "I am beginning to believe in Queen's Weather, myself!"

She was much amused that I should know the London legend about *her* weather, which says that no matter how dreary it may have been for days, the skies will always clear for a royal function. Laughing heartily, she gave me her hand again; I curtsied, and she walked on. She was dressed, as usual, in quite perfect taste but in the style of twenty years before. Wearing a coat and matching toque of beautiful Indian lamé in pastel colors, she was, as always, every inch a queen.

I took this opportunity to listen curiously for "the King's English." The truth is that King George, like Queen Mary, had not a particularly strong British accent. His speech was much like that of any cultured American gentleman. We had a very negative impression of King George V in America, yet really he had great charm and heartiness. I remember his teasing a pretty young English girl with "Don't think I didn't see how you were flirting when you were at Court last week! Come now—tell me when it's going to be announced!" She enjoyed it, blushing.

And speaking of everyday subjects in regal conversations, my next royal topic was, of all things, onions.

It was at another Royal Garden Party several years later, when King Fuad of Egypt was the only royal guest; and as we had met the Egyptian prime minister several times that week, he had me presented to the King by the presenter-in-chief of the occasion, Lord Colebrook.

King Fuad was wearing a gray frock coat with his red fez. He was very stout, but very well groomed, and had the most amazing mustaches, like thin steel wire, which curled around in little curlicues. He was very cordial and very easy to talk to—in French, as he apparently spoke no English (perhaps for political reasons; who can say?)

He began at once to "pump" me about his interests in Washington. "Is my legation really on a good street? You know," he added, "I had to buy it from the photographs! Is it really a beautiful house? Is it really well furnished? Do they entertain well?"

I could honestly reassure him about everything, except that the furniture was still rather sparse. And then he asked if I knew the Minister and Mme. Samy and knew that the Minister had sailed for America the day before, as a special session of the Senate to take up the tariff question was to open the next week. I did; and it also happened I knew that the only item Egypt was vitally interested in was the tariff on onions. They hoped for a seasonable rate that would allow Egyptian onions to flow in free of duty at times when the stream of American onions ran low.

So I was prompted to answer, "Yes, but don't worry, Your Majesty, we'll do all we can to take care of the onions!"

King Fuad laughed so heartily that everyone around was startled. He kept repeating *"Les onions! Les onions!"* in his strange, high voice, the result of a shooting accident to his throat years before.

From the garden of Buckingham Palace to the Throne Room is a long way for most people, and a journey I hardly expected to take. Yet several years later, through chance and the great kindness of Ambassador and Mrs. Dawes, I did make my curtsey in the Throne Room, over which, inconceivably, Hitler's bombs were to burst exactly ten years later.

The Royal Courts are out for the duration; and the "once upon a time" with which all good fairy tales should begin seems worlds ago rather than years. Yet daydreams have been spared even where architecture has not; and what harm if for a moment we take a backward look ahead, to a day when once again Cinderella can bow at the Court of St. James's?

It all begins with months of waiting, punctuated now and then by a polite letter from our Embassy in London assuring you that they are doing the best they can . . .; and finally comes a long letter from the ambassador, beginning: "The number of Court presentations that are permitted this year is limited, and the number of applicants has been unusually large"—which sounds so discouraging that you blink once or twice when you see next, "but I take pleasure in informing you that in accordance with your desire of March 2 I shall be able to include your daughter's name on my list and shall be glad to arrange for her presentation at the Court to be held on May 27."

And with the letter comes this list of Dress Regulations, which you pore over devoutly:

Ladies attending Their Majesties' Courts will wear Court trains, while veils with ostrich feathers will be worn on the head.

Three small white feathers mounted as a Prince of Wales' Plume, the centre feather being a little higher than the two side ones, to be worn slightly on the left hand side of the head, with the tulle veil attached to the base of the feathers.

The veil should not be longer than forty-five inches.

. . . The train, which should not exceed two yards in length, should not extend more than eighteen inches from the heel of the wearer when standing.

. . . Bouquets and fans are optional.

Coming down to earth a bit, you look up the seagoing possibilities to find which boat will get you to London in time to have your gown made and to learn your curtsey; and if you are wise, you will not be tempted by all the dressmakers in Paris put together to go there instead, and so miss the Court atmosphere of London in May. And if you stop to consider that whatever is important enough to be announced by Buckingham Palace—or by the White House, if it happens here—*should* come from them and not from you, you'll resist the temptation to tell either your friends or the ship-news reporters why you are sailing, and get much more thrill out of it for that very reason.

On the boat I found Margaret Halstead, whose father was our consul-general in London, who, of course, had been presented, and who afterwards made a different kind of a debut at the Metropolitan Opera in New York. Since we were then safely past the reporters, I told her "all"; and as Helen Howell, of Chicago, was also on board and going to Court the same night that I was, Margaret gave us both an early lesson on the curtsey: Weight on the right foot while you bend the left knee; shift the weight to the left foot after the curtsey to the King, make the step sidewards—one, two, three—and into position for the curtsey to the Queen; keep your back straight and your head bent until you are almost up again.

First thing on arriving was to call our Embassy. They asked that not a word be given to the press, or to anyone else if I could possibly help it, so I was glad I hadn't talked unnecessarily. The reason, of course, is twofold. For the thirty lucky Americans who can be chosen for the usual five Courts a year, the Ambassador and every Senator are harried with hundreds and even thousands of applicants, most of them on some account difficult to refuse. It eased hard lines for those under pressure if no one made any

Vera Bloom in Her Court Presentation Gown

The Throne Room at Buckingham Palace

announcement until the official one, whereupon everyone would realize that nothing could be done about a finished fact.

The local reason is that every dressmaker, newspaper, Court photographer, Court hairdresser, florist, and shoemaker in London is after the Embassy for the London addresses of the American presentees, and it would take all of a secretary's time just to put them off until the official list could be announced.

You are a very organized Cinderella. There is no way of merely wishing the great experience into actuality. No magic turns a pumpkin into a Rolls-Royce for you. So you must be careful to engage a car, with the necessary chauffeur and footman, in plenty of time. And no fairy godmother supplies a costume at the last minute. Instead, you dash around desperately to all the Court dressmakers, trying to make wisely and quickly the overwhelming decision.

Mother and I finally decided on a long, full-skirted picture dress of ivory-white faille, to be embroidered in silver in exactly the same design with which my cloth-of-silver Court train would be embroidered in diamanté. And had I the choice to make again, no matter how many times, I should still say white, meaning, of course, any white, silver, crystal, or diamanté. Nothing else, except the palest possible green or pale cloth-of-gold, really looks well with the obligatory white feathers and veil. Worth's also had a choice of paste diadems for those of us who lacked diamond tiaras of our own; and instead of a bouquet, I decided that a fan of three long, curling white Prince of Wales feathers—a large edition of the three feathers to be worn in my hair—would be a more lasting souvenir than the flowers so many people carry to Court; for since time immemorial, acrobats and tightrope walkers have known what it means to your balance to have something in your hands in a crucial moment.

Meanwhile, you buy two yards of cretonne, to pin on your shoulders as a practice Court train, and you do your curtsey every spare moment you can, till you feel like a slow-motion jill-in-the-box.

Almost the nicest part about being in London before the Court is the delight of the tradespeople and the servants, who all but walk to the throne with you. Our motherly chambermaid at Claridge's came in one evening in a great flutter to tell us that "another American young lady on the floor"—who happened to be Doris Duke—was just leaving to be presented, and that she had been in to see her in all her Court regalia. I said she must come in to see me, too, when my turn came; and she answered, almost offended that I thought it necessary to tell her, "But, of course, Miss. That is our *privilege*!" Many English families bring all their servants up to London from no matter what distance to see their "Miss" go off to Court. The tradespeople are just as proud and interested. I remember, when we went into Jay's to buy gloves of the special Court length, I looked to see if the buttons were on tight. "But, Miss," the salesgirl said in a hurt voice, "You don't think we would let ladies go to Court with buttons that could *possibly* come off!"

English girls start all these preparations six months or more in advance, most of them taking lessons in the curtsey at Miss Vacarni's, the Court procedure teacher. And for them the prelude usually includes a Presentation Tea, which takes the place of our usual debut tea, when hundreds of apparently admiring friends come in to see the debutante and her mother in full regalia before they leave for the palace.

When, finally, the list of presentees for your Court is announced, you find that your picture has to be taken "exclusively"— meaning separately, for copyright reasons—by every newspaper, news agency, and Court photographer in London, besides every American news service as well. Many English people stay up all night, the night of the Court, going around from one fashionable photographer to the other; but if you are American, you must plan to have your whole costume ready well ahead of time so that news photos can make the fastest boat. The all-important Court hairdresser, who has the magic secret of anchoring your feathers, veil, and bandeau to your bobbed hair so that no conceivable calamity can move them, must be engaged weeks ahead for every time you will need him. And you must "book" the entire day before the court on a fifteen-minute schedule for an endless procession of photographers who come to the hotel, since no one could fly around London quickly enough to go to them.

Then, when you can barely stand and hardly smile, you doff your Court regalia after the last pose and go to a rehearsal at the Embassy that same day before the Court, passing before two empty armchair "thrones," and before eyes which are so particular because they are so patriotic. After tea and final instructions at the

Embassy you go home clutching your "command" and your presentation card, from which the Lord Chamberlain will read your name aloud when he presents you to Their Majesties; and you fall into bed to rest up, wishing with all your heart that the event were safely over, for, say what you please, it is the greatest social ordeal in the world, and a debutante at Court has to "win her feathers" as surely as any knight of old had to win his spurs.

I used to wonder why people had to sit in their cars for hours on end, on their way to the palace, while all London gazed at them, criticizing their clothes and themselves in no uncertain terms. The answer is simple, though longer than it takes to tell. No cars may park in the line until six o'clock. Only the people in the first forty cars will find places right in the Throne Room. So it is only by leaving for the palace at five and maneuvering for a place near the beginning of the line by six that you are able to get inside the gates by half past eight—to wait in the Throne Room, if you are lucky, until the Royal Family enters at half past nine.

The cars are parked in single file, and thus you are subjected to a good-natured double inquisition for all that time: on one side the sidewalk "standees," and on the other side every car and taxi in town passing slowly and critically by. It is considered anything but sporting to pull down the shades of the car, and I really think it may be sensitiveness and not "exhibitionism" that makes people play bridge, read magazines, or listen to a portable radio while all the world looks on.

Helen Howell and I went together. We were fairly early, and so lucky as to come within the first forty. Of course I had modeled at the hotel before leaving, to an audience so delightfully partisan that I was well fortified for the long inquisition of the cars. At exactly half past eight a superb battalion of bagpipers in full Scottish uniform, and a regiment of the King's Guard in their scarlet and gold, marched down the Mall, with pipe and band tones flaring. The gates opened—the motors started—and we were off! I have never sat so still and felt so headlong. We wanted to go on—we wanted to stay back. In a second we were through the gates, under the arch into the inner courtyard, and up to the entrance. Footmen and functionaries in scarlet-and-gold or black-and-silver at every turn made it impossible to go wrong. We reached the Throne Room so soon, and it was so much less glittering than throne rooms on the Continent, that but for the guides I would surely have gone right on.

Because the King was indisposed, there was only one throne. Helen promptly wailed, "That isn't a throne, it's a *chair*!" It was slightly raised on red velvet steps, with seats for the Royal Family behind it. The room was very high, with great arches making a background for the thrones. The decorations were white and gold, relieved by the red satin of the chairs and the red velvet of the carpets.

As we watched and waited, I asked an English dowager next to me how we would be called. The monumental presence remained undisturbed. But a full minute later she answered casually that a functionary would call us, and even added that we could come back to our seats after making our curtsey, if we wished.

At exactly nine-thirty by the Throne Room clock the Court entered. Then "God Save the King," and the Queen, all in cloth of gold, and blazing with jewels and decorations, was entering with the Prince of Wales, while everyone stood.

The Queen herself stood to receive the diplomatic corps. Then the Queen was seated, and all the assembly; and we were called! An officer handed us down the steps from the raised row of seats around the wall, and formed us into a line in the corridor outside the back of the room, our trains still over our arms, our presentation cards tightly in hand. One by one we at last rounded the crucial corner, let fall our trains, which at once were draped into place by at least four ushers, and handed our cards to the first of at least a dozen functionaries, who passed them, stage by stage, to the Lord Chamberlain, who finally called out the name. The moment had come.

To be honest, it is worse than you thought; for you find there is much more to worry about than not falling on your nose doing your curtsey. First, you have to *sense* the right moment to start, so as to be there when the girl before you moves on. Second, you must watch out not to step on her train, at the same time you are judging how many steps will bring you exactly before the Queen. Third, you take up all your remaining energy praying the girl behind you won't step on *your* train. And, as you have to keep your head bent throughout the curtsey till the last moment, you rise as one who "never knew what happened," and are left to wonder for the rest of your life how far down you really got. You walk on, past the diplomats, and at a moment when any help is appreciated, an usher hands you your train.

Thanks to the dowager's advice, we went back to our seats high against the wall, where we had a grand view of everything, especially the Prince of Wales steadfastly studying the ceiling. Later a good intuition of palace geography led us to a strategic spot for watching the Queen's processional to supper. A lane about ten feet wide was cleared; and, preceded by all the Court and about a dozen men in black and silver walking backwards before her all the way, the Queen passed, followed by the Royal Family and then the diplomats, walking two by two to their own supper room. Seeing her at close view meant, actually, seeing a marvelous length of train borne by three pages; for of course we watched from the level of a curtsey.

Gwenda Rogeri had cautioned us that outside the diplomatic supper room we might expect only coffee and biscuits, a prediction happily disproved, for there was everything conceivable for a standing buffet, from chicken jeannette to fruit salad, and champagne for everyone. Then it was time to call the car, which took only a few moments, since they had installed a telephone system from the palace to the Mall. For the sake of completeness we stopped at just one of the photographers' who were going to be open all night. Then home by twelve, like real Cinderellas.

The next day, like any prima donna, you are up early to see your "notices," for the British papers devote page after page to descriptions of who wore what. Then, after a few days' recuperation, you can begin to know it really happened: that in a spectacle you hardly even dreamed of seeing, you have actually had a part; and that in "this realm, this England" you have a wonderful open-sesame.

There was no way of telling how soon Congress might adjourn and Father might join us; so Mother and I decided to stay on in London and see what happened.

"What happened" was three months, and a real London Season. Whether it was because so many diplomats we had known in Washington had been transferred to London, or because of British friends, or through the magic of Court presentation— or because of all three—we had a breathless time of it. Perhaps, too, one ingredient was where we were staying.

I sat next to a most conservative Englishman one day at luncheon, and he was telling me about the annual Caledonian Ball, where all the nobility of Scotland wear their plaids and kilts and dance their reels and flings for a highly exclusive London audience, who have the privilege of paying for their tickets. I asked how the audience was chosen, and he said it was largely by their addresses.

"That would let me out, then," I laughed, "since I have no address at all—only Claridge's."

"*Only Claridge's!*" he echoed, shocked as if I'd been guilty of lese majesty. "Why, *anyone* at Claridge's can go!"

In June came Ascot; and Ascot, from the English point of view, means either the Royal Enclosure or utter darkness. It is almost as hard to get one of those little white and gold "Royal Enclosure" cards with your name, to pin on your coat, as it is to be presented at Court. So hard, in fact, that an American is rather astonished to find that it must nevertheless be well paid for. But the ticket is good for all four days of the races: which to the British means four different costumes and a great sartorial spree. From time immemorial Ascot clothes have been the only fashionable ones that took absolutely no dictation from the current styles. Fantastic and frilly is the word, and nothing can be too extreme or elaborate.

Leaving London about eleven in the morning, we got to Ascot, which is near Windsor, just in time to see and be seen before the Royal Family drove in open landaus around the whole course with postillions in brilliant liveries, black velvet caps, and tightly curled white wigs, perched high on the coachman's box, and still higher on the postillion seat behind. The universal curtsey as the King and Queen drive by made the scene like a garden of flowers swaying in the breeze.

The Royal Family have a huge box banked with flowers and reached by two curving staircases at the center of the enclosure's grandstand, and while the young royalties dashed democratically up and down to place their own bets at the totalizer just outside the enclosure, the King and Queen summoned chosen people to the Royal Box, receiving them as conspicuously as anyone could hope for, with literally everyone they knew watching, but pretending not to, as they strolled up and down, below. To that rare bit of ground are British debutantes brought by anxious mammas, to be paraded where they may be seen, and, perhaps, admired by some eligible peer.

Just outside the Royal Enclosure were the colorful luncheon tents of the smart London clubs, all gaily striped in their club colors, and smothered in flowers, to one of which—the Marlborough—we had the great luck to be invited.

The women's clothes were nothing short of spectacular; but to read the papers the next day you would hardly have known that any woman had attended, they were so busy going into the minutest details about the *men's* clothes. That Lord Lonsdale wore a shirt with *horizontal* stripes, and a carnation exactly matching the stripes, was by far the most important fashion news of the day, except perhaps that the Earl of Harewood's gloves were the palest possible shade of *mauve*.

The next day, all this glory was dimmed in a moment by what everyone there will probably be talking about to their grandchildren in fifty years as the Ascot storm—a thunderstorm that killed a bookmaker, and turned the beautiful scene into a morass of mud from which a few lucky ones in ruined finery escaped across pontoon bridges of chairs, while those who thought themselves terribly bright to take shelter in the underground tunnel from the Royal Enclosure to the paddock were almost drowned.

But the next day England was itself again; the damage had been miraculously repaired, and everyone was back in finer feathers than ever.

Before we knew it, the invitations for the Royal Garden Party, which traditionally closes every London Season, had arrived, just about the same time that Father arrived in London, toward the end of July. "No one"—except about seven million people— would be seen alive in London the day after the Royal Garden Party, so we, too, decided to wind up the Season in the proper way, and left for Paris the morning after.

And in Paris, Father found a royal opportunity. We learned one day that the Infanta Eulalia, the aunt of King Alfonso of Spain had been living quietly for years in her own apartment at the convent at 17 Rue de l'Assomption.

Father immediately knew that, more than anything else, he wanted to meet the Infanta again; for way back in 1893, when, at nineteen, he had taken in hand the lagging plan for the Midway at the Chicago World's Fair and brought it through, the Infanta Eulalia had presented him with a diamond medal on behalf of the fair (where, incidentally, he knew nothing of that legendary lady called "Little Egypt," although he did write a lastingly haunting tune for the Algerian dancers sent over by the French government from the Paris Exposition of 1889, of whom "Little Egypt" was only a later and sensational imitation).

Since the purpose of the fair was to honor Christopher Columbus, who, thanks to Queen Isabella's sacrifice of her jewels, had claimed the New World for Spain, the Infanta had journeyed all the way to Chicago to represent Isabella's successors: the Queen Mother, Maria-Christina, and the very young King Alfonso.

It was easy to understand why Father was so anxious to see her again, and why he still treasured the medal presented by the Midway concessionaires, which he had received from her hand; for he had often told how everyone in this country adored her. And how could they have helped being captivated by a young, blonde, petite Spanish princess of so independent, lively, and informal a temperament that all efforts to make her conform to the rigid mold of Spanish court etiquette had availed not? Which was why, in time, she became a self-appointed and lighthearted exile in Paris, while retaining her rank and privileges. There she had lived happily for many years, when we met her, just before the fall of the Spanish monarchy.

To Father's message asking the Infanta if she happened to remember him, and telling her what great happiness it would give him if she would receive us, an answer came almost at once. Her Royal Highness would be delighted to receive us all the next afternoon at five.

That she lived in a convent was no sign she had taken the veil. I am sure that even at ninety the Infanta would be too young and worldly for that. While it answered to the deeply religious feeling that is part of every true Spaniard's character, it satisfied also the luxury-loving side, for the sunny suite that was her own private part of the convent, reached by a little private staircase to the second floor, was exquisitely furnished.

As a sister led us up those stairs, I could imagine Father must be suffering that special kind of stage fright we all must feel when we are about to meet an idol again after many years, even if it is only across the footlights, or from a distance, and not face to face. But this time, even after forty years, there was no disillusionment. If the *Almanach de Gotha* had not made royal birthdays an open secret to all the world, one simply could not have believed that this small, charming lady, with bobbed blonde hair, could possibly have forty-year-old memories of Chicago.

She came to greet us across a salon filled with people and flowers, introduced us all around, and then asked Father to sit beside her, while she poured out a perfect torrent of questions in rapid, easy English, with just that trace of accent which no charming woman should ever lose. She remembered everything about the fair to the last details—some, I really think, that Father had forgotten himself. And then, when people began to leave, she almost begged us to come in again a day or two later, when they could reminisce to their heart's content.

That next time, when she met us alone, Father could broach an idea that must have been brewing ever since we learned of her whereabouts. Chicago was to hold its Century of Progress Exposition in 1933. How delightful if she would return as its guest to the city whose heart she had won at that earlier fair! But of course he would not suggest this to Ambassador Dawes, the guiding spirit of the Exposition, unless the Infanta would approve.

Oh, she couldn't. To return after forty years—"I should imagine," she said distressfully, "that everyone was saying, 'Is *that* the Infanta Eulalia!' I don't know for which it would be worse —the ones who remembered me so kindly from before, or the ones who had only heard of me. Oh, I *couldn't*!" And although Father could offer reassurances from the one viewpoint, and Mother and I from the other, our pleas were in vain. Vanity conquered, as she herself put it.

The next time I went to the Infanta's, I went alone, as she had asked me to come and have "a little chat" with her before going to a tea near by at which she was to be guest of honor. I arrived to find her obviously suffering from a very bad headache.

"But Your Royal Highness," I said, "do you really feel well enough to go on to tea? And wouldn't you rather that I left now?"

"No, no!" she protested. "Don't you know, my dear, that royalty is never ill? You'll see me at the tea just as if nothing were the matter, and I beg you to stay and talk to me, so that I will forget myself and my stupid head!" She went on to say that this appearing on schedule, no matter what, became a kind of second nature through royal upbringing, and how much sympathy she felt for anyone drawn into the routine of a royal family without that lifelong training.

"May I ask you something I have always wondered about?" I asked then.

"Of course!" she answered.

"I have always wondered what is the first thing a royal princess is taught to do."

"To please people," said the Infanta, promptly and positively.

"To *please* people?" I repeated. "Even at the court of Spain?"

"Yes," said the Infanta, "that is the first thing I remember having ding-donged into me! You see, from every point of view, it is the most important element in a royal person's life. Quite aside from what you might call the political point of view—that of pleasing one's country as a whole—there is the personal element, either with those whom one meets only on occasion, who may be, no matter how unnecessarily, overawed and ill at ease, or with those in the court circle, whose whole pleasure and ease in everyday life depends on the attitude and mood of the members of the royal family.

"I realize perfectly," she went on, simply, "what a great experience it must be for anyone to come in contact with royalty for the first and, perhaps, the only time in their lives. So it is our duty not only to make them feel at ease but to give them, if possible, a happy memory."

And in my sympathy for princesses who must carry on despite headaches and whatever else, I turned to thinking of those easy things the rest of us can do to ease the difficulties of a state occasion. Wherever it may be, in White House, royal palace, or prime minister's office, false pride need not prevent us from asking beforehand of an aide, a lady in waiting, or a secretary how to address the personage giving audience, whether to curtsey, how long one is expected to stay, and—very important—whether one is to take leave or wait to be dismissed, and if the latter, what the sign of dismissal will be. Nothing gives quite such a feeling of security as to know in advance what is going to happen. For every country and every capital has an etiquette of its own, and you are very likely to be heading straight for embarrassing pitfalls if you think that knowing one is knowing all.

"You know," the Infanta went on, "my viewpoint cannot be entirely Spanish, because my husband was a French prince, Antoine d'Orleans, the son of the Duke de Monpensier, and I have lived a great deal of my life here in France."

I thought what a great sorrow it must be to think that both her countries, as well as Belgium, had had to expel her son, Don Luis de Bourbon, for his dark exploits. At the time, he was trying to find a refuge in Italy, and the newspapers were rumoring his engagement to an American millionairess, without his mother's consent.

As if reading my thought, the Infanta said, "You have seen about my son, Don Luis, in the papers?"

I said I had. For a moment she was silent, and then she spoke sadly, "It is a terrible thing for a mother to have to say, but I want you to know that I *couldn't* give my consent to my son's marriage to one of your lovely American girls—for her sake, whoever she might be. Of course, if a woman of the world wished to marry him, I should feel that she knew what she was doing, and I should feel no reason to interfere. . . .

"How strange it is," she added, after a minute, "that my other son, Don Alfonso, should be everything a son, a husband, and a father should be!"

But it was time to remember royal duty. She rose to get ready. "You run along, and tell them I shall be over in a few minutes!" she said.

So I did, and in a few minutes she arrived, radiant and charming; and no one could have guessed that her "stupid head" could be bothering her, or that she had a sorrow in the world.

During another visit, when we were talking of Cuba and Puerto Rico, which she had visited on her American tour while they were still Spanish colonies, Her Royal Highness surprised us by saying reminiscently,

"Do you know that if the Queen Mother of Spain had listened to me, there would have been no Spanish-American War? I see you are astonished!

"But I assure you that, young girl that I was, I saw the writing on the wall—for Spain—and as soon as I returned to Madrid, I begged Her Majesty to either give the Islands their freedom, or sell them to the United States! I told her that the feelings of the people were strong for freedom from the mother country, and that it would not only be the wise but the profitable thing for us to bow to the inevitable.

"But, of course, the Queen Mother and her advisers could not see it that way—and the rest is history!"

Perhaps the most extraordinary royal figure who ever came to Washington was Ras Destu Demtu, the son-in-law of Emperor Haile Selassie of Ethiopia, who came to America to present the Emperor's compliments personally to President Roosevelt, and to return the visit of our special envoys to His Ethiopian Majesty's coronation, just a year or so before Mussolini began his conquest of their ancient African kingdom.

There was much apprehension in high official circles about the success of His Royal Highness' visit to America; as well there might be, when you consider the problem of upholding his proper dignity once the newspapers began making capital and comedy of that exotic headdress made of a lion's mane, which only the bravest Ethiopian warriors were permitted to wear, and the white tunic which appeared below his knee-length black cape, which in the photographs looked strangely like plain American shirttails. But His Highness was coming, and that was that.

Naturally, as a guest of the government and especially one of royal rank, he would be met officially on his arrival in New York, as state visitors have been in every country since history began.

Now, the Ethiopian government had suggested that the State Department might make use of a young Ethiopian medical student in America, Maliku Bayen, as interpreter. I was told that what they didn't know was that young Bayen, who had left Ethiopia as the fiancé of the daughter of the foreign minister, had been hurt at the discrimination shown him at the fashionable Eastern college chosen for him, and had decided to finish his medical course at Howard, the great Negro university in Washington, where he had promptly met and married a pretty colored co-ed —a fact he had forgotten to mention to his fiancée back in Addis Ababa.

No wonder he answered the call to the State Department in fear and trembling. It was arranged that he should meet Jefferson Patterson, the assistant chief of protocol, and Major Brown, whom the Secretary of War had appointed as the Ras's military aide during his stay in America, at the Ritz in New York, at three o'clock in the morning, the day His Highness' boat was due. For some reason, all visitors of state seem to arrive at the crack of dawn, which is probably no pleasanter for them than for those who have to welcome them.

The dusky visitor and his staff were duly greeted, taken off at Quarantine, and whisked back to the Ritz, where their strange Ethiopian costumes, later so familiar to us from the unfortunate Emperor's photographs, created no end of a stir.

They left for Washington almost immediately, and while, of course, the Americans sat at the Ras's table in the dining car, Bayen had to stand behind the royal chair the whole way to Washington, swaying, balancing, and translating all at once. When later during the Ras's visit, Mr. William Phillips, our Undersecretary of State, gave a dinner for him and invited young Bayen out of courtesy, the young man begged to be allowed again to stand behind His Highness' chair all through dinner, although there was a place prepared for him, as he said he could not be seated in His Royal Highness' presence. Apparently he was rewarded for doing the right thing, for after his graduation all was forgiven, and he became the exiled Emperor's personal physician in London.

The next day, the Ras was to be presented to the President, and again it was Jeff who was to escort him. When they arrived at the White House the press photographers had one grand time —for on a hot summer day His Highness wore that whole flowing lion's mane, which I spoke of before, as ceremonial headdress. And one of our more socialistic papers printed the picture of him in all his barbaric splendor, side by side with Jeff, tall and impeccable from top hat to the tip of his patent leather shoes, with a caption posing the question: "Which looks funnier?"

But the end of the story is tragedy; for Ras Destu Demtu died leading a last stand for what seemed a lost cause, against an Italian military patrol in Ethiopia.

Washington knows and greatly admires a sympathetic and magnetic young man who to his own followers and his own family is already "His Imperial Majesty, the Emperor Otto," although the rest of the world still calls him His Royal Highness, Archduke Otto of Austria. He is a frequent Washington visitor, usually accompanied by his younger brother, Archduke Felix, who has made a really remarkable success on the American lecture platform. For after a lifetime of almost unbelievable stress and change, their widowed mother, the ex-Empress Zita, and all but one of her many children, have settled in the New World, to await the time when, they are sure, her eldest son will be called back to the Austro-Hungarian throne.

We first met the two archdukes through Father's attending a stag dinner for them given by former Ambassador Joseph E. Davies, for the Davies' had known the exiled imperial family in Belgium before their escape from their castle at Skenockerzel barely before the Nazis bombed it into oblivion.

Naturally, Archduke Otto's position in Washington is rather unusual, for although there is a great deal of sympathy for his cause, there is no way for our government to recognize him officially. But Father was so impressed with his intelligence and his grasp of world affairs, that he invited him to appear informally before the Foreign Affairs Committee the next time he came to Washington. He had also thought it might be an interesting experience for both Archduke Otto and his brother to lunch at the Capitol after the meeting; but no sooner was it arranged than we got word that the luncheon was "off," as the President had just asked our guests of honor to be at the White House at one o'clock that day!

As it happened, we were able to reach everyone who had accepted except Lilla Moffat, whose husband, Pierrepont Moffat, was chief of the European Division of the State Department; then Mother and I decided to go and meet her at the Foreign Affairs Committee, so that at least we three would not have to miss the opportunity of meeting them.

We waited while the committee was meeting behind closed doors. They said afterwards that Otto answered their questions on the world situation with simply amazing ability and keenness.

Finally the double doors opened and Father came in with two tall, attractive young men followed by the newspapermen and photographers who had also had to wait for the meeting to be over. We were presented in turn to the two brothers, who each shook hands cordially.

Despite having lived almost all their lives in exile, both brothers have that typical Viennese charm, in Otto's case combined with a manner that I can only describe as endearing; and they both cling to a faint trace of an Austrian accent, although their English is quite effortless. They were as easy to talk to as if we had known them for years. But I noticed that Archduke Felix stood or walked the entire time a step or two behind his elder brother, and never joined the conversation until Otto had had his say. Which must have been imperial etiquette, because when we saw him at other times, alone, he was as gay and spontaneous as could be.

We came to know Archduke Otto well, for he has often come to dinner with us alone in the garden on a summer evening, when we would sit for hours listening to his intelligent and fascinating reports of what was going on "inside Europe." He usually drives his little runabout himself, but sometimes he came by bus, and I often wondered whether anyone had the startlement of recognizing a fellow passenger as a prince who might even some day become the emperor of a restored empire.

During the war Washington was to play host to three crowned heads: Queen Wilhelmina of the Netherlands, King George of Greece, and young King Peter of Yugoslavia. But the climax of climaxes remains the historic visit of King George and Queen Elizabeth in the summer of 1939, an event whose effects were certainly realized when after the outbreak of war only three months later, American feeling for Britain showed in early aid and grew to comradeship in arms.

"Three cheers for the King—and four for the Queen!"

That was how one of the bewitched Washington newspapermen—with, I'm afraid, a faint flavor of lese majesty—saluted King George VI and Queen Elizabeth, as they left the Capital after those two June days that climaxed six solid months of preparation and excitement. For there was no doubt that, while the King looked on in smiling agreement, Washington had given the lovely little Queen of England the new title of Queen of Hearts.

Probably there never was such an avalanche of words about a happy happening: usually it takes battles, murder, or sudden death to make conquest of edition after edition of the newspapers and broadcast after broadcast of the radio chains. And yet I think the royal visit can bear another telling, from the viewpoint of someone who not only shared the general excitement in the city where naturally it was most intense, but who also watched and shared in the long preparation.

There were several reasons why we had a vantage spot in the wings while the stage was being set and the great scene being played. After nearly fifteen years on the Foreign Affairs Committee, Father was called on to be acting chairman—and within a month, chairman—during the most dramatic days the committee had known in years. For just as the struggle over his bill to revise the neutrality law reached its first great climax came the outstanding social event in Capital history. Since the chairmen of the Foreign Relations Committee of the Senate and of the Foreign Affairs Committee of the House automatically represent the Congress at all international state occasions, it was inevitable that Mother and Father would attend all official entertainment for the King and Queen. Also, because I was one of the few people in Washington who had been presented at Court, and because every Washington newspaperwoman was told to have a new and different story with a royal flavor every day for at least a month before the King and Queen arrived, it was only natural, I suppose, that they should think of me as a source of London lore. Day after day someone would telephone in desperation for a "new slant." Finally, after I had given almost my last crumb of Court procedure, someone was grateful just to know that the London papers speak of The King, in capitals, like that, even in the middle of a sentence.

From the moment the royal visit came in prospect, a storm raged over Washington that made the Dolly Gann–Alice Longworth feud look like a gentle breeze. The storm center was the garden party to be held at the British Embassy the day Their Majesties would arrive. There were three questions that almost shook the Washington Monument for weeks.

First, who was to be or not to be invited.

Second: to curtsey or not to curtsey. Far from being a poser only for the women concerned, this frightful issue not only agitated the whole country right down to its grass roots, but racked Washington's male officialdom nearly as much as its ladies. Father actually received a stern letter from a constituent containing a not very veiled threat of what would happen to him at the next election if he should send the wrong answer, and demanding that he return the letter with the one word Yes or No to the question: "Will you curtsey to the King and Queen?" Of course, since a man never curtseys, he was able to write a very large NO in red pencil, so his political career was saved.

One of the big news services telephoned Mother weeks before to ask her point-blank whether or not she would "bend the knee," since the garden party would take place on British soil. She seemed to make a very popular answer when she said that, though she followed the custom of the country and curtsied in England, she felt that the King and Queen would approve of Americans following their own custom, and would not expect a curtsey in America. As it happened, that was how the overwhelming majority of official wives decided the question.

The third burning question—although not so packed with political dynamite as the curtsey—was whether or not to wear a long, garden-party frock, that Washington usually ridicules even for the annual British Embassy garden party on the King's birthday. A long skirt seemed appropriate to the unprecedented great occasion; but many staunch democratic hearts trembled at the thought that this, too, might be looked on as "kowtowing" back home. A universal solution was not attained without some good old American log rolling. Eventually even the wildest Western Senators allowed their ladies to appear in long, frilly frocks, while they proclaimed their democracy by clinging to their ten-gallon hats.

The papers had a lot of fun when they discovered that the Capital's Court presentees—including me, under the No Daughters ban—had not been "commanded" to the royal garden party, although we would automatically have been on the list for the one at Buckingham Palace every year. They enjoyed themselves even more when they had figured out, by the next edition, that since Mrs. George Barnett, the Duchess of Windsor's cousin, was one of the few on the list, very likely we had all been "penalized" so that Their Britannic Majesties need not receive her. (Later, Mrs. Barnett remarked cheerfully that she thought she really might have rated a private audience, as the King and Queen owed so much to her family!)

One or two of the victims, taking it hard, wailed to the press about the injustice and ingratitude of it all, when they had spent so much money in the London shops on their Court costumes. A day or two later Mother ran into Lady Lindsay, who had been paying heavily for being the British ambassadress by having all the wrath poured on her, at a garden party in Virginia, where all the talk was of nothing but The Garden Party, which was still a week or so away.

"I only wish I could take care of everyone," Lady Lindsay said. "What must Vera think of me!"

Mother relayed what I had said when the newspapers insisted on a statement: that England, I felt, owed me nothing; being presented had been a wonderful experience, and as for helping the London shopkeepers, almost every woman in America seemed to be begging for the chance! And that these wails of ingratitude reminded me much too much of a woman crying about "giving that man the best years of my life." Lady Lindsay laughed, and was grateful for one kind word.

That same afternoon Father gave her the laugh on us, by broaching a helpful idea. His own sphere of agitation in the great events was the reception to be given the King and Queen at the Capitol on the morning of the second day of their visit, for which he had been put in charge of arrangements by a joint House and Senate committee. He equipped himself with special blueprints of the rotunda made by the Capitol architect, upon which everyone, to the last cameraman, was put down in blue and white. And after much poring over the situation, it had been decided that only the actual members of the House and Senate could be presented to Their Majesties. This was a crushing blow not merely to their wives but to all the sisters and the cousins and the aunts who had been hoping "somehow" to go along. The responsibility for the safety of the King and Queen while they were the guests of the nation, however, was an even heavier consideration. Marines were to be stationed from the dome to the sub-basement so that no one without the special admission badge could pass. Other Marines were to escort the cooks to the Senate and House restaurant kitchens, and to stand guard so that no substitutions of the regular staff could be made. But the best of such precautions would lose their sureness if a number of people not thoroughly familiar around the Capitol were to be included. Hearts were very heavy over the deprivation to the ladies, however; and Father had an idea.

"What do you think," he suggested to Lady Lindsay, "of having a place outdoors in the Capitol plaza, so that the Congressional wives and daughters and other official families can see Their Majesties when they come to the Capitol?"

Naturally, Lady Lindsay, harassed and hounded as she was, was more than enthusiastic about the idea. For one thing, here was a case when the onslaught for invitations would turn to someone other than herself.

And did it turn! From the moment the papers got hold of the story, and announced that there was room for several thousand seats in the plaza, we had a taste of what the Lindsays must have been going through. Don't let anyone ever tell me again that Americans are indifferent to royalty! If they are, why did our telephone start ringing at seven in the morning with someone saying sweetly, "You don't know me, and my husband has no official position. But I do so want to see the Queen, and I think you could arrange it—because I have so much fine old English furniture!"

Eventually each member of the Senate and the House was given five tickets for whichever lucky ladies or children he chose, and at the end there were four thousand people seated in the plaza. It was difficult to decide who would enjoy it most, and it was even easy to guess wrong entirely, as we did with a friend of ours. "Oh, my dear, how sweet of you!" she said, when I telephoned about it. "But I really think you should ask someone who would appreciate it more. Now, if I could see the Duchess of Windsor, *that* would be romantic!"

Could anything, I wondered, be more romantic than to see the first "commoner" Queen of England—even though she is the daughter of a hundred earls—since Henry VIII wound up his career by marrying Katharine Parr? But I didn't ask out loud. There were, in a way, already too many who thought Queen Elizabeth "romantic" enough!

Meanwhile Father's worst problem in the production department concerned a rug.

The rotunda, the huge circular hall under the Capitol dome, had been chosen for the reception rather than the chamber of the House (where all joint sessions of the Congress are held) because of the ancient British tradition that the monarch may not enter the House of Commons, for fear that such close association with royalty might undermine its independence of thought; and it was feared that holding the reception in the House, here, might

257

be misunderstood in London. The plan was for Vice-President Garner to stand beside the King and Queen while Senator Pittman, as chairman of the Foreign Relations Committee, presented the members of the Senate. Then Speaker Bankhead was to take the Vice-President's place while Father took the Senator's place and presented the members of the House. The British Ambassador and American-born Lady Lindsay, and the lords-and-ladies-in-waiting, were to stand in the background.

So it wasn't the problem of finding a large rug, once it had been decided that the royal couple should have a carpet underfoot no matter what problems were involved, but of seeing to it that the color had no political significance. A "red carpet"— symbol of royal pomp the world over—was definitely out. What the newspapers could say about American legislators standing on a royal red carpet under the dome of the Capitol with the King and Queen of England would surely have meant more than one defeat at the next election. Emerald green might have been interpreted as a political gesture by the Irish Americans in Congress. Purple . . . oriental . . . trouble lurked on every side.

One day as we were talking over this basic problem in our little library upstairs, it dawned on me that the solution might be under our very feet—a good, plain gray-green eight-by-twelve carpet, fortunately of American make. The committee accepted it gratefully, so it was sent off to be cleaned, and Father's own trusted messenger delivered it the day before the reception.

The newsmen, quick on the scent of any possible copy on the royal visit, had asked Father for all details about the carpet, which no doubt they hoped against hope would be a red one. He told them everything, except that it was ours. They also wanted to know if there would be a carpet on the front Capitol steps; to which the answer was, it had been vetoed as possibly dangerous. There would have been no way to attach it securely to the steps except by the very undemocratic method of having two soldiers on each step hold a rod across the carpet with their heels.

Thus the rug question was well disposed of; or so we thought. But Drew Pearson still wasn't satisfied, and a week or so later his daily Washington Merry-Go-Round divulged lengthy fact and fancy about "the historic Bloom carpet." Various papers throughout the country actually boxed the story on the front page. Whereupon there was more to-do. Rug manufacturers wrote begging to know whether or not the rug was their product; the head of the carpet cleaning company wrote and telephoned begging for a letter confirming the story. He solemnly promised never to use the letter as a "testimonial"; it was only wanted as an heirloom for his grandchildren, real proof that the King and Queen of England had actually stood on a carpet that grandfather cleaned!

By now you have at least a sketchy idea of the inch-by-inch planning necessary for the Capitol reception, which was to occupy exactly forty-five minutes of rigid royal schedule. You can therefore imagine how busied the State Department was for every separate second the King and Queen were on American soil. The Secret Service actually investigated every foot of railroad track over which the royal train was to pass from the Canadian border.

Meanwhile the battle for garden party invitations still went merrily on. We even heard that one Washington official cabled to Lord Lothian, who had just been designated in London to succeed Sir Ronald Lindsay, soon to retire as British Ambassador, to beg him to "use his influence on Sir Ronald!"

And there was one group who exerted influence en masse. At first it had been decided that from Congress only the members of the two committees dealing with foreign affairs could be invited. At that such a wail went up from the Senate ladies (and the bill for neutrality revision hadn't yet passed the upper house, you should remember) that at the last minute the entire Senate received those precious pasteboards with the golden G.R.E. under the British crown.

All the while, the papers were keeping up a crescendo of excitement. It was like one of those old-fashioned band concert pieces where the finale goes on and on, when you think no composer could possibly think of any more endings. Society editors had sent out long printed questionnaires to everyone who might possibly be on the list for one of the great occasions, asking in detail what not only the ladies but the men would be wearing to each. Washington merchants had that same all's-well-with-the-world expression that the London merchants have at the height of the Season.

But all this was only the overture, after all. The symphony only really started when the Marine Band broke into "God Save The King!" as Their Britannic Majesties, accompanied by the Secretary of State and Mrs. Hull, who had gone to the Canadian border to greet them as they stepped on American soil, stepped from their train at Union Station at eleven o'clock the morning of June eighth, and walked down the broad blue carpet to the beautifully redecorated Presidential waiting room where, for the first time in history, a President of the United States was waiting to welcome a reigning British monarch to American soil.

Besides the Roosevelt family and the entire staffs of the British Embassy and the legations of the British Dominions, there were waiting, of course, the Garners, the Bankheads, all the Cabinet and their wives, the Pittmans, Mother and Father, and a few others, including the Undersecretary of State and Mrs. Welles, the nearly exhausted chief of protocol of the State Department, George T. Summerlin, and the chiefs of the armed forces, who were all presented to Their Majesties by the President with a few special, cordial words about each one. These were the official group who were to make up, with Mrs. Woodrow Wilson and a few additions, the guest list at the two state dinners—the first at the White House for the King and Queen, and the one at the British Embassy, the second evening, when the King and Queen were hosts to the President and Mrs. Roosevelt.

And with those moments at the station and the procession along crowded avenues to the White House, there began in earnest the Queen's complete conquest of America, already in its prologue on the journey from the border: a capture evident not only in the time of her presence but continuing long afterward as America paid her the supreme compliment of suddenly making soft femininity rather than brittle sophistication the fashion in women themselves as well as in their clothes.

We had had several good opportunities, in London, to see the Queen as Duchess of York, and we could appreciate the almost miraculous blossoming out of her personality since she had come to the throne. From a sweet and smiling but rather passive personality, the Queen, as she neared her fortieth birthday, had suddenly become a person completely enchanting. Her own qualities, plus the glory of the throne, and the complete and constant devotion of the King, had combined now to make her the very essence of a woman lovely, lovable, and beloved.

One thing that impressed Mother immediately, and to which one of the royal party agreed when she spoke to him of it at the White House dinner that night, was that Queen Elizabeth has the rare asset of being able to give her utter attention to the person who is with her at the moment—the highest form of flattery, they say, in any woman; much more in a queen.

As for the King, though he might lack that electric glamor his brother Edward had flashed as Prince of Wales, he showed himself to be extremely kind and keen, distinctly better looking, and so obviously and unselfishly delighted with the Queen's tremendous triumphs, that it warmed your heart to see it.

Not that anybody or anything needed warming! I cannot tell you why this great visit took place in a tropical Washington June, or whether the monarchs knew what they were likely to get into. One can only say that they suffered, and with unfailing grace. Before the long-awaited garden party, a storm came up, cleared just in time, and left the city hotter than ever. And Father, who after all had once demonstrably turned off the rain when he tested the loudspeakers for the President's speech at the Washington Monument, said to the Queen,

"You see, Your Majesty, I stopped the rain for you!"

"Indeed you did," the Queen agreed. "But," she added laughingly, "didn't you forget to turn off the heat?"

From the Embassy garden party the King and Queen returned to the White House in time to rest a bit and change—the fourth time that day—for the dinner in the state dining room, at a table almost completely hidden by the thousands of white orchids that had been a gift to Mrs. Roosevelt for the occasion from one of the great orchid growers of the country. Everything that could possibly have been planned had been planned. No one could foresee that the air cooling system, so confidently installed in the White House not long before, would contribute nothing but nerve-racking noises to one of the rarest occasions in all White House history!

It was easy to see, Mother told me afterward, how the Queen must have been suffering, no matter how gallantly she carried on. In her wide crinoline gown of white and gold, her heavy ruby and diamond tiara, necklace, and earrings, and all her orders, and with the torture of a Washington sunburn on her fair, Scottish skin, it was no wonder that, as Mrs. Roosevelt disclosed later, the Queen had begged for a few minutes alone in the garden with the King after dinner, to revive her for the musicale which was to follow, and for which additional guests were beginning to arrive.

It was well they refreshed themselves, because—as nearly everyone who was there privately agrees—if ever there was a trial under the name of amusement, that was it.

For more years than anyone in Washington seems to remember, Steinway and Company have had charge of the musicales that invariably follow state dinners at the White House; and by an unwritten rule, none but great artists of world-wide reputation —a Paderewski, a Kreisler, or a Tibbett—appeared on those programs, for which their only material recompense would be an autographed photograph of the President and the First Lady, and an invitation to dinner.

With the second Roosevelt regime, however, all this began to change. There was a New Deal in musicales, too. In Mrs. Roosevelt's opinion all native American music belonged in the White House, and it soon became a usual thing for the crystal chandeliers in the East Room to shiver and shake to hillbilly bands, and to the stamping of backwoods dancers in ginghams and overalls. And with the musicale for the King and Queen of England came the climactic collision of the two schools of thought.

To be sure, Lawrence Tibbett and Marian Anderson (then more than ever famous because the D.A.R. were alleged to have forbade her appearing in Constitution Hall on grounds of color and not of art) were on the program. But with them were to appear, beside Kate Smith, who as radio's "Songbird of the South" stood somewhere midway of the artistic scale, the most touchingly untamed and untrained groups of hillbillies and revival-meeting singers that could probably be found in the entire country. They would have been thrilling and stirring against their own background, as, indeed, all folk music is throughout the world, but the effect in the East Room was a trial for the audience that I think really broke the heart of poor, old Mr. Junge of Steinway's, who had arranged the White House musicales for all those years, and who had counted on the one for King George and Queen Elizabeth to be the climax of his career.

After the musicale (two solid pages long) the King and Queen had to stand in line again to receive each and every one of the musicians, including the Marine Band; and upstairs in the private apartments, it is said, the King and the President talked confidentially for an hour or more after everything else. Yet both the King and Queen looked radiant and refreshed the next morning when they arrived at the Capital at exactly eleven o'clock, already having journeyed to the Embassy to receive all the British subjects living in the Capital.

Not so their audience for the Congressional reception! Or at any rate not the distaff side of it, who, thanks to Father's inspiration, were privileged to watch from the Capitol plaza. We had had to come early, of course, to be sure of getting through traffic and police lines in time; and we broiled, with no protection from the blistering 99-degree sun but here and there a few parasols, which the Queen had made fashionable again overnight.

Just before eleven o'clock the committee of the two Houses, escorted by Colonel Jurney and Kenneth Romney, the Senate and House sergeants-at-arms, appeared at the door of the rotunda, where the Vice-President and the Speaker waited to receive their royal guests, and walked slowly down the steps. They were, on the whole, resplendent in formal morning dress, with the two exceptions supplied by the minority leaders of Senate and House, Senator McNary unconcernedly wearing a collapsible opera hat, and Congressman Joe Martin a derby.

Senator Pittman and Father had thought out every move they would make from the moment when the royal car drove up until it rolled away again. Just one question had agitated Father at the last. Should he or should he not support the Queen's arm as she mounted the long stairway? He had decided to leave that to the King; and was surprised to see later by the photographs that he had done so anyway, as he would have for any lady he had been escorting on such a climb. But it was quite unnecessary. In fact, the one comment I heard most often afterward was on the simply extraordinary grace and ease of the Queen, especially as she came down that long stairway while thousands of eyes looked on. It was, exactly, what the novelists used to mean when they described their matchless heroines as "floating on air."

As they reached the first landing, going up, Father said to Her Majesty, "Perhaps you would care to turn now, Ma'am, and see the crowd?" (He meant, of course, "and let the crowd see you!")

The Queen said something to the King, and they both turned around to face the delighted ladies below. The King gave a wave of the hand that seemed to have caught already some of the American breeziness of the President, and the Queen, exquisite in a simple, all-white street costume with touches of silver, and a large white hat, smiled and made that slow, indescribably graceful gesture of her hand.

The King wanted to know just how many members of Congress there were, and Father supplied the statistics. After the reception, I saw His Majesty turn to Father, say something, and laugh heartily. Later, I learned that he had flexed his right hand ruefully and laughed, "Did you say there are *only* five hundred and thirty-one!"

But it was surely worth everything it had entailed, for as the King and Queen turned to leave the rotunda, the members of Congress broke into such spontaneous cheering that the royal visitors, accustomed to continuous ovations as they are, were taken completely by surprise. The Queen turned to Father and asked him whether or not she was expected to acknowledge it; and when, on his assurance, she bowed, and waved, and smiled her lovely smile, the enthusiasm doubled. The British had taken the Capitol by storm a second and better time.

The enthusiasm grew as they came down the steps and passed between us down the center aisle to the far side of the plaza where their car was waiting. There was a crescendo of applause, coming, oddly, from an audience still seated; for the Secret Service men, who made no effort to disguise themselves that morning, insisted that no one should rise, since any remotely possible "incident" would be less likely to occur and far easier to foil in a seated crowd than in a standing one. There was no incident, however, but the main one; and now it was over, as Their Majesties, smiling and waving, drove off to meet the President and Mrs. Roosevelt for the trip down the Potomac to Mount Vernon.

The Embassy dinner, in contrast to the White House dinner the night before, was really small: in fact only sixteen couples sat down that night with the First Gentlemen and First Ladies of the two most powerful nations in the world, and only the Embassy staff was commanded to come in after dinner.

As the guests arrived, it was Ambassador and Lady Lindsay who received them; but when Their Majesties entered the drawing room, the Lindsays stepped back and became merely guests, while the King and Queen, naturally, became host and hostess on British

"Three Cheers for the King—and Four for the Queen!"

At Dinner Given by H. M. King Peter of Yugoslavia at Royal Yugoslav Legation (l. to r. from foot of table) Yugoslav Minister Fotitch, Assistant Secretary of State Berle, Vera Bloom, Mr. Snoj, Mrs. H. H. Arnold, Senator Connally, Mme. Fotitch, Soviet Ambassador Litvinov, Lady Halifax, Vice President Wallace, Mme. Litvinov, and Speaker Rayburn soil. And it was fascinating (as Mother and Father told afterwards) to see how the atmosphere immediately reflected their kind and charming personalities, just as every party, everywhere in the world, is made or marred by the host and hostess. Suddenly it seemed not a stiff state function, but like a friendly gathering.

The King chuckled as a man does over an old joke, when, making the "royal circle" among the guests, he came up to Father. "*How* many members of Congress did you say there were at the Capitol this morning? Don't you think some of them must have gone through twice?"

The Queen wore the most beautiful costume, undoubtedly, of all those created for her New World visit. It was one of the huge crinolines she revived so charmingly, with an off-the-shoulder bodice, of rose-pink tulle, embroidered all over as exquisitely as an eighteenth-century fan with Queen Alexandra roses of tiny rose-colored sequins outlined with gold and silver threads, and just here and there a touch of aquamarine blue stones, which matched her eyes. She wore marvelous jewels of diamonds and pearls, and the tiara with the straight rows of diamonds like icicles, that she wears on the coronation stamps, on her dark hair.

And she presented a rose-pink problem to Speaker Bankhead. For when he went to take his place at the Queen's left at the table, he saw that his chair had quite disappeared under the enchantment. Her Majesty's crinoline had acted as crinolines will, and, indeed, often did in olden days when it was not surprising for each lady of fashion to require three chairs for herself alone.

The Queen was already deep in an animated conversation with the President, who was, of course, seated at her right. So the Speaker stood and waited until she should turn around to him.

When she did, she looked up at him in surprise, and he, with a gesture toward the chair, explained in his courtly Southern way, "Your Majesty, I am indeed at a loss to know what to do—"

The Queen laughed, expertly handled the situation, and the Speaker took his place beside her.

Mother made a souvenir of the Queen just as she was that night, to the last diamond, in one of the really exquisite little figurines which she created by a process she was able to patent as her own, of setting jewels into clay. To be sure, the "jewels" she used were only make-believe gems; but even these were becoming rare after Hitler's seizure of Czechoslovakia, where most of the best imitation gems came from.

While she was making her little six-inch Queen in the Virginia Blue Ridge mountain place we took for that summer, one of the little barefoot, bashful mountain girls came to the door one day with a pail of berries to sell. After the berry sale was consummated over some cake and milk, it suddenly occurred to Mother that the child might like to "see" the Queen. So she took her in to her work table, where the figurine still stood with piles of "diamonds" and "pearls" around it.

"And this is the Queen of England!" said Mother, as the little girl, more speechless than ever, stood with her eyes and mouth making three complete circles in her astonished little face. I think she was nearly as enchanted as Secretary of Commerce Harry Hopkins' little daughter, Diana, had been when she saw the real Queen as she was leaving the White House for the Embassy dinner. It had been Her Majesty's suggestion that Diana have the chance to see her, dressed "as a little girl would expect a queen to look."

For Mother, the loveliest picture of that evening was when, after dinner—while the gentlemen, in the English fashion, stayed behind in the dining room where the port and cigars had been placed on the shining, doily-decked table before the King, who had moved around to the place beside the President—the Queen stepped out alone through the French doors from the drawing room onto the portico, and stood, in her wide, shimmering dress, in the doorway, with the dark garden as background.

After a moment the Queen went on down the garden steps to the lower terrace, while Lady Lindsay hastily instructed some of the footmen to follow with a sofa—the traditional "royal sofa"—and some chairs from the drawing room.

Miraculously, after those two dreadful days, the Embassy garden was cool.

Mrs. Roosevelt followed, and took her place beside the Queen on the sofa, and Lady Lindsay plied between the upper terrace and the garden, bringing one lady or two at a time with whom the Queen wished to chat for a few moments. The same procedure had been followed at the White House dinner the night before; and Mother said the Queen had been so helpful and spontaneous that, when her turn came, she hadn't even realized that in obedi-

266

ence to protocol she was only speaking when the Queen spoke to her.

After a while, probably when the King had suggested, "Shall we join the ladies?" the gentlemen came out onto the portico. The President, who is, of course, under the unwritten law that the occupants of the White House can never, in ordinary circumstances, visit an embassy, was enchanted with the beautiful setting.

The royal train was to leave Washington for New York and the homeward journey to England, over which war clouds were already beginning to gather, before midnight that night; and accordingly, the President and Mrs. Roosevelt departed early. Their Majesties made the circle again, with a personal word of thanks and good-by to everyone, and disappeared, and the guests left immediately after.

Everyone thought the Queen had probably gone upstairs to change for the train; but in a final endearing gesture, she had decided to go right on to the station as she was, only throwing a rose-colored feather cape around her shoulders, so that the thousands and thousands who lined the streets and crowded the huge station for a last glimpse of the King and Queen could remember her, too, "as a queen should look."

And I wonder if she and the King, riding by, did not feel a lump in their throats as group after group of good Americans, standing under the lamplit green arches of Washington's trees, spontaneously began singing "God Save the King!"

II. Wartime Washington

There were really two wartime Washingtons: the one when the rest of the world was already at war, but we were still trying to convince ourselves it was no concern of ours; and the one after Pearl Harbor, when everyone had to realize that it was.

Strangely, the first period was in many ways the hardest, especially for those of us who saw the writing on the wall. This was the heyday of America First, when the slogan, "We must not send American boys to die on foreign battlefields!" was constantly and shrilly reiterated against anyone who dared to think that the Axis threat had grown to where we could no longer save our lives by not risking them, or appease the unappeasable.

It was not at all a question of political party lines but of personal convictions. For instance, I remember that one night Mother was seated at dinner between Senator McNary (then the Republican leader of the Senate, and soon to be Wendell Willkie's running mate) and a former fanatical New Dealer who had been one of the President's closest advisers but now was a rabid American Firster.

So rabid, in fact, that as the dinner progressed he attacked the President's sincerity on his foreign policy in language that left Mother in horrified silence. And then Senator McNary proved what a really fine American can be, and why he was so beloved and respected by both parties, when he, who if he had been a lesser man might have been delighted at such a defection from the Democratic ranks, suddenly said: "If you continue to insult the motives of the President of the United States that way, I shall have to leave the table!" The tirade stopped.

At a dinner at Mrs. McLean's one time the wife of that same man was holding forth on what she called the Japanese incident in

China. She turned to me and asked, in that infuriating more-in-sorrow-than-in-anger tone they all used with the rest of us, "Don't you *believe* in Asia for the Asiatics?"

"Of course I do," I answered; "but I also believe in China for the Chinese!"—to the obvious delight of others at the table who had been waiting to get in a word for our side.

This was the sort of verbal dueling that went on everywhere with growing tension, until even lifelong friendships broke under the strain.

The isolationists had the immeasurable advantage of being able to appeal directly to the most fundamental fears, especially of those who had husbands or sons of military age; while those who saw the situation realistically could only try to appeal to people's reason. I do not deny that there were some fine and sincere patriots in American First; but they were unconsciously being swayed, nevertheless, by the persuasions Dr. Goebbels and Co. had been spreading everywhere through long years of brewing mental poison.

Those they could not appeal to through "patriotism" they tried to reach through social ambition, for they made practically a person-to-person campaign with invitations to teas and parties, and such lures as: "Couldn't I just arrange for you to sit down and have a nice little private chat some day with Mrs. Champ Clark, the chairman of our group, so you could *really* talk things over?" Or they appealed to those who fancied themselves as the intelligentsia by showing them that all civilizations had their rise and fall, and that it was indeed "progress" for France and England to make way for a New Order under which the few really intelligent people in each society would be the leaders.

I heard that kind of talk in the most incredible circumstances from friends of ours I had always thought too intelligent to be taken in by that sort of thing, after a small dinner we gave on the hot June night of 1940 when the Nazis were marching into Paris. No one knew yet whether the Germans would spare the city or destroy it as an "example" to the rest of Europe; and as we listened every few minutes for the latest bulletins, it seemed exactly as if a beautiful and beloved friend were dying.

Some of our friends said placidly: "Who knows? Maybe it's all for the best! After all, the Nazis are strong and vital; and even though some beauty and some 'civilization' has to be sacrificed, it may be the only way for them to bring about a better and a brighter world!"

That they could have such thoughts, and could voice them to us, was bad enough; and doubly unforgivable in the presence of our guest that evening, Archduke Felix of Austria, whose family had escaped from Nazi benevolence only in a matter of inches and seconds when Belgium was invaded. I decided then and there that it was no use trying to keep on pretending close companionship with people who felt like that. You might have been really fond of them; but where there is no meeting of the minds, how can there be a meeting of the hearts?

The only person in Washington who continued to mix us all up "irregardless" was Evalyn McLean; which made her famous Sunday night dinners more famous than ever. For years, people and the press have attributed every kind of motive to her in doing it, from being the leader of America's Cliveden Set to a simple urge for bigger and better publicity. Personally, I think it's just that Mrs. McLean honestly believes "once a friend, always a friend," and the fact that for years her invitation list included a grand melange of the Barkleys, the Wheelers, the Peppers, the Champ Clarks, the Guffeys, the Tafts, the Fishes, and the Blooms was all the reason she needed to keep on asking them together. She has a heart as big as a house—even a house as fantastically big as "Friendship"—and while no one else would have dreamed of asking the Finnish Minister and Mme. Procopé to sit at the same table with the British Ambassador and Lady Halifax when their two countries were at war, the mere fact that she is godmother of the Procopé children would have made the Procopés part of the family and not a political problem in her eyes.

And then, there's no denying that she has inherited a strong streak of Irish perversity; and just as she enjoys wearing the Hope Diamond to the most unlikely places, like Petticoat Lane, the thieves' hangout in London, I suspect she takes an impish delight in her dinner lists just because no one else would have the courage to concoct them. Her "informal little dinners" of a hundred and twenty-five or so are seated at small tables of eight or ten in rooms scattered all over the rambling house; and even though you find yourself, as you probably will, next to your pet political peeve, you are just as likely to have a bulwark of the administration, like J. Edgar Hoover or Charles Michelson, on the other side.

I suspect, too, that it is that same perversity that made her keep on with her parties after food rationing, the pleasure driving ban, and all other wartime restrictions had brought Capital entertaining (except state functions) to a standstill. No coffee? All right, no coffee. No meat? All right, no meat. The limousine-lazy would have to transfer to three buses to get to Friendship? All right, too. And somehow or other all the "regulars" were always on hand.

There was a dinner at Friendship the night France fell; the bulletin came over the radio while we were dressing. Somehow I felt it was awful to be going to a party after that. But what could you do, telephone and say, "I'm so heartbroken about France, I just can't come"?

The first person I met there was Lord Lothian, who certainly would have more reason to stay home mourning England's last ally than anyone else. He just said, "Bad news—bad news. Well, from here on we carry on alone!"

The only time I've ever seen Mrs. McLean in the role of guest instead of hostess, except long ago at the White House (for she never goes to any parties but her own), was at a dinner Elsa Maxwell gave for her in New York. It happened to be the night that Stalin abolished the Comintern; and it also happened that, because Miss Maxwell wanted to give Mrs. McLean a dinner that even she couldn't produce in Washington, she had invited all the star columnists and commentators in New York.

After dinner she slyly started a free-for-all discussion between Dorothy Thompson, William Shirer, Anne O'Hare McCormick, John Gunther, Major Eliot, George Sokolsky, Larry Le Sueur, and a dozen more, who soon had themselves and each other in a fine frenzy about what Stalin's motives really were. The amazing and amusing part of it was that no two of these people, whom we listen to night after night with bated breath as the fount of all wisdom, could agree. Well, it was all brilliant, if not conclusive, and a mental menu few hostesses could produce.

Wartime Washington even before Pearl Harbor began to take on the new personality that was to blossom fully in the not-so-distant days when the real-estate agents simply put signs in their windows, "No Vacancies," and the domestic employment agencies wouldn't even bother to answer the phone. The time of tragicomic overcrowding was still to come; yet with the neutrality revision

271

and lend-lease already setting war-goods production in motion, bringing in a stream of technical experts, manufacturers, dollar-a-year men, and just plain white collar workers, Washington was acquiring a perpetual convention-city atmosphere. And for the first time in Capital history it became a conversational tidbit to boast that you had been able to get a drug store sandwich in less than an hour.

In its social tone Washington was like a sheltered woman suddenly pushed out into a tough world, who tries to put on the veneer of a ruthless career woman to convince people that she can hold her own with the best or the worst of them. But the veneer kept chipping off. Even today, with transportation on streetcars and buses at the same sardine-can stage as the subway rush hour in New York, and with Capital cocktail bars (where no one who was anyone would be seen before the war, for fear people would think they hadn't been *invited* anywhere) so jammed you would think the drinks were being given away, Washington still hasn't achieved the authentic glossy sophistication of "21" or the Stork Club, and I don't think it ever will. I still have a sneaking suspicion that it will go right back to all the dear old folderol as soon as things are normal again, just as I suspect that even the blitz has not fundamentally shaken England from the old-school-tie state of mind.

Functionally, however, Washington was coping with the hard realities. I have mentioned that it was my father who led the hard fight in the House for revision of the Neutrality Act in the summer of 1939, when there were still so many in the Capital and throughout the country who were hoping "somehow" for peace. Even though the Senate failed to act on the bill before Congress recessed, its passage in the House that June was a victory against odds, in which Father could take solid satisfaction.

We rented a house in the near-by Virginia mountains hoping he could restore strained energies during the recess; but he enjoyed very little of the mountain air except when he was asleep, for he went back and forth to the Capital every day. Only on Thursday, the last day of August, did he declare that he was going to take a few days' real vacation, and that nothing would get him back to the office until Monday.

At three o'clock in the morning the telephone shrilled. It was the State Department. Hitler was on the radio announcing the invasion of Poland. Of course there was no thought of sleep for any of us from that moment on, and no more vacation hopes for Father in years. News services and radio chains had him on the wire off and on all night; then came the summons to be at the White House as early as possible; and before seven o'clock he was away on the fifty-mile ride back to Washington. Congress was called into special session; the Senate passed the new Neutrality Act; and by winter the bitter struggle over lend-lease was on.

That the Lend-Lease Act did become law nearly a year before Pearl Harbor showed that the majority of Congress and the country were taking a realistic look at that tough world. But the America Firsters and similar groups were still doing all they could to build up the Great Divide, and with too much success. Now, no longer having to rely only on memory and imagination, they could point out in the daily papers what horrors we would invite if we were so mad as to ignore the fact that Providence had given us two great oceans to insulate us from a world at war. Remember all that talk about "if a madman like Hitler can see that he can't get twenty miles across the English Channel, surely he can't dream of declaring war on us across two thousand miles of ocean! And as for Japan—my dear, have you ever really *looked* at the Pacific on a map?"

But no words, no matter how lulling they might be nor how logical they might be made to sound, could hold back December 7, 1941, for a single second.

It seems to me that no one could have lived through these times, either at the Washington crossroad or in a remote-seeming village, without having his sense of values change deeply. In our case the difference was even more profound because, while the universal tragedy deepened, our own private world was plunged in darkness at the same time.

Mother, who had always been so radiantly alive that people all over the world who didn't know each other called her "Sunshine," suddenly and almost imperceptibly began to fail. At first we thought it was only the effect of her worrying about the war, as a whole, and of Father's heavy responsibilities in particular. When someone has always been so well, somehow you just can't believe that it can be "anything serious." But then one day in May of 1941, Dr. Salzer, who is the best friend as well as the best physician anyone could have, came down to Washington to surprise us for breakfast, and incidentally to escape for a few hours from his heavy schedule in New York. As soon as he saw Mother—he knew. But he didn't tell Father and me; he only said he wanted her to come to New York for a complete rest in the hospital, where he could see her every day, and of course we went along.

Our family had led a charmed life in many ways, but in none more so than in our total inexperience with hospitals and serious illness. The Doctor was solicitude and wisdom personified, and he called the greatest medical minds in New York in consultation; but almost before we knew it, she was gone, and Father and I were left numb and unbelieving, to face a world without her. . . .

Deeply as we appreciated the overwhelming expressions of sympathy—separate messages from the President and Mrs. Roosevelt; others from the Apostolic Delegate, Archbishop Cicognani, whom we had come to know when we were neighbors in the Blue Ridge, from royalty, from diplomatic friends scattered everywhere; indeed, thousands of messages from people in every walk of life from all over the world—there were two that touched us more poignantly than any others. Why, I can't say, except perhaps that people in high position often do kind and thoughtful things as a natural result of lifelong training, while simple people do them entirely from an overflowing heart.

The first happened the night we came back to Washington from New York. The Doctor had come back with us, and after dinner he went to see his son, Bob, who was then an ensign at the Navy Department. On the way back, stopping at a drugstore to get some cigars for Father and some candy for me, he saw the young man who was waiting on him had obviously been weeping. At first he thought perhaps he should pretend not to have noticed; but then he changed his mind and, mentioning that he was a physician, asked if he could help in any way.

"No," the clerk said sadly, "there's nothing anyone can do. It's only that I just heard of Mrs. Sol Bloom's death. I used to wait on her sometimes, and she was the kindest and loveliest lady that ever lived."

Then, of course, the Doctor told him that his purchases were for us, and that he would surely tell us of their strange and touching encounter.

The other thing that stands out especially of all those messages was the one from Mr. Harrison, the dining car steward on the train we took back from Mexico a few months before, which was signed by every one of the colored waiters and all the cooks. We had stopped in the kitchen to thank them for a special turkey dinner they made for us one night. It was beautiful to know that the kindness and warmth that Mother gave out so unconsciously left such lasting memories wherever she went.

From all our years in Washington I can think of only three other women who have had that same quality of spontaneous friendliness toward everyone, from a king to the cop on the corner; and they are Mrs. Coolidge, Mrs. Borah, and Bee Sokolowska.

Bee was to prove my closest friend in sad days, as she had been in happy ones; and her being near enough to help was not at all a matter of course. She and Peter and the boys had barely escaped from Poland; in fact when they arrived in New York the end of November, Peter still had on the sport jacket and white trousers he had been wearing that terrible Friday, September 1, when Hitler began the invasion.

By a strange twist of fate they had been waiting at a summer resort near Warsaw to leave for Copenhagen as soon as the King of Denmark returned there from the country; Peter (everyone forgets his real name is Wladislaw) had been appointed Polish Minister, and wanted to be able to present his credentials immediately on arriving. Everything they owned was packed and ready for shipment at a storage company in Warsaw; and if the summons had come a few days earlier, they would undoubtedly have reached Copenhagen safely with all their belongings.

Instead, they were lucky to escape with their lives and the clothes they had on; and Bee firmly believes that the only thing that kept the family together was the American car they had taken back to Poland. The four of them could return to it, slowly making their way to Rumania, between the incessant Nazi air raids which constantly strafed the pitiful lines of escaping refugees, who had to hide in the vegetable fields like animals while the Germans tried to pick them off with machine guns one by one.

As they crossed the bridge into Rumania, fourteen-year-old Ducky made a vow that he would be back—but on the giving end next time. And he is on his way back: as a pilot with our Army Air Corps. He couldn't even wait for his eighteenth birthday to join up; and one of the most touching moments of the war, to me, was when his father went to a notary public to sign the necessary papers for a minor, and the notary refused to accept her fee, saying, "If you can give your son to America, surely you will let me do my little share to make it possible for him to go."

One of the great trials for the Sokolowskis, when they first returned, was that they simply couldn't make people here believe the truth about the Nazis: the reality of their determination to exterminate all Poles regardless of religion, and of their fiendishly thorough tactics of invasion, which have since become all too familiar. And like all diplomatic refugees, they had a very difficult period of readjustment, until Peter's appointment as Polish Consul General to San Francisco.

A diplomatic refugee friend of mine summed it up one day when he said, "I'm lucky—I have no wife or children to take care of; a man alone can always manage to exist somehow, and like all of us, I am so grateful to be in America that nothing else really matters. But the truth is that the mental readjustment we have to make is really harder, in a way, than the matter-of-fact problems of daily living. I mean, aside from the 'glamour,' a diplomat, like an army or navy officer, has—or thinks he has—one thing that is certain in life, and that is financial security. He knows he will never have an opportunity to make big money, but he can look forward to a gradual advancement as he goes on from one rank to another, and there is always the pension to look forward to when he reaches retirement age. So that the feeling of security becomes a part of you, and suddenly to find that there is no security—well, that seems the most unreal part of the whole thing."

A very tragic element for all of our diplomatic friends who were trying to readjust themselves was that the more cultured and distinguished a man was, the harder it was for him to make a livelihood, no matter how humble he was about being willing to take any kind of a position that would be offered. People simply couldn't believe that a man who knew six languages and had a string of scholastic degrees and a row of decorations would be not only willing but eager to be an elevator man or a shipping clerk to support his family. I know that one unhappy diplomat, whose country had been swept into oblivion by Hitler, sent literally hundreds of applications to firms in New York, Chicago, Philadelphia, all without success. He had a wife and several children, and the German Embassy had magnanimously offered to give them passports back to Europe, where they could live with his family, if he would be willing to fill them out as "a citizen of the Reich," and that his birthplace was "in Germany." He was an ardent patriot, and at first he swore that he would rather die than make such a statement. But finally the pressure of failure became too great, and the last we heard of them they were on their way back to—what?

The most harrowing part for most of those who escaped from Europe is the not knowing what has become of the relatives they had to leave behind. A Greek friend of mine heard that his mother had died of starvation; he has not had a word of the rest of his family in years.

And then there is the less tragic but still frightfully difficult situation of diplomatic husbands and wives who find themselves "enemies," no matter how much they love each other, if their countries are at war. I've often wondered what happened to Gwenda Rogeri, as an Englishwoman in wartime Italy. And a Canadian friend of mine who was married to someone at the Italian Embassy, could not go home to visit her mother, who was very ill, because of course she was technically an enemy alien.

To me the most touching story of all was one I heard at a dinner where I was placed next to a man here temporarily on a war mission. I knew from what had happened to his homeland that he must have lived through terrible tragedy, and I was marveling that he could keep up the old game of polite dinner-partner conversation, when he suddenly turned from the lady on his left, and said to me with the most tragic expression in his eyes, "How can I sit here eating Lobster Thermidor, when my wife and child may be starving?"

And then the whole story came out. His wife, with whom he was obviously desperately in love, had been expecting their first child just when Hitler invaded their country. His duty was to escape with what was to be his government-in-exile, and though he tried to convince his wife, and himself, that his first duty was to stay with her, she finally prevailed on him to go.

For nearly two years the poor man didn't hear a single word from home. He didn't know if he had a son or a daughter, or even if his family were alive. And then at last, somehow, through the underground, he received some snapshots of his wife and their son.

They were, naturally, the most precious things in the world to him; and to preserve them, at least, there were some things he could do. He had duplicates made, and he sent them to be put into safe-deposit boxes in London, in South Africa, in South America, in India, and in New York, so that even if three continents should be destroyed, there would still be copies somewhere in the world.

While so many of our friends were readjusting themselves to their changed lives, Father and I were trying to do the same to ours. The Doctor had wisely decided that Father's greatest help was in getting back to his duties at the Capitol, where Hitler's invasion of Russia had created a new crisis.

Bee and Peter were living at the Polish Consulate in New York, and the boys, through the marvelous work of the interdenominational committee to place the children of political refugees, had been going to a fine school in Pennsylvania, and now had summer jobs in the country. Though Peter certainly needed Bee's courage and companionship as much as we did, as his family in Poland were in the path of both armies, he unselfishly let her spend most of that summer in Washington with us, off and on.

I remember particularly that Fourth of July, for both a personal and a historic reason. Like all holidays, when one is sad, it seemed interminable. On that broiling Sunday afternoon Bee and I were sitting in the patio while Father was upstairs in the library alone. Suddenly I said to her, "Oh, if only something really urgent would happen! If he would only get a call from the White House, it would take him out of himself completely. But I saw in the paper that the President is at Hyde Park."

At that very second the telephone rang, and though it was almost too hot to move, I rushed into the house to see who it was. A man's voice said, "This is a message for Congressman Bloom from the White House, highly confidential. The President wishes him to be here for a conference at eight o'clock this evening. Thank you. Good-by."

When I came back outside, Bee took one look at my face and said, "Of course I can't ask you, and of course you can't tell me— but that could only have been one message!" She and I stayed up until after midnight listening to the radio, hoping for some news bulletin to come through. But when we finally went to sleep, there was still no news, and Father had not returned.

She was leaving on an early train the next morning, and although Father took us to the station, of course we couldn't ask him anything about the night before. She told me later that when Peter met her at the other end, instead of saying hello, she demanded to know what the latest headlines were.

"Why, don't you know?" he answered. "The American troops have landed in Iceland!"

"That was it! That was it!" she cried, and Peter thought she must have lost her mind.

The reason the conference had lasted so late was the grave apprehension caused by Senator Wheeler's statement to the press a few days earlier predicting a landing in Iceland. No one could tell whether or not the Nazis would use the information to make a U-boat attack on our troopships, and everyone in the know was on tenterhooks until they had landed safely.

The strange part of the story was how the advance information had reached Senator Wheeler. It seems that one of our soldiers on furlough mentioned thoughtlessly to someone that the orders were to take along winter underwear, in the midst of a heat wave. "We must be going to Iceland!" he wisecracked (of course he had no idea what the destination really was); and that was passed on as "inside information" to Senator Wheeler, who promptly and characteristically gave it to the press. It could have served, all right, as inside information; but the Nazis must have decided it was too good to be true, and did nothing about it.

The isolationists proceeded to outdo themselves in their accusations against the President; but all he and his advisers cared about was that the Nazis wouldn't have a base halfway across the Atlantic. Still, there is no denying that the isolationist arguments had their effect—"Why should we pull England's chestnuts out of the fire?"—when one recalls that the extension of the peacetime draft passed the House, that summer of 1941, by exactly one vote. If a war declaration had been proposed in Congress on December 6, there would probably not have been half a dozen votes in favor in both houses.

Then came Sunday, December 7.

Everyone in the country must have his own special, ineradicable memory of the news of Pearl Harbor. I remember that Father and I had turned on the two o'clock news, which featured the bulletin that Secretary Hull was receiving the two Japanese envoys at the State Department. We were just warming the radio up again for the two-thirty news, when the telephone rang—and never stopped ringing for six solid hours. I think it was the Associated Press that called first with the horrible, the incredible news. And requested a statement from Father.

One of the most difficult things a man in public life is expected to do is to give a well-judged comment to the press at the very second he is overwhelmed by the news of some great disaster. In this case, there was still the remote chance that it might be a false report, or even Axis propaganda of some kind to affect the "peace talks." In any event, Father decided he could not give a statement to the press until he had received official confirmation from the White House or the State Department. But apparently every single newspaper in the United States was determined that he should, from the *New York Times* to papers we had never heard of in towns we didn't know existed. They kept phoning and phoning at shorter and shorter intervals all afternoon, so that it was almost impossible for us to make an outgoing call. I volunteered to be the "buffer" until Father was ready to speak; and by the time the message came through from the White House that the President wanted Father there at eight o'clock for a conference with Congressional leaders on the declaration of war, I hardly knew what was happening, I was so dazed from the shock, and from the endless repetition of, "I'm sorry, but Congressman Bloom cannot give a statement now."

By then it was almost dinnertime, and we were expected at Mrs. McLean's. Of course Father, like all the men in official or military circles, dropped out automatically, and I suppose the last thing I should have wanted was to go out to dinner. But I felt I simply had to get away from the house and from the telephone (which, perversely, rang not once after Mr. Crawford, Father's secretary, who had been kept from the scene of action by car trouble on a Virginia back road, came to take over; doubtless because the newsmen knew that the White House conference was on).

Apparently most people react the same way in a crisis. Friendship was filled with official womenfolk, all with the one desire to "talk it over with someone." It was quite a different reaction from the one we had on the night France fell. I don't know why; perhaps that was felt as the end of an era, and this as a beginning.

But the party broke up early (the usual after-dinner preview movie was omitted), and when I got home, Mr. Crawford was still sitting faithfully by the silent telephone; Father hadn't returned. He got back around midnight, for it had taken all that time to work out the details for the President's appearance at the joint session of Congress the next morning to declare war on Japan.

Father had suggested (although it meant foregoing the honor of having his name on the House resolution) that the best way of cutting through all the parliamentary red tape involved in the usual procedure, that would have routed two resolutions through the Foreign Relations and Foreign Affairs Committees, was to have the majority leaders in each house introduce a joint resolution to declare war; and that was the procedure that was followed. Of course I was in the House Gallery on Monday and heard Father make the most quoted speech of his career, when he rose and said, "Mr. Speaker, speedy action, not words, should be the order of the day," and sat down.

On Thursday came the declarations of war against Germany and Italy. Early that morning Archduke Otto had telephoned to find out if there was any possibility of his getting into the House Gallery; but from the experience of Monday's session I couldn't offer him much hope. However, he agreed to come to Father's office and see, and we were lucky enough to find him a place. And for me it certainly heightened the experience of that unforgettable morning to have been with the heir of the Austrian Empire when war was declared on his arch enemy and ours.

America at war. The tremendous, incredibly complex job of mobilization was under way; and for those who had responsibilities at the core of the effort, the December 7 sense of shock must quickly have disappeared in action. To many of us, remnants of daze persisted. Would Washington—could it—be bombed? Everyone put up blackout curtains as hastily as possible, and first aid courses were so besieged it was hard to get in. Wherever you went, people were sure to be talking about whether the Germans would consider "suicide raids" on Washington worth while for propaganda purposes. We all acted very casual and British about it, but I don't think we felt as brave as we sounded.

At first it seemed that actual war must bring an end to the pre-Pearl-Harbor cleavages uniting us all in the one great task. But finding one's war work was no more automatic for Washingtonians than for anyone else, and, as we found, unity of purpose was hardly complete. America First had promptly disbanded; and yet some of the things you still heard from former America Firsters would make your hair stand on end. I actually heard one of them argue at a luncheon a year later that "we could have avoided Pearl Harbor if we had wanted to—and of course, even if we win, we lose"! Nor was she the only one. Many times one had to wonder if some people even knew the meaning of the word patriotism.

Of course, some women started carrying patriotism to hysterical extremes, such as vowing not to have their hair set or get a manicure until the war was over. They couldn't have been numerous, though; you have to make an appointment at almost any Washington beauty shop two weeks in advance: which suggests that all women are sisters at least skin deep, since even during the worst of the London blitz, when the beauty shops were forced to move into air-raid shelters, they still did a land-office business.

Fortunately there were plenty of others who went about things practically. The Senate Ladies Luncheon club, which had formed during the First World War to make Red Cross dressings, had continued ever since, when the Senate was in session, to work for some charity after a Tuesday snack lunch which the ladies took turns providing in one of the large rooms in the Senate Office Building. But the House wives had never done any war work as a unit until after Pearl Harbor, when Mrs. Charles Dewey, whose husband is the only Republican Representative from Chicago, organized their group; and I was glad they decided to include one daughter among the wives, when I was asked to be secretary of the Unit. Mrs. Dewey had a hard time securing a workroom for us, but finally the Librarian of Congress, Mr. MacLeish, gave us a fine big room in the Library Annex, where we have turned out even more than our quota for the Red Cross.

I still felt there must be something I could do on my own to contribute to war relief. The answer came in an unexpected way, through a letter of introduction to me for Belle Fenstock, a well-known New York composer, who was doing war work in Washington. Almost before we knew it we had written and placed eight popular songs, and I could turn my royalties over to whatever charity happened to be having a drive when a check came in.

Meanwhile Washington had donned its helmet. The Army took over the Capitol in grim earnest at four o'clock every afternoon, with sentries on the roof as well as pacing the entrances; and the White House was under military patrol day and night. The beautiful night lighting of the Capitol dome, the Washington Monument, and Lincoln's brooding figure at the Memorial became a peacetime memory; and the streetside color scheme became more and more a matter of khaki and navy blue.

The war effects came by stages. I don't remember any of the wartime restrictions or rationing that first winter, and I can't recall just when the hotels put their five-day rule into effect: the rule that led to the legend of the big shot who has spent the war shuttling across the street between the Carlton and the Statler every five days.

As it happened, I was to see wartime Washington with an unexpected fresh perspective, because I spent the second war winter in California, on doctor's orders. I had had absolutely no respite from new problems and responsibilities, and the Doctor decided I must "get away from it all," literally, and the farther the better. While I was reluctant to travel so far when transportation was overburdened, the presence of so many relatives and friends in San Francisco and Los Angeles made California the logical haven.

Bee and Peter had established themselves in San Francisco several months before, an event that for me meant mingled feelings. I was happy that they had found security and recognition at last; but Bee and I had been through so much together that it felt more as if I were saying good-by to a sister than to a friend. California seemed very far away.

Yet six months later there I was, staying with Anita and Walter Newman, Mother's favorite cousins, and mine, who lived, as Anita put it, only "half a hill" away from the Sokolowskis, and shared the same breathtaking view of the Golden Gate, through which an apparently endless stream of convoys passed day and night. At first it was hard to understand why you were never to mention that you had seen one, when a million other people could look out of their windows and see it, too: for unlike New Yorkers, San

Franciscans can see their bay from every part of town. But as I soon learned, experience had proved the value of keeping quiet on the thousand-to-one chance that the wrong person hadn't been looking at the right time. And I became convinced that the very fact that you do see the war moving ceaselessly out to the Pacific with your own eyes has a great deal to do with making San Francisco the most war-conscious city in the country, as everyone agrees it is.

Bad luck would have it that Bee, who had escaped from Poland without a scratch, was quite badly hurt when they ran into a parked car in the dimout the very night before I arrived, and was laid up almost the whole time I was in San Francisco. But she was able afterward to carry out our plan for a few weeks together in Los Angeles. The magical San Francisco air, the complete change, and everyone's boundless kindness had made an entirely different person of me; and if anything else had been needed to restore both Bee and me completely, the right medicine was that trip to Hollywood, which turned out to be a most exhilarating cross between a Marx Brothers movie and *Alice in Wonderland*.

Bee's sister, Margaret King, who, never having worked in her life, was now a riveter at Douglas Aircraft, came to spend her day off with us; but after a few hours of hearing both our telephones going incessantly—"This is Miss Louella Parsons' secretary." . . . "Can you lunch at M.G.M. on Tuesday?" . . . "Miss Gracie Fields would like you to be her guest at her broadcast honoring Poland, Thursday at seven." . . . "Oh, Cobina, it sounds wonderful!" . . . "Mr. Hays was thinking you might like a guest card for the Beach Club at Santa Monica." . . . "This is Whitney Bolton at Warner Brothers. If you want to see Bette Davis and a scene from *Mission to Moscow* the same day, you'd better come on Wednesday . . ."—she declared she was going back to her riveting for some peace and quiet.

We took it all in our stride. That is, until we were invited to luncheon at the Faculty Club at California Tech to meet the great Dr. Millikan. Cary Grant hadn't fazed us a bit, but Dr. Millikan really got us down. We even tried practicing on each other, "Oh, Dr. Millikan, do tell us how you split the atom! You *did* split the atom, didn't you?" And then he turned out to be the most disarmingly easy person to talk to one could imagine, and one more unpredictability in our grand tour of Wonderland.

The Washington I came back to in February hardly seemed the same place I had left around Thanksgiving. True, Father's letters had prepared me somewhat for the change. I knew that all but one room of our house downstairs was closed off to save fuel, and I expected to stay glued to the fireplace. I knew there was no pleasure driving in the East. I knew that food rationing, not a major problem to a traveler, would be making some difference in everday life.

But the streets looked like a deserted village! This I was not prepared for. And all of Washington, like a city full of medieval monks disputing over how many angels could stand on the head of a pin, was arguing with zeal and with finespun distinctions, "Just what *is* pleasure driving?" Eventually it was decided that if you were going to a party where it was your official duty to go, this did not come under the ban. Even so, some high officials felt they should go by bus, and I remember the Vice-President and Mrs. Wallace arriving at a very grand state dinner after transferring three times, carrying Mrs. Wallace's evening slippers in an old-fashioned slipper bag.

The snoopers—both the official O.P.A. ones and the unofficial busybodies—had their innings on Sunday nights at Mrs. McLean's, where they would wait to see if any official cars were used for what unquestionably was unofficial pleasure, and the story was always sure to make the front page of Monday morning's papers.

Naturally, Washington women, like others everywhere, couldn't be together for two minutes without talking "points," and Capital hostesses who used to be famous for their elaborate tea tables were now boastful if they managed to save up enough cheese and crackers to ask a few friends in for a drink, since tea, though unrationed, was practically impossible to get.

Diplomats are rationed too. (Not their presences, but their cuisines!) The only difference is that if they have to entertain officially for their visiting chief of state, the State Department gives them special ration points for the occasion.

And nothing has been quite so significant a sign of Washington's new role of world capital as the endless series of good will state visits that have gone on all through the war. Both in purpose and in atmosphere they have been the greatest possible contrast to those prewar visits to Berchtesgaden, when the whole world held its breath while Hitler entertained one doomed "guest of honor" after another.

The President, who has such a strong feeling for the personal, human element in every situation, felt he should know the leaders of the United Nations in the most real and direct way possible, so he invited them one by one to come to Washington. For some reason I have been unable yet to discover, about everyone except Prime Minister Churchill and Mme. Chiang Kai-shek has arrived at the height of a heat wave, and not a single one has been here in the spring, when the blossoms make Washington incomparably beautiful. It may be because flying is safer in the summer; or just for mysterious "reasons of state." Under wartime travel difficulties almost all of the official guests have come without their wives. There was one exception when the Prime Minister brought Mrs. Churchill and their daughter Mary along; but they stayed quietly at the White House and accepted no official entertaining.

The Latin American chief executives came so thick and fast that we can remember them only as a sort of grand presidential parade. The schedules of their visits called for the first night to be spent at the White House, where a state dinner was always given, usually stag, attended by nearly the same group of ranking Cabinet, Congressional, and military guests in each case. The Protocol Division did relax enough to institute a Good Neighbor policy in its own sphere: by revising the usual law of seating arrangements so that the guest of honor and his party would find themselves placed with at least one Spanish-speaking neighbor; and Secretary Hull followed the same rule at the dinner he invariably gave the following night at the Carlton. In the meantime the visitors had moved from the White House across Pennsylvania Avenue to Blair House, the beautiful historic home the government bought especially to lodge official guests; for besides the Churchills, only Queen Wilhelmina and Mme. Chiang have stayed at the White House all through their Washington visits. The third night usually found the guests of honor entertaining at dinner at their own embassy or legation, with a large reception to follow, which gave others besides the one small official group their only chance to meet the state visitor.

Not only chiefs of state but foreign ministers came in a seemingly endless stream. They went directly to Blair House, and did not rate a state dinner at the White House; otherwise the schedule was the same familiar one. Perhaps it sounds like much ado for wartime; but really it was by no means overfestive. All our official guests had made long and dangerous flights to come here, and naturally wanted to meet as many people and get as many impressions as possible during their three or four days in Washington. Surely these were "parties with a purpose," as all wartime entertaining should be.

All the visits took place in a bright blaze of publicity except one, and that had all the elements of a first-rate mystery story. On Decoration Day, 1942, Father had a message from the White House that the President wished him to be there for luncheon that day; he hoped the short notice on a holiday would not disrupt his plans; he would understand when he came.

At the front door the chief usher murmured, "The luncheon is in honor of Foreign Commissar Molotov!"—the very first inkling he, or anyone else, had that Molotov was in Washington. The luncheon lasted until long after four o'clock, and turned into an informal round-table discussion on all Soviet-American problems, led by the President and the Commissar, and joined in by the Congressional and military leaders. In spite of language difficulties, Father told me, it was one of the most illuminating discussions he has ever heard.

The precautions for Molotov's safety were probably the most elaborate that Washington ever knew. Not only were all the luncheon guests pledged to secrecy, but so were all the newsmen and photographers, and even the chauffeurs waiting outside. Our colored chauffeur, Starks, who is very news-minded, recognized Molotov as he went into the White House, but said not a word to anyone until the story broke after the Commissar was on his way back to Russia.

He stayed at Blair House for several days, and then at the Waldorf in New York, but he was simply a "Mr. Brown," in case anyone was interested. Of course he accepted no invitations except for the President's luncheon, but he did manage to do some sightseeing both in Washington and New York. The whole visit was the most superb job of voluntary censorship. Dozens, if not hundreds, of people could have spilled the news, but not one did. Father said he was almost afraid to think the word Russia, the whole time Molotov was here, for fear someone might read his mind.

The arrival of King Peter of Yugoslavia had a touch of mystery, too, beyond the usual wartime precaution of never announcing flight arrivals or departures in advance.

The King was expected in Washington on a Wednesday, when the usual schedule was to begin. On the Sunday afternoon before, the telephone rang, and a friend of mine at the Yugoslav Legation said mysteriously,

"Monsieur est arrivé!"

For a minute I couldn't imagine what "Monsieur" had arrived. And then it dawned on me that it could only mean the King! After cautioning me "not to breathe it to a soul," my friend rang off, and I felt just as Father had about Molotov. But to my relief the State Department announced the King's arrival late that night, adding that His Majesty had left for Hot Springs to rest until Wednesday.

It wasn't he who needed respite, however. What had happened was that the King had an unexpected chance to fly in an Army bomber rather than by clipper; and having a normal eighteen-year-old love of adventure, he couldn't resist it. The carefully worked out schedule could not be changed at the last minute, so the King had to "rest" at Hot Springs until the time for his official arrival, although a rest was probably the last thing he wanted.

For King Peter's visit to the Capitol, Father, as usual, was in charge of the arrangements; he also attended the White House dinner, and we were both invited to the Legation dinner where the King was host.

There, after dinner, and before the reception guests began to arrive, the Minister and Mme. Fotitch took some of us, one or two at a time, to chat with the King informally. I found him very easy to talk to—of course, he speaks perfect English, as he has lived in England for years—and he was particularly interested in what to do in New York, if "they" would let him. I suggested, for the already long list of musts, going up to the top of the Empire State Building just at twilight, when the lights are coming on all over the city. What gave him the greatest thrill, Father learned when he went to see him at the end of the New York visit, was being asked to toss the first ball at the Polo Grounds.

The next royal visitor was King George of Greece, who after the tragedy of Crete had escaped disguised as a peasant, with the Germans hardly a stone's throw behind. His modesty and matter-of-factness about the story of danger and heroism were extraordinary. He has lived so long in England during the years of his two exiles that he might be taken anywhere for an Englishman, and one felt that great strength of character and a realistic outlook were his dominating qualities.

The White House dinner for him has a special place in my memory because it was the first one I attended there, after becoming Father's official hostess. As I have mentioned, in wartime these dinners have been simplified in several respects. They are black-tie, and the formalities of presentation and procession-forming have been much shortened. Dinner ends with a toast by the President to the visiting monarch or chief of state, who responds; and then the party goes upstairs to the private apartments, where a movie is shown. For all except those who are seated near the guest of honor during dinner, this schedule permits no more than a brief greeting and leavetaking. Thus embassy or legation dinners on the second nights afforded a better chance for getting a real impression, since both King George and Queen Wilhelmina, whose visit was to follow, chatted with the guests by ones and twos after dinner, as King Peter had done also.

Both evenings Queen Wilhelmina wore a simple, high-necked and long-sleeved black dinner dress, the only regal touch a magnificent diamond stomacher. It was hard to believe that the Queen, who looks and acts as much as anyone could like a modern, middle-aged reincarnation of Queen Victoria, could actually have been the heroine of that flight across the Channel when she escaped to England in a plane under incessant Nazi bombardment all the way.

When my turn came to be summoned to the Queen after dinner at the Embassy, I found that although she was as kind and gracious as could be, you felt that, like Queen Victoria, she could show very plainly if she were "not amused." No doubt it was sheer nervousness that made one lady, who was taken in to the small drawing room where the Queen was sitting at the same time I was, plunge into a long recital telling Her Majesty how she had lost her maid, and what a terrible time she was having to get another! If the Queen was a bit startled at this unroyal conversation —especially as one is supposed to wait for royalty to choose the topic—she didn't give the slightest sign; but somehow, without our quite realizing how it happened, the subject had been changed and the Queen was asking questions about the old Dutch legends of the Hudson River Valley, which evidently the President had been telling her of. After a few minutes Mme. Loudon came in with another group of ladies, and the Queen wished us good-by.

All these royal visits were in utmost contrast to the excitement and pomp with which King George and Queen Elizabeth had been greeted so short and yet so long a time before. The Netherlands, Yugoslavia, and Greece all lay prostrate under Hitler's heel, and Queen Wilhelmina as well as King Peter and the King of Greece had shared the tragedy of invasion with their unhappy peoples. I've heard it argued that they should have stayed on to the bitter end; but that is really a ridiculous argument from every point of view. After all, they are not only the symbols of their countries but the legal chiefs of state, and once they fell into the Nazis' hands, even if they resisted every "persuasion" the Germans might have used on them to do their bidding, who knows how long they could have withstood the pressure of the inhuman retaliations the Nazis could have taken on their helpless people if they refused to "co-operate"?

Certainly Washington's most frequent wartime visitor, and its most welcome one, has been Prime Minister Churchill, who almost rates as a commuter now. And yet during all his four visits he has never accepted any formal entertaining; there has not been a single state dinner or reception in his honor. But Father saw him often, as the President asked small official groups to meet him at luncheon or dinner at the White House, and Mr. Churchill gave the same sort of stag parties at the British Embassy, so he could really get to know and exchange views with the key men in the government. Otherwise, the only invitation he has accepted, so far as I know, was the luncheon Senator Connally and Father gave in his honor at the Capitol after he addressed the special joint meeting of Congress on May 19, 1943.

And I'm sure that no one was more stirred by his superb speech that morning than Lieutenant the Honorable Richard Wood, the Halifaxes' modest hero son, who had only recently come to Washington after losing both legs in the North African campaign, and who had a place of honor in his wheel chair on the floor of the House. For myself, I shall never cease to be grateful for the opportunity to see as well as hear the Prime Minister, for the only way to appreciate fully his matchless oratory is when his facial expressions and his gestures do their share.

Mrs. Connally and I had been doing our persuasive best to have ladies included at the luncheon, as we knew it would probably be our only chance to meet Mr. Churchill. But when the Secret Service, who had charge of the Prime Minister's safety, looked over the situation at the Capitol and decided that the Foreign Relations Committee Room, just across the corridor from the Senate Restaurant, could most easily be closed off completely, with Senator Connally's private office to be used as a reception room, we knew we didn't have a chance. The committee table only seats twenty-two when set for luncheon, and the Prime Minister's party and Lord Halifax, with Vice-President Wallace, Speaker Rayburn, and the Congressional leaders quickly filled up the list. Even at that, there was one prime minister too many!

Prime Minister Mackenzie King of Canada was a most welcome guest at that luncheon; and I doubt that anyone realized he was also a quite unexpected one. Father had no idea he was even in Washington (although of course he frequently is) until he saw him drive up to the Capitol with Mr. Churchill. Very likely Mr. Churchill had told him there was to be a luncheon after his speech, and he had naturally taken it for granted that he was expected, as of course he would have been if it had been known he was in town. Anyhow, at the very last second, in he walked, and in a flash Father realized the situation. It was too late to reseat the table —most of the guests were already taking their places—so Father did the only possible thing, which was do a sleight-of-hand trick with his own place card and give the Canadian Prime Minister the place between Lord Halifax and the Speaker, while he hastily had a chair squeezed in somewhere at the bottom of the table.

After luncheon the Foreign Relations and Foreign Affairs Committees met Mr. Churchill, who had gladly agreed to hold an informal discussion with the two groups. Mrs. Connally and I were among the few others who were asked in for a few minutes before his off-the-record talk to the committees got under way, and I found him at close range the endearing blend of belligerent little boy and jovial John Bull that has made him just "Winnie" to all of Britain.

But perhaps no wartime visitor has aroused the same pitch of interest and curiosity as Mme. Chiang Kai-shek. Here was an almost legendary lady, symbol of a beloved and indomitable people, who came surrounded by suspense and pathos. No star ever had a more perfect entrance on the stage than Mme. Chiang on the Washington scene. You remember that after her arrival in America, she disappeared completely for several months. All anyone knew was that she was recuperating from the six-year ordeal she had gone through in China. While I was in San Francisco, a picture appeared of her surrounded by a group of Chinese nurses, and everyone there concluded that she must be at the local Chinese hospital, which is the only one in this country. But finally it was disclosed that she had been in the Medical Center in New York, and that at last, though still weak and delicate, she would be able to pay her long-looked-for visit to Washington, where she was to be the President and Mrs. Roosevelt's personal guest.

Appealing and spellbinding as she was, she was also, to tell the truth, a problem; for she was the only one of the Capital's wartime guests who had absolutely no official position of her own, and whatever was done for her would set a precedent for all future visiting dignitaries' wives. If there is one thing Congress and the Protocol Division see eye to eye on, it is their absolute horror of setting a precedent.

Mme. Chiang soon let it be known that she hoped to address Congress—a thing which no foreigner but a reigning monarch, a president, or a prime minister had ever done before; the very acme of an unprecedented occasion. Furthermore, Madame was known to be as unpredictable as she is eloquent, and there was no way of knowing what she planned to say, or where her oratorical chips might fall. But on the other hand, she was the one woman in the world whom everyone was most anxious to see and hear. So the arrangements were made; and since Mme. Chiang was her personal guest, Mrs. Roosevelt took care of every detail herself, as I happen to know because she telephoned Father often about the arrangements.

Madame was anxious also to meet the Congressional leaders, so Senator Connally and Father gave a luncheon for her after her speech, and, since Mrs. Roosevelt was also to be a guest of honor, it was only natural to include other ladies too. The papers said that Mrs. Connally and I acted as hostesses, but we were really just guests like all the others, with the Senator and Father as hosts.

I doubt that there was ever a greater scramble for seats in the House Gallery than on that morning of Mme. Chiang's speech; and she certainly lived up to expectations. Beautiful, brilliant, forceful, exotic, fiery, and poignant all at once—what more could be asked of one woman? She is the result of the strange fate that has made her really two personalities in one; she can interpret China to America and America to China with almost equal insight, and has a command of English which is matched only by Winston Churchill's. But I can't say she aroused the same warm enchantment that Queen Elizabeth did. She is both too zealous and too fabulous for that. You felt rather, as you would feel if you were meeting Joan of Arc.

Since the Secret Service precautions for her safety were careful in the extreme, it was arranged to have the luncheon in the Foreign Relations Room again. Before luncheon Madame sat on a couch with Mrs. Roosevelt, and you could tell how spent she was after her scheduled broadcast speech in the House and her extemporaneous talk to the Senate. In fact, all through her visit she spared herself as much as possible between speeches. She asked Father to come to see her at the White House several times, and each time he found her resting on a sofa, storing up her strength for the heavy strain of her appearances all over the country.

The Chinese Embassy had sent out invitations for a colossal reception at the Shoreham in her honor: the one chance that most of Washington would have to meet her. Except for the luncheon at the Capitol there had been no entertaining in her honor, even at the White House. But Madame must have overestimated her strength when she allowed the Embassy to send out over three thousand invitations to the reception, and she told Father she did not see how she could remain standing all that time and shake all those thousands of hands.

He suggested that she take a leaf from Martha Washington's book—surely a good American precedent if ever there was one—and remain seated all afternoon. And to avoid any awkwardness about shaking hands, he suggested she could keep her hands in a muff, which was just what she did. Even so, the strain of greeting and bowing to that long stream of guests must have been terribly exhausting. It took over an hour to get from the door of the hotel to where she was sitting, and most of the guests had only a moment's glimpse of her famous face, a huge corsage of orchids on a blue Chinese gown, and a sable muff.

Not long after Madame's visit Father found, to his amazement, that he was doing some wartime flying of his own. The honor of being a Short Snorter was not one he had aspired to; in fact he had always flatly declined to fly at all. But now I think there is nothing he takes more pride in than that dollar bill signed by the President, Mr. Churchill, and other illustrious ocean hoppers, which he earned en route to the Refugee Conference in Bermuda in 1943. The advisability of his taking to the air for the first time at seventy-three was something I hadn't escaped a few doubts about; but the purpose of the conference was very close to his heart, and Dr. Salzer gave his approval. Almost before I knew it, he was off.

War, that brings so many kinds of new comradeship and interchange, also brings terrible isolation. It is a strange feeling when one really grasps that all Europe under Nazi occupation was as cut off from the rest of us as if telephones, cables, and radio transmitters didn't exist. Or when one thinks how isolated the front line army units must be in the crucial times of battle. Or realizes how many of the people we see every day cannot speak of the war-secret concerns that are their deepest interest. Once Father had taken off for Bermuda and was under Navy regulations, I felt that isolation very keenly. Even official radiograms took several days to be cleared; and although he managed to telephone once, after careful prearrangements, there were so many forbidden topics in transocean conversation, because of wartime security, one had little left to say. There was the wonderful comfort of hearing for myself that he was really all right; in fact, thriving on the experience. Even so, as long as there is an area any place in the world where wires are down, I shall know how to feel for those who are cut off.

And what will Washington be like in its next chapter, I wonder, after victory, when travel lanes and talk lanes are open again for peacetime comings and goings? Will we ever take our white kid gloves and our card cases out of moth balls to set out on the old prewar routine? Or have war years turned our backs forever on the days that seem so frivolous and empty to us now, but which seemed so happy and satisfying to us then?

I should like to think that we have all really changed for the better, and that we will keep a soldierly single-mindedness in right-ing the peacetime world. But if straws show which way the wind blows, I'm afraid that what happened after our first taste of interim victory only proves that something's to be said in praise of folly.

For a few jubilant hours the day of Italy's unconditional surrender most of us imagined that all Italy was already ours, and that our armies would be marching under Rome's triumphal arches in a matter of days; not guessing that Salerno and Cassino and Anzio lay between, and as bloody a progress beyond. I suppose that people should feel like celebrating a great milestone in some high-minded way; but as far as I can discover, there are two principal reactions: to go out and get tight, or to buy a new hat.

On that day, following my own normal response to almost any extraordinary excitement, I started down Connecticut Avenue to the nearest milliner; but by the time I got there, I was feeling pretty shamefaced about my impulse. And then whom did I see, trying on a mad bit of millinery, but Mme. Fotitch, the wife of the Yugoslav envoy, whose feeling of the momentousness of that day would surely be as intense as anyone's in Washington. We looked at each other and said, "You, too?" and confessed the sameness of our reactions.

Then I recalled a little incident of a year or so before, when a few of us were talking after a small wartime dinner, and one very serious woman said she had promised herself not to buy a single hat that was frivolous instead of functional until the world was right again; in fact she doubted that we could ever go back to a frivolous outlook after the tragedies of this war. Whereupon Genevieve Forbes Herrick, the brilliant newspaperwoman who was nearly killed in the automobile accident in which the first Mrs. Harold Ickes lost her life while they were motoring in New Mexico, made a surprising comment.

"I don't know if you're right or not, my dear," she said thoughtfully, "I'm inclined to believe that frivolities are a sure sign that things are right; and I'll tell you why.

"When I lay in the hospital all those months not knowing if I would live or die, I didn't know or care whether there was such a thing as a hat in the world. Later, when I began to take an interest in the papers and magazines, I got many a chuckle out of those bits of nonsense women seemed to be buying to put on their heads; but as I didn't need a hat, and still didn't know if I ever would, they still had no real meaning for me. They were something from a most fanciful storybook. And then suddenly I was told that I could leave the hospital soon, to go home. And believe it or not, my very first thought was, 'I must get a hat!' I mean, you see, that I was part of normal life again, and all at once a pretty hat was something vitally important!"

So perhaps among the freedoms we have all fought for is the right to be happy and carefree again. And it wouldn't surprise me too much if Washington's particular version of happy folly turned out to be very much like the dear old days. After all, the states and the nations will still have to work together; pleasure will still be a duty, and duty a pleasure.